CRADLES OF CIVILIZATION

CHINA

CRADLES OF CIVILIZATION

CHINA

ANCIENT CULTURE , MODERN LAND

General Editor: Robert E. Murowchick

University of Oklahoma Press
Norman, Oklahoma

NOTES ON ROMANIZATION AND PRONUNCIATION

This volume uses the pinyin *romanization system, the official transcription system of the Chinese mainland. In those cases where another spelling might be more familiar to readers, both spellings* *are given at the first occurrence, e.g. "Guangzhou (Canton)." The basic* pinyin *pronunciations (followed by some examples) are provided below.*

BASIC PRONUNCIATIONS IN THE PINYIN ROMANIZATION SYSTEM

Vowels:

a	*as in* father, *but not as in* tank *(e.g., Ma, a surname)*
ai	*as in* why *(Shanghai city)*
an	*pronounced as* **aun**t *(Anhui province, Han dynasty)*
ang	*as in* **ang**le *(Shang dynasty)*
ao	*as in* ou*t (Chairman Mao)*
e	*as in* her *(Henan province)*
ei	*as in* **eig**ht *(Wei dynasty, Beijing)*
en	*as in* den *(Shenyang city)*
eng	*as in* **y**ou**ng** *(Zhengzhou city)*
i	*generally as in* mach**i**ne *(Jilin province, Xi river); although the pronunciation varies depending upon the consonant preceding it*
ia	*pronounced* **ya** *as in* Mala**ysia** *(Xia dynasty)*
ian	*pronounced* **yen** *(Dalian city)*
ie	*as in* **ye**llow *(Xie, a surname)*
iu	*pronounced* **yo** *(Liu, a surname)*
o	*as in* n**o**r *(Boyang Lake)*
ong	*as in* l**ong** *(Longmen grotto)*
ou	*as in* s**ou**l *(Zhou dynasty)*
u	*as in* cr**u**de *(Suzhou city)*
ü	*as in the French* t**u** *(Lü, a surname)*
ua	*as in* w**a**ffle *(Hua, a surname)*
uai	*pronounced* **why** *(Huai River)*
uan	*as in* w**an**d *(Sichuan province)*
uang	*pronounced* **wong** *(Guangzhou city, Huang River)*
ui	*pronounced* **way** *(Guizhou province)*
un	*pronounced* **oon** *(Changchun city)*
uo	*pronounced* **wo** *(Zhongguo, or "China")*

Consonants:

b	*as in* **b**oat *(Beijing city)*
c	*as in* ha**ts** *or* pa**ts**y *(Cui, surname)*
ch	*as in* **ch**air *(Changsha, a city)*
d	*as in* **d**oor *(Dunhuang caves)*
f	*as in* **f**og *(Fujian province)*
g	*as in* **g**irl *(Guangdong province)*
h	*as in* **h**ouse *(Hunan province)*
j	*as in* **j**am *(Jiangsu province)*
k	*as in* **k**ing *(Kunming city)*
l	*as in* **l**amp *(Liaoning province)*
m	*as in* **m**any *(Ming dynasty)*
n	*as in* **n**ot *(Nanjing city)*
p	*as in* **p**oor *(Pan, a surname)*
q	*as in* **ch**air *(Qing dynasty)*
r	*as in* **r**ight *(Rao, a surname)*
s	*as in* **s**imple *(Sichuan province)*
sh	*as in* **sh**ame *(Shenzhen city)*
t	*as in* **t**own *(Tianjin city)*
w	*as in* **w**ar *(Wuhan)*
x	*as in* **sh**e *(Wuxi city)*
y	*as in* **y**ellow *(Yang, a surname)*
z	*as in* a**dz**e *(Zuo River; Mao Zedong)*
zh	*as in* **J**oe *(Zhou dynasty)*

In the pinyin *system, apostrophes are used only to separate two syllables that might otherwise be confused (e.g., xian is a single syllable meaning "county," while the two syllables Xi'an refer to the capital city of Shaanxi province).*

Published by the University of Oklahoma Press, Norman, Publishing Division of the University

Produced by Weldon Russell Pty Ltd
107 Union Street North Sydney NSW 2060 Australia

Copyright © 1994 by Weldon Russell Pty Ltd

China : ancient culture, modern land / general editor Robert E. Murowchick.
    p. cm. -- (Cradles of civilization)
    Includes bibliographical references.
    ISBN 0–8061–2683–3
    1. China--Civilization. I. Murowchick, Robert E., 1956-
II. Series.
DS721.H6918 1995
951--dc20
                        94-13366
                        CIP

Managing Editor: Ariana Klepac
Project Coordinator: Margaret Whiskin
Copy Editor: Yani Silvana
Assistant Editor: Libby Frederico
Picture Researchers: Anne Ferrier, Jane Lewis
Designer: Catherine Martin
Design Concept: Kathie Baxter Smith
Illustrators: Mike Gorman, Jan Smith (maps)
Seal Carving and Calligraphy: He Wan Guan
Indexer: Garry Cousins
Production: Dianne Leddy

Produced by Mandarin Offset, Hong Kong
Printed in China

FRONT COVER: Close-up of Beijing architecture.
LEO MEIER/AUSTRALIAN PICTURE LIBRARY

ENDPAPERS: Han dynasty (206 BC–AD 220) silk manuscript from the Mawangdui tomb, Changsha, Hunan province. WENWU PUBLISHING

PAGE TWO: Lama monks in Ganze, Tibet. LEO MEIER/WELDONS

PAGE THREE: Northern Dynasties (c. last half of sixth century). Warrior made of gray clay with red pigments. It stands 35 inches (88.9 cm) high.
ASIAN ART MUSEUM OF SAN FRANCISCO, THE AVERY BRUNDAGE COLLECTION/B60 S498

PAGE FIVE: Yangshao culture (c. 4800–3600 BC) painted earthenware bottle.
ASIAN ART MUSEUM OF SAN FRANCISCO, GIFT OF HANNI FORESTER/1992.2

PAGE SIX: Ksitgarbha with ten Kings of Hell, Five Dynasties (c. tenth century). BRITISH MUSEUM, LONDON

PAGE SEVEN TOP LEFT: Peasant farmers in Guilin, Guangxi Autonomous Region, with karst limestone peaks in the background. THE IMAGE BANK/TADAO KIMURA

PAGE SEVEN BOTTOM LEFT: Dawenkou culture (c. 5000–3000 BC) ceramic pot. WENWU PUBLISHING

PAGE SEVEN RIGHT: The Temple of Heaven in the Forbidden City, Beijing. PETER EASTWAY

PAGE EIGHT: Fan painting by Shen Zhou (1427–1509), who was a foremost painter of the early Ming dynasty Wu school.
ASIAN ART MUSEUM OF SAN FRANCISCO, THE AVERY BRUNDAGE COLLECTION/B81 D39

PAGE NINE: A bell from Shang dynasty called a nao, *with a dragon mask design.* METROPOLITAN MUSEUM OF ART/HUNAN PROVINCIAL MUSEUM

SERIES PREFACE

Timothy Potts

Cradles of Civilization is a new series which aims to provide a reliable, up-to-date, and well-illustrated account of the world's great civilizations. Each volume is written by a team of leading international experts, building into an authoritative review of the cultures which have shaped the course of human history around the globe. Exploring the patterns of the past as brought to light by the findings of archaeology, the books lead the reader on a journey through one of the major scientific and humanistic achievements of our age.

In a new departure, *Cradles of Civilization* brings together geographers, anthropologists, archaeologists, and historians to form a rounded picture of life in ancient times, one that seeks not only to describe the past but also, as far as possible, to explain it. Taking as its theme the juxtaposition of "Ancient Culture, Modern Land," each volume examines the civilization in the context of its environment — the physical and cultural landscape which molded lifestyles and formed the foundation upon which empires were to rise and fall — while special features look at the arts, sciences, and great personalities of history.

The legacy of the past is very much apparent in the way we live today, and each volume traces the history and culture of a particular region up to modern times, building into a concise, but comprehensive, overview of human achievement through the ages. Both individually and as a series, *Cradles of Civilization* will form a valuable guide to the cultures which not only represent the highpoints of antiquity around the globe but have also done most to shape the face of the modern world today.

CONTENTS

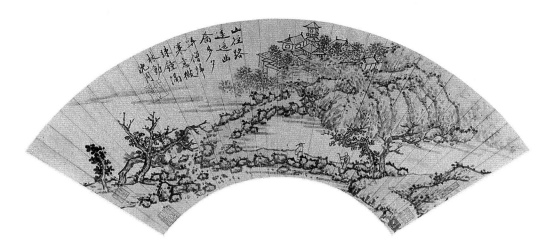

SERIES EDITOR

TIMOTHY POTTS

Deputy Director and Co-ordinating Curator of International Art, National Gallery of Victoria, Melbourne. Formerly Research Lecturer and British Academy Post-doctoral Fellow in Near Eastern Archaeology, University of Oxford, UK

GENERAL EDITOR

ROBERT E. MUROWCHICK

Associate Director, Fairbank Center for East Asian Research, Harvard University, and Associate in East Asian Archaeology, Peabody Museum, Harvard University, USA

CONTRIBUTORS

TIMOTHY H. BARRETT
Professor of East Asian History, London University, UK

KWANG-CHIH CHANG
John E. Hudson Professor of Archaeology, Department of Anthropology, Harvard University, USA

TIMOTHY CHEEK
Assistant Professor of History, The Colorado College, USA

PATRICIA EBREY
Professor of East Asian Languages and Cultures and of History, University of Illinois at Urbana-Champaign, USA

ELIZABETH ENDICOTT-WEST
Former Associate Professor of Chinese and Inner Asian History, Department of East Asian Languages and Civilizations, Harvard University, USA

LOTHAR VON FALKENHAUSEN
Associate Professor, Department of Art History, University of California, Los Angeles, USA

GRACE S. FONG
Associate Professor, Department of East Asian Languages and Literatures, McGill University, Canada

CHRISTOPHER FUNG
Doctoral Candidate, Department of Anthropology, Harvard University, USA

DAVID N. KEIGHTLEY
Professor of History, University of California, Berkeley, USA

MICHAEL LOEWE
Retired. University Lecturer in Chinese Studies (1963–90), Cambridge University, UK

RHOADS MURPHEY
Professor of History, University of Michigan, USA

RICHARD J. SMITH
Professor of History, Rice University, USA

JAMES L. WATSON
Fairbank Professor of Chinese Society and Professor of Anthropology, Harvard University, USA

ROBIN D. S. YATES
Professor of History and of East Asian Languages and Literatures, McGill University, Canada

INTRODUCTION

Robert E. Murowchick

EVEN THOUGH CHINA'S major historical events and achievements are familiar to most Western readers, as we enter what many have called The Pacific Century, a deeper understanding of China and its neighbors is required, not only by specialist scholars, but by all who will be affected by the rapid economic, social, political, and environmental changes that are taking place there.

While China has an ancient tradition of historical study, over the last few decades the study of China has entered something of a Golden Age, with exciting new research providing a better understanding of where China has been and where it is going. This volume brings together many of the world's experts to present the latest research on this flow of Chinese history. Although this presentation is organized chronologically, recurring themes that appear throughout China's history are carried across the chapters: long-standing attitudes of "us" versus "them," or "center" versus "periphery," continual attempts at unity amidst rich diversity; physical and political isolation in the face of constant cultural interplay; and repeated efforts at modernization within a society restrained by traditional conservatism.

We can also trace a series of recurring questions throughout the volume: how does one define "Chinese," and at what point can we discern a "Chinese civilization?" What has held China together in the past, and what will continue to hold China together in the future? Will China, with its vast population and enormous reserves of natural resources, emerge as the dominant world power at some point in the future, or will it continue to be beset by the same kinds of obstacles that have burdened it repeatedly in the past?

As it has many times in the past, China today faces a huge challenge in a rapidly changing world. China is experiencing an economic boom that has made it become one of the fastest growing economies in the world. These heady days of regional economic success are straining the existing infrastructure: transport systems, telecommunication, banking, and even the generation of power can scarcely keep up with demand. Moreover, this rapid but localized economic boom is quickly leading to a country of "haves" and "have nots," producing a time bomb of potential civil unrest in many interior "have not" regions. Two thousand years of traditional Confucian society and fifty years of Communist rule are once again facing the challenge of rapid change, and it is not at all clear what form the inevitable changes will take. What is clear is that China will be a dominant player in the developing Pacific world, and the choices that China — perhaps radically reorganized, perhaps basically unchanged — makes today and tomorrow will affect the world in very substantive ways.

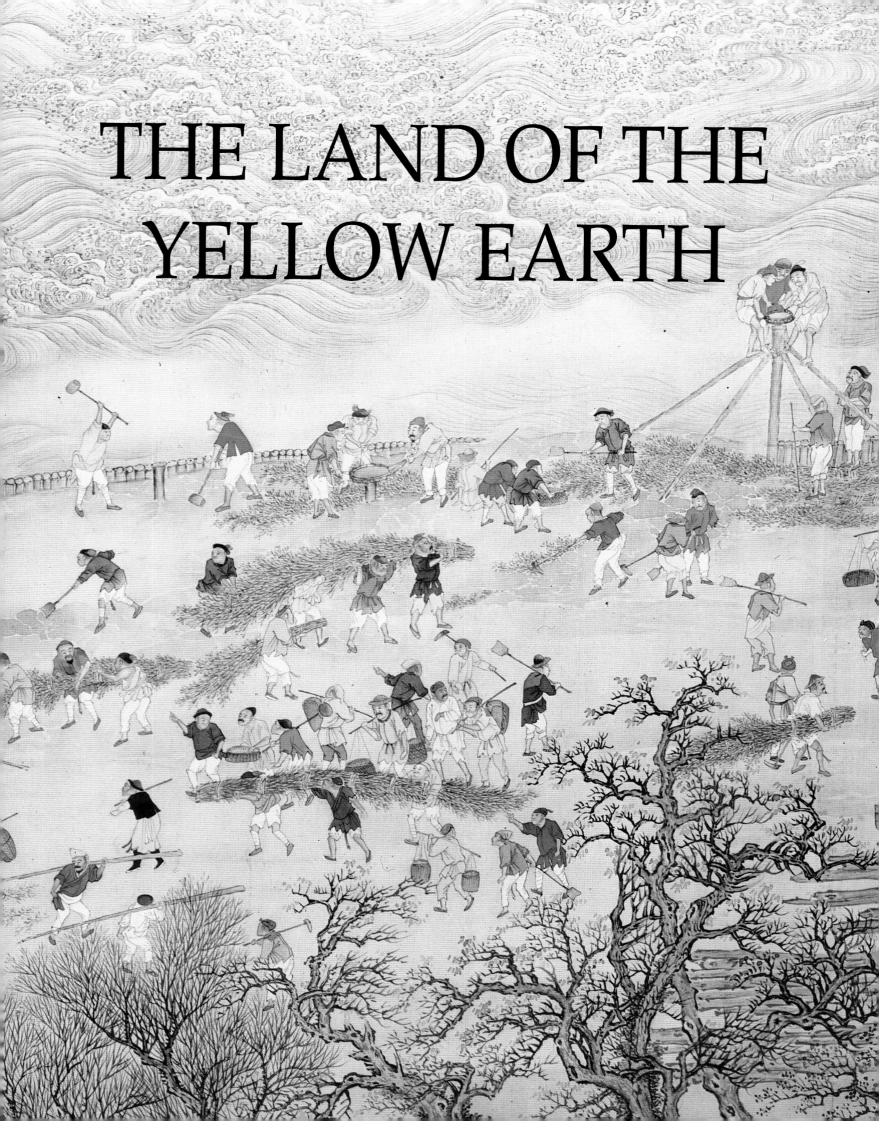

THE LAND OF THE YELLOW EARTH

THE LAND

Rhoads Murphey

THE MODERN NATION OF CHINA SPANS a vast territory particularly notable for its geographic diversity, ranging from the broad, fertile lowlands in the southeast to expansive deserts and mountains in the northwest, from snowy mountain forests in the northeast to subtropical jungle in the southwest. It is often helpful to divide this huge territory into two large zones: Inner China, or China Proper, a fertile and densely populated region lying within Outer China, a large western and northern arc presented by the mountains and deserts of Tibet, Xinjiang, Inner Mongolia, and Manchuria.

Chinese civilization arose in close association with agriculture and formed its major centers in the areas where agriculture was most productive. This left out most of the outer areas that were mountainous, cold, and dry, and underlined the attractions of the river valleys and flood plains: fertile alluvial soil, possibilities for irrigation, and a generally warm climate with long growing seasons and adequate rainfall. In addition, the rivers enabled easy and low-cost movement of people and goods by early-developed water transport or along the natural routes provided by valleys and flood plains. Even today the densest areas of population still coincide with the rivers and their deltas, where

agricultural advantages are maximized.

China is underlain by a floor of very ancient and hence highly metamorphosed rock, some of which has been exposed by weathering in the north and in Inner Mongolia. The most dramatic part of the landscape is, however, the great Tibetan massif and its surrounding ranges which are the highest in the world. They include the peak called Everest by Westerners and Zhumulangma (Qomolangma) by the Chinese, which is over 29,000 feet (nearly 10,000 m) high. It lies along the rather arbitrary border between Tibet and Nepal which attempts to follow the highest ridge line of the Himalayas along the southern edge of the Tibetan plateau. The plateau averages well over 10,000 feet (3,500 m) above sea level but is considerably lower than the ranges that form a rim around the plateau: the Karakorum and Pamirs curving around from the Himalayas at the western end, and the Kunlun along the northern edge. Most of Tibet is an alpine desert, too high, too cold, and too dry for farming except in a few lowland pockets, such as those around Lhasa, the capital. The dominant form of land-use is thus pastoral nomadism based on the yak, a long-haired bovine suited only to high altitudes and hardy enough to survive bitter cold and sparse forage. North of

OPPOSITE: By intensive cropping China manages to sustain more than one billion people — almost a quarter of the world's population — on less than one tenth of the planet's arable land.
LEO MEIER/AUSTRALIAN PICTURE LIBRARY

ABOVE: The Karakorum range forms a natural border between China and northern Pakistan and includes some of the world's highest mountains.
JULIA WATERLOW/TRIP EYE UBIQUITOUS

PREVIOUS PAGE: This section of a seventeenth-century scroll illustrates the massive earthworks that were necessary to build and maintain the dykes to stop the Huang (Yellow) River from breaking its banks.
MUSEE GUIMET, PARIS (CLICHE MUSEES NATIONAUX)

Tibet the Tarim Desert of Xinjiang lies in the basin between the Kunlun and the Tian Shan range along Tibet's northern border. The desert is even more inhospitable to agriculture than Tibet, except for a few scattered oases where streams drop down from the basin's surrounding mountains before they lose themselves in the desert sands. North of the Tian Shan the region of Dzungaria is far better watered, enough to sustain the Ili River and to support extensive pasturage as well as some irrigated agriculture. To match the dramatic uplift of Tibet, Xinjiang includes the Turfan Depression, which is over 500 feet (nearly 200 m) below sea level.

The heart of China is its three great river valleys and plains: the Huang in the north, the Yangzi occupying most of central China, and the Xi (West) in the south. The first two rise within a few miles of each other on the eastern slopes of the Tibetan plateau, but soon diverge. The Xi is a much shorter stream rising in the confused mountain mass of southwest China and entering the sea near Guangzhou (Canton). It was in these valleys and their flood plains in north, central, and south China that China's early civilizations first emerged, and over the succeeding millennia matured into a distinctive culture. With the coming of empire under the Qin (221–207 BC) and Han (206 BC–AD 220) dynasties the Chinese state reached out to conquer first Xinjiang (Chinese Turkestan) and subsequently Inner Mongolia, southern Manchuria, and Tibet, although these conquests fell away from Chinese control after the fall of the Han and were reconquered only under the Qing dynasty (1644–1911). Manchuria was their home base, and as an originally pastoral tribe they were the longest lasting non-Chinese group to rule the whole empire, the other being the Mongols whose control of China lasted less than a century. Together these outer regions make up more than half the area of the modern state, but except for Inner Mongolia and Manchuria they are still inhabited largely by non-Chinese people (Uighur, Khirghis, and Tibetan, for example) and in any case their population totals remain a small fraction of China Proper's.

ABOVE: *Stock graze on the high plains flanking the road from Lhasa south to Gyangze in Tibet or the Xizang Autonomous Region.* MIKE LANGFORD/AUSCAPE

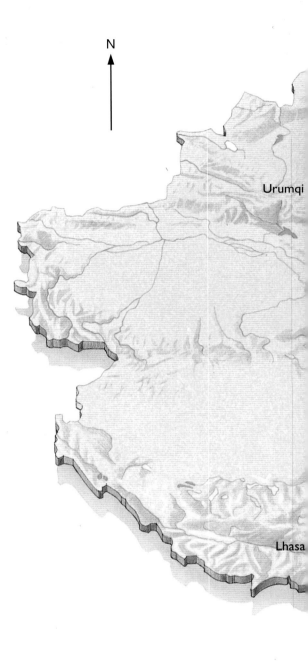

N

Urumqi

Lhasa

380 miles
610 km

CHINA'S TOPOGRAPHY

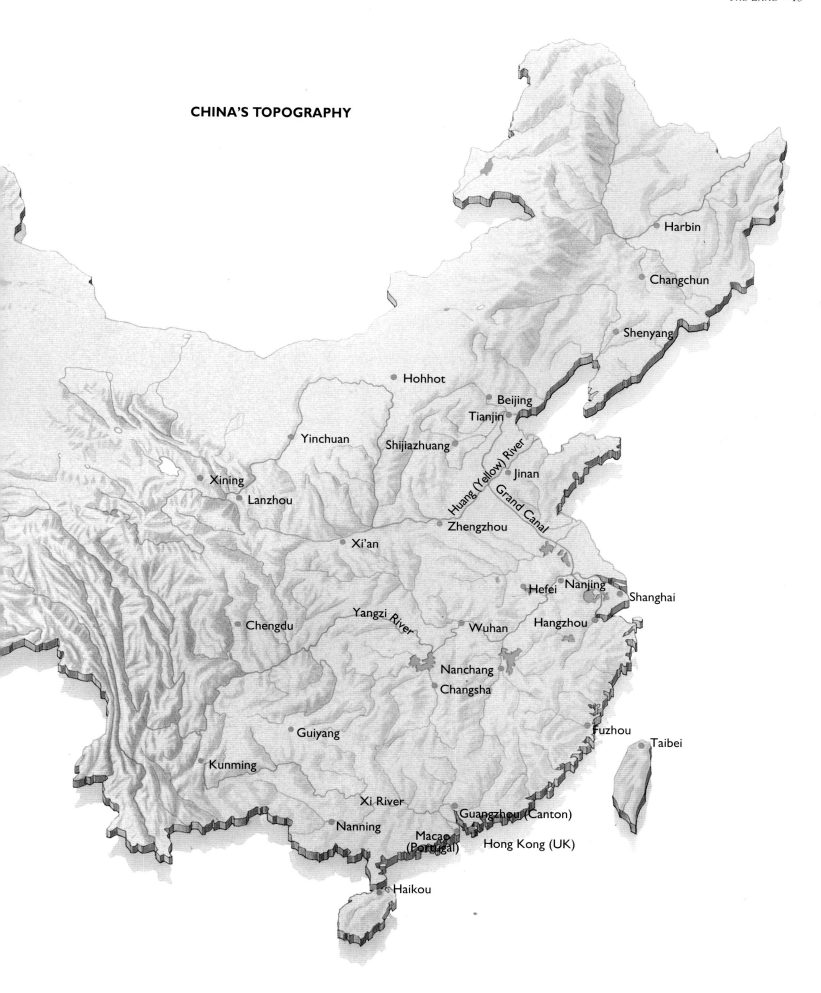

ABOVE: *One of the major bridges spanning the Huang (Yellow) River near Lanzhou in the western province of Gansu.* PETER EASTWAY

BELOW: *Procession of donkey carts in the lee of the Flaming Mountains, a ridge of heavily eroded sandstone which extends across the northern edge of the Turpan depression in Xinjiang Uygur Autonomous Region where China's highest temperatures are frequently recorded.* CHINA PHOTO LIBRARY LTD

East of Xinjiang, along the northern edge of China Proper, lies the vast steppe of Mongolia, traditionally divided by the Gobi Desert into better watered Inner Mongolia to the south, and Outer Mongolia to the north. Much of Inner Mongolia is a long-grass steppe ideally suited to grazing. Traditionally, it served as the basis for pastoral nomadism based on flocks of sheep and goats, but most of the area is now farmed, especially where irrigation is available from wells and canals. Inner Mongolia has been under Chinese domination since the collapse of the Mongol empire of Chinggis and Khubilai Khan in the fourteenth century. Since the advent of railroads, dams, and power-driven pumps in the late nineteenth century, Chinese farmers have become the great majority of the population and now outnumber Mongols by more than ten to one. What grazing economy remains is no longer nomadic but commercial, feeding its animal products into the huge Chinese market. The same long-run trends have more recently become clear in independent Outer Mongolia, although it is generally much drier and offers only limited agricultural potential. Taken together, Inner and Outer Mongolia (the latter known since 1921 as the Mongolian Peoples' Republic) are about the size of the whole of Europe west of Russia. East of Mongolia, across the line of the Great Hinggan Mountains lies the region known to Westerners as Manchuria (Country of the Manchus) but in China simply as the Northeast. Its northern and eastern parts, framed as they are by mountain barriers, are marginally too dry for farming, and bitterly cold in winter. Roughly the southern half, especially the valley of the Liao River, is milder and better watered; its fertile alluvial soils have been intensively cultivated since at least Han times, although, like north China, it suffers from periodic drought. A low saddle of hills divides the Liao drainage of the south from the Amur drainage of the north. The Amur River forms the boundary between China and Russia; its tributaries the Songhua (Sungari) and Ussuri drain roughly the northern half of Manchuria.

Southern Manchuria is linked to north China by a narrow coastal plain known as Shanhaiguan (Mountain Sea Gate), between the southern extension of the Da Hinggan Ling (Great Hinggan Mountains) and the sea. This plain was the route of successive invasions and of the mass migration of Chinese since the latter part of the nineteenth century into Manchuria. This migration welded Manchuria firmly into the Chinese polity despite first Russian and then Japanese domination

(until 1945). Manchuria proved to be richly endowed with coal, iron ore, and petroleum and its rivers had hydroelectric potential. These resources came to support the largest single industrial complex in Asia, centered especially in the Mukden (Shenyang) area. Commercialized agriculture also boomed in Manchuria, generating a surplus of wheat and soybeans for export after 1949 to periodically food-deficient north China. The border with Korea on the east is marked along the boundary line by the Yalu River and also by the Changbai shan (Long White [snowy] Mountains), which support one of the few remaining forest stands in China.

China Proper still includes most of the agricultural land, the majority of the Chinese people, and the roots and body of Chinese civilization. Most of north China is drained by the Huang River, running north in a great loop through the steppe-desert of the northwest, into the Ordos Desert of Inner Mongolia, and finally down across the semiarid north China plain to the sea. Much of eastern north China is in effect the flood plain of the Huang, which has entered the sea both north and south of the Shandong peninsula at different times in the past and is still extending the coastline; in relatively recent geologic times, Shandong was an island in the Yellow Sea. The high silt content of the Huang, great seasonal fluctuations in its volume, and recurrent changes of its course (all typical of arid-climate rivers) severely limit navigability and have led to disastrous floods, earning it the sobriquet "China's Sorrow." Natural and artificial levees or dykes along much of the river's lower course have prevented the regular

ABOVE: *The Yangzi divides the mountains that ring the Red Basin of Sichuan in a series of deep and steep-sided gorges.*
CHINA PHOTO LIBRARY LTD

release of silt, with the result that in many places the river's bed lies above the level of the surrounding plain. The ultimate escape of pent-up floodwaters through breaches in the dykes has drowned both people and land over extensive areas. Silting has also damaged or ruined countless irrigation works, but silt deposits, spread widely over the plain, have helped to make this China's most fertile major agricultural area and its largest single cluster of dense population. The river's course has seldom been constant for more than a century, so its delta and flood plain are very widespread.

Of the three river systems that form the heart of China Proper, the Yangzi is by far the most important. About half of China's people (about 600 million) live in its basin, which includes the most productive half of the country, and its delta, from Nanjing to the sea, is especially densely settled.

LEFT: *At the Gezhou hydro-electric plant in Hubei province below the Yangzi gorges, twelve turbines provide electricity for China's central provinces.*
ROBERT E. MUROWCHICK

The river's usefulness for transport is greatly increased by the navigable tributaries that enter it from both north and south in an alternating pattern, each draining its own productive area. This river pattern plus the natural reservoir provided by Dongting and Boyang lakes in the central Yangzi basin, has helped to reduce flooding on the Yangzi by feeding peak flows into it at different times. With the use of the tributaries, much of the trade of north, south, and central China moves interregionally on the Yangzi system. The Yangzi is navigable for ocean-going ships as far as Wuhan, 630 miles (1,010 km) from the sea, during most of the year. Steamships, launches, and motorized junks use about 20,000 miles (32,000 km) of waterways in the basin. The physical head of ocean navigation (beyond which deep-draft ships cannot go) is at Yichang at the downstream entrance to the famous Yangzi gorges where the river has cut a deep and steep-sided gorge through the mountains that ring the Red Basin of Sichuan. A huge dam, long planned at Yichang but not yet built, would raise the water level enough to cover the many rapids and rocks in and beyond the gorges and permit deep-draft shipping to reach Chongqing or beyond.

The Yangzi is not immune to disastrous flooding — as was shown in 1931, 1954, and 1984 — and the water level often rises 200 feet (60 m) or more at Chongqing, and over 100 feet (30 m) even at Wuhan between winter and when the rains come and the snow melts (from its upper reaches) in spring and early summer. As deforestation has spread in the Yangzi basin, at an accelerating rate since 1949, erosion, silting, and hence flooding have greatly increased. Until about 1960 the river was clear green in winter until the spring floods, but thereafter mud and silt washed into it from denuded slopes left it muddy year round. However, the Yangzi is not as heavily silt laden as the Huang, whose silt content has often reached 40 percent.

The Yangzi delta (the triangle bounded by Nanjing, Hangzhou, and Shanghai) too

has continued to grow seaward as the river drops its silt load with the fall in its velocity over this flat plain. A huge bar off the river's mouth requires continual dredging, and the estuary itself contains many shoal areas. But the delta as a whole is very fertile and is intensively cultivated. It is China's most densely settled area of comparable size. The delta landscape is covered with an intricate pattern of navigable waterways, most of them artificial or artificially deepened, linking every village and town by water transport. This has aided the growth of commerce and its chief centers at Suzhou, Shanghai, and Hangzhou, making the delta for many centuries China's major commercialized and urbanized area. Shanghai, near the river's mouth, remains the country's largest city (urban area population about 8 million) and major port, serving the world's most populous hinterland in the Yangzi basin.

The Xi River in the south, with its mouth below Guangzhou, is a much lesser stream and its watershed is restricted by the high-relief characteristic of south China. It also lacks major tributaries on the scale of the Yangzi, and its basin, much of it mountainous, is far less productive. But as the largest river of south China it is heavily used for transport in its navigable lower half. The Xi has also built a delta in the Guangzhou area that, though smaller than the Yangzi delta, rivals its productivity and population density. Guangzhou itself, in combination with nearby Hong Kong as its outport, is the dominant port for south China as a whole.

China has often been divided into the mountainous south and the more level north, but topographic distinctions are also clear between east and west. The north China plain reaches westward from the sea less than 400 miles (640 km) for the most part, and beyond are the rugged uplands of the northwest. In central and south China there are only occasional breaks in the jumbled sea of mountains west of the Wuhan area, especially south of the Yangzi drainage, while to the east are extensive lowlands. South China as a whole is a land of mountains, which does contrast sharply with the brown level plains of the north. Well-defined mountain ranges are few in China Proper, but where they occur their effects are pronounced.

BELOW: The Yangzi River and a string of lakes provide the water supply which supports intense agriculture and doubles as a transport network in the coastal province of Jiangsu.
WU YIU BO/CHINA TOURISM PHOTO LIBRARY

BELOW: Intense farming continues in spite of heavy erosion near Linxia in the western province of Gansu. In one reforestation program in this region, the denuded hills have been dug with catchment basins to capture the rain and nourish young trees.
PETER EASTWAY

CLIMATE

The most important part of China's physical framework is probably climate: there is an overriding contrast between the dry north and the wet south and a similar west–east distinction. The source of most of the country's rain is the monsoon of spring and summer, but it weakens both northward and westward, especially as mountains hamper its passage from the sea. North China as a whole has cold, dry winters and hot summers with periodic drought when the monsoon rains fail or are delayed.

ABOVE: The climate in the northeast is harsh, with oppressively hot summers and long, freezing winters heralded by dehydrating autumn winds.
CHINA PHOTO LIBRARY LTD

Farther from the sea, in the northwest, semiaridity merges with desert conditions, as it does in northwestern Manchuria. Variation in rainfall from year to year is much greater away from the sea, and in the northwest rainfall varies by up to 40 percent from one year to another. For north China as a whole, roughly one year in three produces less than adequate rainfall, with severe drought one year in ten; both inadequate rainfall and drought are most pronounced west of Zhengzhou.

Roughly along the line of the Qinling and the Huai River to the east, the drought-prone north — with an annual rainfall of only about 20 inches (508 mm) — merges with the green, warm, humid, hilly south, which receives over 40 inches (1,016 mm) of more reliable rain a year. South China pays for its ample rainfall (which reaches over 80 inches/2,032 mm from Guangzhou south) with soils that are heavily leached outside the alluvial areas. This process is hastened by the higher temperatures, so that heavy fertilization is necessary. However, milder winters and longer growing seasons mean that the south grows two or even three crops a year. Rice takes the place of the drought-tolerant wheat, millet, and sorghums of the north, but it is supplemented by beans, vegetables, maize, mulberry (for silkworms), and cotton. Because the southwest (the provinces of Yunnan and Guizhou) is more mountainous and farther from the sea, it is much drier. Thanks to its moist climate, the south overall has a better vegetation cover so erosion is less of a problem than in the deforested

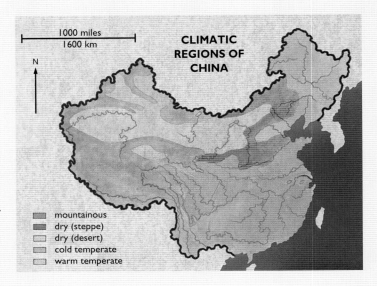

CLIMATIC REGIONS OF CHINA

1000 miles
1600 km

N

- mountainous
- dry (steppe)
- dry (desert)
- cold temperate
- warm temperate

north. However, erosion has increased greatly in the last few centuries as the once luxuriant forests of the south have been cut, a process that still continues.

BELOW: The mountain ranges near Guilin in Guangxi Autonomous Region are reminiscent of many Chinese landscape paintings — steep camel-hump hills of grey limestone dropping away to fertile valleys.
HARALD SUND/THE IMAGE BANK

The Qinling range running roughly east-west from southeastern Gansu province to central Henan marks a sharp physical and cultural line between the dry, brown plain of the north and the green hills of the south. The Qinling contributes to the agricultural productivity of the Red Basin of Sichuan by shielding it from the cold winter winds that sweep across the plain to the north. Truly level land is scarce in Sichuan, but many slopes are gentle enough for terracing.

The north–south contrast is re-emphasized by the change in the nature of the coastline at about Hangzhou, just south of the mouth of the Yangzi. North of Hangzhou Bay is a long sandy coastline with shallow water and few good harbors except for the rocky peninsula of Shandong. To the south is a rocky coast where mountains come down to the sea and have in effect been drowned by a rising sea level as the coastline has tilted (during the past million years) on both sides of the Hangzhou fulcrum. South China, with its highly indented coast, has almost endless natural harbors including Fuzhou (Foochow), Xiamen (Amoy), and Shantou (Swatou), though Guangzhou, some 50 miles (80 km) inland, beyond the head of the Xi estuary, is small and troubled with silting.

From at least the time of the Tang dynasty, southeastern China has been the country's maritime region, with extensive coastal and overseas shipping and numerous port cities dominated by ocean commerce. This was also for many

centuries the chief base of extensive piracy. Pirates sheltered in the countless smaller harbors on this mountainous coast where they could conceal themselves from government forces, build ships with the timber from the forested mountains, and plunder a golden stream of waterborne trade passing just off the coast. It was here too, in these southern harbors, that the Ming dynasty admiral Zheng He built and manned his huge fleets of oceangoing ships, which in seven successive expeditions in the early part of the fifteenth century explored Southeast Asia and India and voyaged as far as the Red Sea and the coast of Africa (see page 157 for more information on Zheng He).

ABOVE: Hong Kong, with its deep and spacious island-shielded harbor at the seaward end of the Xi estuary, is China's premier deep-water port and serves as an entrepôt for eastern China as a whole.
IAN LLOYD/WL/AUSTRALIAN PICTURE LIBRARY

LEFT: The face of agriculture has changed little in centuries. The checkered pattern of the paddies, the plough yoked to the buffalo, and intense manual labor have characterized rice production since the beginning of the Song dynasty, when southern China took over as the nation's major cereal producer.
SALLY & RICHARD GREENHILL

LOESS AND THE HUANG (YELLOW) RIVER

LEFT: The loess soil is easily worked, and cave dwellings — such as these substantial structures in Shaanxi province — are made by tunneling into the hillsides. WANG MIAO/ CHINA TOURISM PHOTO LIBRARY

BELOW: Loess, the deep layer of limestone silt that covers much of northern China, is fertile and provides an easy base for agriculture. Attempts to stabilize it include terracing, such as on these hillsides in Shanxi province. SALLY & RICHARD GREENHILL

North China is sometimes called the "Land of the Yellow Earth," because of the yellowish color of the deep layer of fine limestone silt called loess that covers most of it. The river that runs through it and drains most of north China has acquired the same color and so is called the Huang (Yellow) River. Yellow was often designated the imperial color, and a (now superseded) account of the origins of Chinese civilization referred to the Chinese as "Children of the Yellow Earth," alluding to their supposed origins in the loess country, not their skin color. Although the largest amount of early evidence of the rise of Chinese civilization (settled agriculture, metals, writing, and walled cities) and the creation of the first states (followed by the first unified empire that included most of the present day territory of China) comes from north China, more recent evidence brought to light since the 1950s suggests equally early origins of civilization in central and south China, well beyond the Land of the Yellow Earth. However, the term is still used by some, and it is certainly true that the first authenticated dynasty (the Shang, c. 1600–c.1050 BC) and the first empires (Qin, Han, and Tang, 221 BC–AD 907) originated in north China and that it remained China's dominant area economically, politically, culturally, and demographically until the latter part of the Tang dynasty, about the ninth century AD.

It is also true that the loess offered an easy base for agricultural beginnings, and for the steep rise in productivity from about the fourth century BC which provided the support for empire. Its highly fertile alluvial mix, calcareous nature, and easy workability

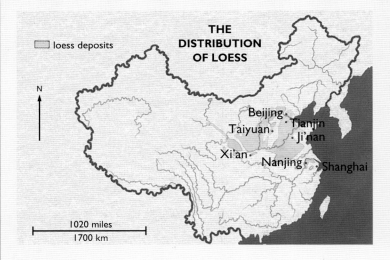

THE DISTRIBUTION OF LOESS

loess deposits

N

Beijing
Taiyuan · Tianjin
· Ji'nan
Xi'an ·
Nanjing · Shanghai

1020 miles
1700 km

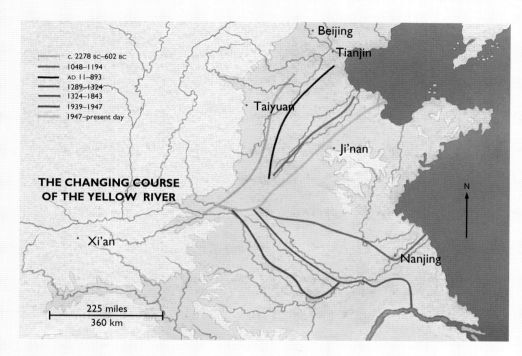

THE CHANGING COURSE
OF THE YELLOW RIVER

c. 2278 BC–602 BC
1048–1194
AD 11–893
1289–1324
1324–1843
1939–1947
1947–present day

225 miles
360 km

very large area to the southeast and east. This would presumably have discouraged forest growth, as did the low rainfall. Over succeeding millennia the Huang and its tributaries became heavily silt laden through massive runoff from the largely unforested slopes in the watershed, acquiring their yellow color. Much of what they carried was redeposited over a wide area in northeastern China and augmented by increasingly frequent flooding of the Huang as its silt load rose with the spread of tree cutting and farming on the hillsides. Most of the eastern part of the north China plain is deeply covered with loess left behind by Huang flooding and course changes as its bed was periodically choked by silt. All of this was fine for agriculture, but the destructive-ness of Huang floods which clearly took place in the centuries before the Han, increased over the centuries until they were largely controlled by a series of dams and siltation basins constructed under the Communist government after 1955.

BELOW: Huang (Yellow) River flooding the loess plateau. The fine alluvium that gives the river its color and name has been redistributed through the millennia due to floods, changes in the river's course, and an increase in cultivation. In recent decades, the destructiveness has been curbed by a series of dams and siltation basins. WANG MIAO/CHINA TOURISM PHOTO LIBRARY

offered few obstacles to early agriculturists, as long as it was given adequate water. North China is climatically marginal and still suffers from periodic drought, but the early concentration of farming in the flood plain of the Huang and its tributaries meant that there was a relatively high water table and ample opportunities for supplemental irrigation. The loess cover is very deep — up to 600 feet (200 m) in some areas and mantling most of the mountain regions — and its loose structure means that fresh nutrients are continually brought to the surface, making it virtually inexhaustible. Its chief disadvantage is that wind and water erode it easily, on even gentle slopes. At the same time it is very easily worked, and dwellings have long been made by tunneling into hillsides to create relatively spacious caves that are warm in winter and cool in summer. The vertical cleavage of the loess makes this practicable, but may expose the occupants to catastrophe in earthquakes, which are regrettably common in the northwest of China.

One further advantage of the loess area for early farmers was its largely treeless nature, or at least the absence of the dense forest cover that retarded development farther south beyond the immediate river valleys and deltas. Goods and people could move freely over the generally level plains of the loess area without forest barriers, making the growth of regional exchange and

specialization much easier. It is thought that the loess was originally deposited (as in north Germany, where the term originated) by strong winds blowing out from the retreating ice sheets that once covered northern Eurasia. The winds picked up finely ground sediments from the glacial outwash plain, and dropped them progressively over a

THE PEOPLE

Rhoads Murphey

THE CHINESE STATE AND EMPIRE AROSE on the flood plain of the Huang (Yellow) River near where it emerges from the mountains of the northwest, in what is now the province of Henan. The Shang dynasty (and probably the still unauthenticated Xia before it) built successive walled capitals in the area between modern Luoyang, Zhengzhou, and Anyang. Anyang, which was the site of the final capital of the Shang, was destroyed by the army of the Zhou in league with a great slave revolt, about 1050 BC. The Zhou had been a Shang feudal dependency entrusted with guarding the western frontier of the Shang domains with their base near modern Xi'an in the valley of the Wei River, a Huang tributary. As the Zhou dynasty, they retained their capital there, moving it in 770 BC to Luoyang at the edge of the north China plain. Thereafter Zhou rule broke up increasingly into a number of warring states, from which the Qin, occupying the same Wei River base as the Zhou had earlier done, emerged victorious to found the first empire in 221 BC. The Qin unified the north and much of the south under a single rule for the first time, but was displaced by the Han dynasty in 206 BC. The Han built a new capital named Chang'an (Long Peace) near the site of the Zhou's capital in the Wei valley and, like

the Zhou, moved to Luoyang in AD 25. They consolidated imperial rule and unification of north and south and extended Chinese rule into southern areas (including what is now northern Vietnam) not conquered by the Qin, or that had fallen away from Chinese control.

The best known project of the Qin was the building of the Great Wall (actually its consolidation from a number of earlier walls) in an effort to limit raids and invasions by a variety of nomadic steppe peoples, most importantly the Xiongnu. The wall was never very effective as a protective barrier — it was too easily infiltrated or bypassed — but it served as a line of demarcation between the steppe, where agriculture was not permanently possible without irrigation, and the better watered areas south of it, where Chinese culture and methods of land-use reigned. However, there have always been wetter and drier than average years in this notoriously variable climatic zone, so there was a wide area of transition between farm and nonfarm cultures, sown and steppe, and Chinese and barbarian (as the Chinese called all nomadic, nonagricultural people). During successive wetter than usual years Chinese farmers often cultivated land farther out into the steppe, where there are the remains of several walls beyond the major line. However, this

ABOVE: *The line of the Great Wall, especially its eastern half, still approximates the annual average rainfall line that determines the distinction between the dry, harsh north and the moist, cultivated south.* JAY FREIS/THE IMAGE BANK

OPPOSITE: *A recent view of Nanjing Road, Shanghai, gives some indication of the population density of urban China. Shanghai is the business and industrial center of the lower Yangzi region.* JON BADER

PROVINCES AND THEIR PRESENT-DAY CAPITALS

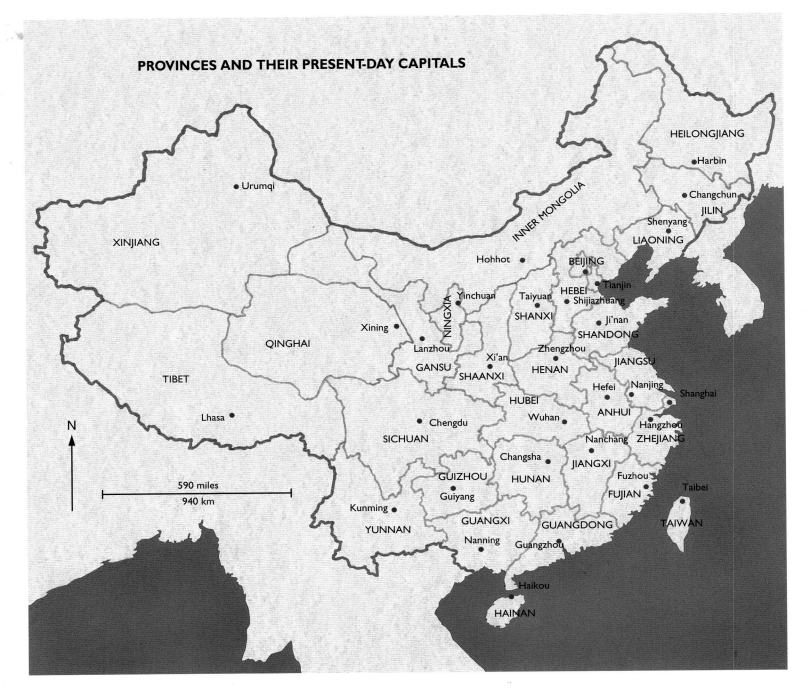

extended cultivation was wiped out and abandoned with the return of the normal drier weather pattern. Han rule collapsed in AD 220, to be followed by over three centuries of political disunity in which the north was controlled by a series of non-Chinese, originally steppe nomads. But at the end of the sixth century an all-China empire (the area within the modern borders of China) was reestablished by the Sui dynasty and reaffirmed by the Tang, which ruled until AD 907 with its capital also at Chang'an.

The impact of the Chinese on their landscape has been perhaps the heaviest in the world, due to the large population, 4,000 years of Chinese agriculture, and massive industrialization since the mid-twentieth century. Already by Shang times the originally sparse tree cover of north China had been heavily cut into, resulting in serious erosion, siltation, and flooding. The development of iron tools, which replaced bronze, beginning in about the sixth century BC, made it easier to clear land for cultivation and so hastened the assault on remaining forests in the north and accelerated the same process in central and south China. With more land producing crops, population rose steeply, from perhaps 5 to 10 million for all of China in Shang times to roughly 60 million under the Han; that in itself added enormously to pressures on the land, as trees were also cut for building and for fuel as well as to clear the land of wild animals. By Tang times most of the north was effectively deforested and much of the original cultivated area was eroded, silted up, or forced out of use by the siltation of the irrigation works that had provided it with essential water.

By the mid-Tang period, the south, below the Qinling mountains and the Huai River, held more than half of the Chinese people. The old northwest, where state and empire had been born, had become economically marginal. South China presented a sharply different environment, and it took time for farming techniques developed in the dry and cold but level and fertile north to be adapted to the wetter, warmer, hillier, more forested, and poor soiled south. The alluvial areas in the immediate river valleys and deltas were of course settled earliest, and it was there, in both the Yangzi and the Xi valleys, that late Neolithic cultures merged with those working metals, producing consistent food surpluses, using writing, and building walled towns or cities. This merging happened probably about as early as in the north, although this is uncertain as archaeological remains are fewer and less well preserved in this more humid and warmer climate. The south probably benefited earlier from the northward diffusion of rice, water buffalo, tropical root crops, chickens, and pigs — all of which were native to Southeast Asia and earlier domesticated there. It is hard to imagine Chinese agriculture without even one of these elements, even though they were understandably slower to reach the north where the dominant early crop, millet, was probably native to north China. Wheat came in later, probably during the Shang period, from its original home in the steppes of southwest Asia, hence a plant well suited to north China and still its principal crop. Rice was grown by the Shang in better watered or irrigated areas, but the chief rice-producing areas of China have always been the Yangzi and Xi valleys and deltas, including the lowlands around Dongting and Boyang Lakes in the central Yangzi basin, now known as "China's rice bowl."

In the political chaos following the fall of the Han dynasty in AD 220, many Chinese fled south, where a series of Chinese states or would-be dynasties vied for power or succeeded one another. Southern areas began to fill up, as more forests were cleared and cultivation spread beyond the immediate river valleys to the gentler slopes. One can trace the southward spread of Chinese settlement through the successive establishment of *xian* (county) capitals, first along the Yangzi, then southward following its major tributaries, and finally into upland areas adjacent to them. By Han times most of south China was still occupied by a great variety of non-Chinese people, some of them still preagriculturists. In the centuries following the Han dynasty these people were conquered, slaughtered, or displaced (although there was doubtless some integration) and their lands that were suitable for Chinese-style wet-rice agriculture, or could be made so, were taken. This process has continued for some 2,000 years and is still going on as Chinese agricultural land-use and timber cutting continue to displace the original inhabitants, whom they so vastly outnumber. Along the edges of the Tibetan massif in mountainous western Yunnan and Sichuan and in much of Guizhou, the

ABOVE: Rice will not grow in stagnant water as the plant requires constant oxygenation to thrive. The advent of the hydraulic pump in the Song dynasty and the arrival of the faster-growing Champa variety from Annam (Vietnam) around the turn of the tenth century marked the modern turning point for rice production.
GUIDO ALBERTO ROSSI/THE IMAGE BANK

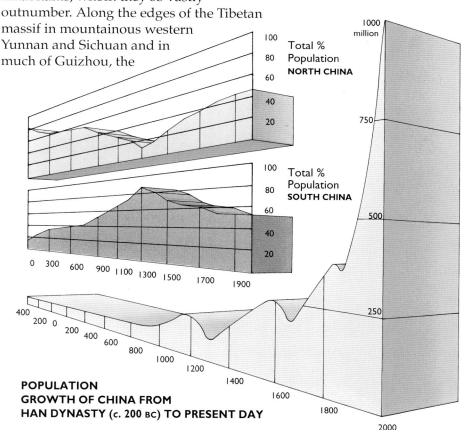

POPULATION GROWTH OF CHINA FROM HAN DYNASTY (c. 200 BC) TO PRESENT DAY

RIGHT: *Flock of ducks on the road in Sichuan province, perhaps destined to end up as the local specialty, duck smoked with tea. Ducks are efficient scavengers, and most paddies support a flock.*
TONY WALTHAM/ROBERT HARDING PICTURE LIBRARY

BELOW: *Horses and camels are used for transport in the western deserts and the north where roads are easily made across the loess plains. These beasts of burden also provide fresh milk and a number of curd or yogurt-based foods. Marco Polo described the Mongols' use of fresh and dried milk products along with a fermented liquor called* kumiss *(from mares) or* kephir *(from camels).*
GUIDO ALBERTO ROSSI/THE IMAGE BANK

original inhabitants are still in the majority, occupying land which has proved to be too steep for Chinese-style farming.

By the end of the eighteenth century, traditional Chinese agriculture had reached a peak of efficiency and of yields, which rose as population increased — the source of both night soil and of intensive labor — but it could increase yields and output further only by the use of new technologies (as used in Europe) such as artificial fertilizers, the development of better strains of crop plants, power-driven pumps, and large dams — none of which

it generated. The traditional system left only marginal place for animals, unlike Europe, since population pressure encouraged only the most productive use of land and discouraged less productive uses for pasture to support animals. Draft animals, primarily water buffalo, were never raised for food and were eaten with a show of reluctance only when they died naturally. Pigs, chickens, and ducks could however exist as scavengers, picking up what they could or living on anything the people would not eat, which was very little (including some "night soil"). Sheep and goats, voracious grazers, were kept largely to the steppe borders and beyond, though horses and camels were used for transport in the north. In the south, goods and people moved almost everywhere by water, and where that failed, by human porter or pack animal on mountain trails that excluded wheeled vehicles.

The Qing dynasty (1644–1911) brought a long period of peace, prosperity, and rising commercialization. With the additional stimulus from the sixteenth century of productive New World crops, especially potatoes and maize, population doubled or tripled, reaching some 430 or 440 million by 1850 and 500 million by the dynasty's end. Agriculture and the much smaller nonfarm parts of the economy lost the ability to increase output further, and as population rose and the imperial government began its long deterioration, China slowly sank from its traditional

TERRACING AND RICE CULTIVATION

The whole system of terracing was a triumph of preindustrial engineering and successive generations of labor built and maintained the terraces in this monsoonal climate and worked the fields thus created, sometimes moving up and down the slope by rope. The warm wet climate was ideal for rice and it yielded more food per acre than any other cereal crop. The Chinese had a strong habitual preference for rice so that when potatoes were introduced from the Americas via the Spanish in the Philippines beginning in the sixteenth century, they were relegated to poor soil, sandy, or unirrigable areas, despite their high calorie yields.

Rice is a demanding crop in its need for water, fertilization, and cultivation, but in the environment of south China it repays the labor-intensive care it is given. Two or even three rice crops are grown per year in many areas south of the Yangzi. Fertility has been maintained, despite this often single-crop system on the same fields of soil leached already by heavy rainfall, primarily by repeated applications of human manure ("night soil" as the Western missionaries called it) which is carefully collected and aged so as to avoid burning the crops. Night soil has made it possible for yields to rise along with the population. Some crop residues and of course animal manures are also given to the soil, and in the deltaic areas mud from streams and canals, enriched by the refuse that has collected there, is regularly dug out and distributed onto the fields.

Paddy fields are finely prepared, often by driving a buffalo through it, to puddle and

BELOW: Every aspect of rice production remains highly labor intensive. In a field in Yunnan province, west of the city of Kunming, a group of workers husks the dry rice. ROBERT E. MUROWCHICK

pulverize the flooded soil to the consistency of thick cream. Puddling also compacts the subsurface and helps the paddy to hold water. Rice was originally a swamp plant, but its yields are increased if the water level in the paddy is slowly raised as the rice gains height,

and then drained dry for the last period before harvest in order to hasten the ripening of grain heads. Each paddy thus requires careful engineering and immense amounts of labor. The irrigation water does bring in with it a variety of soluble minerals which augment fertility, and the strong sun on the water in the paddies promotes the vigorous growth of blue-green algae. When the paddy is drained before harvest, the algae and the small water creatures such as snails, crabs, and small fish decay and boost soil fertility further.

LEFT: Traditional Chinese agriculture is perhaps better described as gardening, with each plant given careful attention and regular weeding to optimize the growing environment. Rice seeds are sown first in a specially prepared bed. Here, in the countryside near Kunming in Yunnan province, they are being transplanted as individual seedlings to the larger field or paddy.
LEO MEIER/AUSTRALIAN PICTURE LIBRARY

BELOW: Beyond the river flood plains and deltas, terracing was used to cultivate the slopes that dominate the southern landscape. In time, much of this area was artificially reconstructed in a series of stepped patches carved out of hillsides, such as these terraces in Guangxi Autonomous Region. Each is more or less level but arranged so that every paddy can be irrigated and subsequently drained in a controlled flow of water from the highest to the lowest.
JULIA WATERLOW/TRIP EYE UBIQUITOUS

ETHNIC MINORITIES AND AUTONOMOUS REGIONS

For centuries, China has been inhabited by a mosaic of different ethnic groups. After 1949 the predominantly Han Communist government officially recognized many of these "national minorities" and even created so-called "Autonomous Regions" for some of the larger groups. However, the hand of the Chinese state and of Chinese culture remains all-powerful. The Chinese, labeled Han people (from the Han dynasty) by the Communist government to distinguish them from the non-Chinese minorities, account for about 95 percent of the total population (although the non-Han proportion is rising as more Hans marry them or claim their status in order to avoid the one-child limit from which they are exempt). It is really only from Han times that one can speak of a Chinese people as a single

Uighurs who cultivated the oases. (Autonomous Areas are usually smaller than Autonomous Regions.) Inner Mongolia, despite its over-whelming preponderance of Chinese settlement after the late nineteenth century, formed another Autonomous Area, but as with the Autonomous Regions in parts of the mountainous south, this was more window dressing than political or cultural reality.

RIGHT: "Yunnan" means "south of the clouds," a poetic description for this ethnically-mixed province which, until migration was encouraged post-1949, was mainly non-Han. Here, in the village of Dali, Bai women sell baskets at market. CHRISTINA DODWELL/HUTCHISON LIBRARY

BELOW: An idealized poster in Kunming, the capital of Yunnan province, shows China's various ethnic groups united under the Chinese Government. ROBERT E MUROWCHICK

cultural unit: before then what became China with the Qin conquest (where the name China probably comes from) was occupied by a number of separate cultures (quite apart from the aboriginal inhabitants of the hilly south), speaking different languages (such as the ancestors of Cantonese and Fujianese) and with separate states, writing systems, and societies. These were forcibly merged in the empire by conquest and over time absorbed in a greater Han Chinese whole. The original differences still show in the south, in areas such as Guangdong and Fujian provinces, in language and other aspects of culture. Tibet, with its wholly different culture and history and its late conquest by the Qing dynasty in the seventeenth and eighteenth centuries, was labeled an "Autonomous Area," as was Xinjiang, which is inhabited by a mix of non-Han people, most importantly the Turkic

RIGHT: The Kirghiz are a traditionally nomadic Turkic people from the former Soviet Union who form part of the non-Han population of the Xinjiang Autonomous Region. NEVADA WIER/THE IMAGE BANK

Miao–Yao	Mongolian
Han	Kazakh
Dai	Uighur
	Tibetan

CHINA'S MAIN ETHNIC GROUPS

ABOVE: *Parade at the opening of the Little Flower Miao Festival, where husbands are chosen.*
ROBERT HARDING PICTURE LIBRARY

RIGHT: *A woman milks a yak in Tibet, or the Xizang Autonomous Region.*
LEO MEIER/AUSTRALIAN PICTURE LIBRARY

ABOVE: *A birth-control poster spreads the message of the national policy of one child per family which was imposed in 1981.* SALLY & RICHARD GREENHILL

position as having the wealthiest and most highly developed economy and technology in the world into mass poverty as well as technological backwardness.

Since 1949 the Communist government has tried to attack these longstanding problems, although progress has been hampered by repeated disastrous policies that were especially damaging to agriculture. Population about doubled between 1949 and 1990, despite the belated imposition of a policy of one child per family in 1981. This is reasonably well enforced in most urban areas but much less so in the countryside where nearly 80 percent of Chinese still live. There is still only a precarious margin between total food supply and total consumers, although famine has largely been eliminated (after disastrous years from 1958 to 1963, when over 30 million Chinese starved to death in the worst famine in world history). Apart from the food-supply problem, agriculture still directly or indirectly employs over half of the work force and thus remains the heart of the economy. There is no substantial new land to be brought under cultivation; land that would pay to farm has long since been pressed into use, and in many areas, such as steeper slopes and the drier margins of the north and northwest, cultivation has been extended well beyond economic rationality. Most of the country is too dry, too steep, too cold, or too high

ABOVE: *Tackling the traffic and air pollution are daily hazards for commuters in Beijing which has been the national capital several times, most recently since 1949. Rapid expansion of industry, including iron and steel, machinery, and textiles has occurred in its recent history.*
PETER SOLNESS/AUSTRALIAN PICTURE LIBRARY

THE SILK ROAD

The Han dynasty had reached out to conquer most of Xinjiang in the second century BC, as part of the military expansion that also absorbed southern Manchuria. In Xinjiang this was to protect China's profitable trade with areas to the west along the famous Silk Road, which was vulnerable to chronic nomadic raiding, usually from Mongolia. The route left China Proper through the desert Gansu Corridor along the edge of the Tibetan massif and following the western extensions of the Great Wall. At Yumen (Jade Gate), the traditional frontier of

ABOVE: The Silk Road became a vital trade route to the West. The Romans called China "Seres," their word for silk, and some authors blamed the drain of gold in exchange for fabric and other Chinese luxuries for the weakening of their empire. TOM NEBBIA/ASPECT PICTURE LIBRARY

BELOW: The ruins of this ancient city of Jiaohe date back to between 1300 and 200 BC. It is on the Silk Road in the Turpan Depression. ANNE RIPPY/THE IMAGE BANK

China, the route diverged, one branch following the northern edge of the Tarim Basin of Xinjiang and its scattered chain of oases, and the other following the similar southern edge. A third route to the north followed the Ili valley of Dzungaria, and a southern route branched off at Hetian (Khotan) in southwestern Xinjiang to cross the Karakorum Pass into Kashmir and India.

Beyond Xinjiang various routes ran west across the dead heart of central Asia, via Middle Eastern trade centers such as Babylon/Ctesiphon, to ports on the eastern shore of the Mediterranean, from where high-value goods such as silk, spices, and lacquer were carried to Rome and elsewhere in the Roman empire. Chinese merchants turned over their goods at Yumen, or at the old imperial capital of Xi'an, to Turkish or

Arab middlemen, a long series of whom transported it to the borders of Syria and the Greco-Roman world. Western buyers were obliged to pay for Chinese goods in gold, since they produced nothing the more highly developed Chinese market wanted. Upper classes clothed themselves in Chinese silks, drank and ate from lacquer cups and bowls, and perfumed themselves with Asian fragrances. The Romans knew little or nothing about China and the Chinese were equally ignorant of Rome, though they heard travelers' tales of a great empire on the shores of a western ocean.

for crops, and only a little over 10 percent is cultivated, despite the pressures caused by high population.

China has large deposits of coal, especially in the north and Manchuria, and has large reserves of oil (primarily in Manchuria, northeastern China and offshore, Sichuan, and Xinjiang), with some surplus for export, although refining capacity is more limited. There are substantial known deposits of iron ore in Manchuria, central China, Hainan Island in the extreme southeast, and Inner Mongolia. Aluminum ores are at least adequate, and there are ample supplies of tin, tungsten, and antimony, of which

China has very large reserves and an export surplus. Hydroelectric potential, especially on the Yangzi system, is immense but is expensive to develop. In general, the resource base is favorable to industrialization, but the needs of a population now well over one billion will strain many aspects of its natural resources and may require expensive imports of some items. China still lags behind technologically in nearly all fields, thanks in part to its self-imposed isolation from the rest of the world from the 1950s to about 1980, and the government still regards foreign ideas and influences as a threat. This has retarded the quality of

industrial output and the increase in the number of appropriate technologists, trained workers, and managers adequate to the scale and urgency of the problem, but some progress has been made.

Since at least Han times China has had more and larger cities than any other part of the world, but the urban proportion of the population approached 10 percent only by the Qing dynasty, and even then probably only in the most highly commercialized and urbanized areas such as the Yangzi and Xi deltas. The Han and Tang capitals at Chang'an each boasted a population of well over a million, as did the Song dynasty (AD 960–1279) capitals of Kaifeng and Hangzhou and the Ming and Qing capitals of Beijing. Administration of the empire rested on a hierarchy of cities

from the imperial capital through provincial and regional urban centers to the *xian* (county) cities, each ringed by imposing walls as a symbol of authority. The Chinese word for city (*cheng*) has also always meant wall. But China remained predominantly agrarian and most people probably never saw a city, living instead in peasant villages linked with each other for trade and marriage arrangements through periodic markets or fairs meeting in different villages in a regular rotation.

Late in the nineteenth century, with the beginnings of industrialization, manufacturing and mining cities began to grow more rapidly, first in Manchuria under Russian and then Japanese management, and subsequently in northeastern China where large coal deposits helped to fuel industrialization. But the largest single industrial center remains the city of Shanghai, dominated by foreigners under the so-called Unequal Treaties from 1843–1949. Shanghai has no local raw materials, but its unmatched water connections via the Yangzi system and the sea, plus its function as the country's leading commercial center, continue to give it cost advantages for assembly and distribution. Skilled labor and technicians, managerial talent, and financial services add to its industrial leadership. Smaller industrial centers also under foreign domination grew up at

ABOVE: *Street scene in the old city of Shanghai, China's leading commercial center.* AUSTRALIAN PICTURE LIBRARY/DAMM-ZEFA

LEFT: *China is well-endowed with coal. Modern technology may have reached the mining industry but not the railways, and China remains the last nation still building steam engines.* PETER CARMICHAEL/ASPECT PICTURE LIBRARY

POLLUTION AND LAND DEGRADATION

LEFT: In industrialized cities such as Beijing the "yellow dragon" often obscures the sun. TRIP/KEITH CARDWELL

RIGHT: The search for timber has gobbled up what little remained of China's forests. PETER CARMICHAEL/ASPECT PICTURE LIBRARY

Pollution and the forced pace of industrialization since 1950, and the heavy if understandable use of coal — most of it unfortunately highly polluting soft coal — plus the relatively crude technological level, have produced perhaps the worst air and water pollution in the world, although procedures to measure and monitor this pollution are still inadequately employed. All urban and many rural water supplies are heavily polluted, including dangerous amounts of heavy metals from industrial effluents. Water supply is totally inadequate in the larger cities and urban air is choked with a variety of mainly industrial pollutants that often obscure the sun. The Chinese call air pollution "yellow dragon," and its pall hangs also over many rural areas where industrialization has spread. There is some environmental legislation, but it is seldom effectively enforced and offending factories usually just pay a fine but are not obliged to clean up their operations. Like most developing (that is, poor) countries, China appears to feel that antipollution measures are for the rich, already fully industrialized countries and would slow China's growth and add to its costs. The Japanese experience with controls imposed in the 1970s makes it clear that this is not so and that the cost is minimal. It is China's people who are paying the price in damage to their health.

Equally serious is the accelerated removal since 1949, in the age of the chain saw and the logging truck, of most of China's remaining forest cover to feed rising demands for wood for new construction, and in rural areas for fuel. The search for timber has gobbled up most of what few forests remained where they had previously been protected by isolation and steep slopes, such as in originally heavily forested Sichuan. Removal of tree cover on slopes is often disastrous and produces the inexorable consequence of soil loss through erosion, siltation, flooding in the stream courses, blocking of irrigation works, and loss of moisture-retention capacity. More and more of China's topsoil is being carried into already silt-laden rivers and dumped into the sea. There have been some efforts at reforestation, especially in the denuded loess highlands of the northwest and along the steppe margins, but far from enough to replace what is still being cut. Reforested areas are raided for wood by local peasants, and new plantings suffer from drought in the absence of adequate watering.

RIGHT: It is hoped that these trees planted on terraces in Shaanxi province will provide windbreaks and stabilize the soil. JULIA WATERLOW/TRIP EYE UBIQUITOUS

BELOW: China's people do what they can to protect themselves from daily exposure to air pollution. P & G BOWATER/THE IMAGE BANK

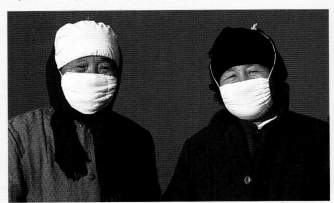

Tianjin (the port of Beijing), Wuhan, Canton, and other treaty ports.

With the expulsion of foreigners and the end of the Unequal Treaties in 1949, the Chinese Communists came to power with a legacy of distrust of all cities: they were such obvious bastions of foreign privilege and ready targets for a peasant-based revolution. For a time there was talk of dismantling Shanghai, the leading treaty port, and redistributing its factories in the underdeveloped hinterland. That did not happen, but there was a new emphasis on promoting urban industrial growth in poorer and more remote areas and in achieving a better national–regional balance, with new industrial centers in cities as distant from the coast as Lanzhou in Gansu, Luoyang in Henan, Kunming in Yunnan, and even Ürümqi in Xinjiang. Shanghai has remained China's largest and most advanced industrial center, followed by Tianjin, another ex–treaty port, but their former dominance has been greatly reduced as new inland centers have grown: Wuhan in the central Yangzi basin, Chongqing in Sichuan, Taiyuan in Shanxi province, and many others. The Manchurian industrial complex originally built up by the Japanese has remained a major element, primarily in the Shenyang area but also at Changchun at the northern end of the Liao valley and Harbin on the

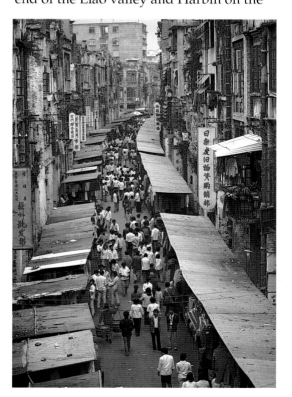

Sungari. Oil found in the 1950s at Daqing in Manchuria supported a large refining center there. Beijing, the capital and second largest city of this huge country, has grown enormously, with its swollen bureaucracy that attempts to regulate everything, in the Communist mode, in a highly centralized system. Beijing has also become a major industrial center, straining the limits of its water supply and producing fearsome pollution, while demolishing most of the remains of its imperial past and expanding outward. However, the inner part of the old capital, called the Forbidden City, has been preserved as a symbol of imperial greatness, and it still has the power to awe those who visit it.

Even though China's industrial growth rate has been rapid since 1949, the major problem will remain producing enough of almost anything to satisfy the needs of an immense and still growing population, especially as its expectation levels rise, an inevitable consequence of economic development everywhere. The bottom quarter or more of the population remains poor by world standard, especially in the more remote and mountainous areas, while at the top there is a rapidly growing group of new rich, encouraged by "market-oriented" policies since about 1987. Government controls (although some people are able to evade them) still restrict migration from countryside to city which is where most people seem clearly to still want to be despite their crowding and despite the anti-urban rhetoric of the revolutionary years. What began as a revolution against cities, capitalism, and "bourgeois values" may end up succumbing to all of them.

LEFT: A street scene in the village of Wuyuan in Jiangxi province. There is a growing gap between urban and rural living standards, an ironic sequel to an originally peasant revolution. TAI CHI YIN/CHINA TOURISM PHOTO LIBRARY

ABOVE: Badly overcrowded and inadequate housing in many Chinese cities is giving way to new construction. In Shekou, new apartment buildings tower over the rapidly disappearing older neighborhoods. MA PO SHIUM/ASPECT PICTURE LIBRARY

LEFT: Street market in the industrial city of Wuzhou on the border between Guangdong and Guangxi provinces. The former garrison town now has thriving silk-textile, chemical, and engineering industries. MIKE LANGFORD/AUSCAPE

A VIEW OF THE PAST

REDISCOVERING THE PAST

Lothar von Falkenhausen

THE PERCEPTION, BY PARTICIPANTS IN Chinese civilization, of continuity with the past has been of tremendous importance in determining how, over the centuries, they chose to structure their lives. Throughout Chinese history the use of political power has been legitimized by reference to precedent. This necessitated the keeping and manipulation of historical records, which gave rise to a rich tradition of historical and philological scholarship.

Written records and objects from earlier epochs were used from early on as tokens bearing the force of tradition, inspiring the scholarly study of ancient artifacts and inscriptions. Traditional antiquarianism (*jinshixue*, literally the "Study of Metal and Stone") has significantly informed the practice of modern field archaeology (*kaoguxue*) in China, introduced from the West during the early twentieth century. Fused somewhat uneasily with preexisting modes of scholarship, archaeology has been a tremendous stimulus to the study of Chinese history.

EARLY STAGES

Collecting and ritually using ancient objects may have been an elite concern as early as the Shang dynasty (*c.* 1600–1050 BC).

Some of the magnificent jade objects found in late Shang tombs at Anyang have been assigned to northeastern Neolithic cultures predating the Shang by more than 1,000 years. Throughout the Bronze Age, paraphernalia of ancestral worship (ritual bronzes, jades, lacquer vessels, and textiles) were handed down within lineages. Even after the founding of the Chinese empire by the First Emperor of Qin in 221 BC, ritual bronzes of previous dynasties continued to be transmitted from dynasty to dynasty as tokens of sovereignty. Accidental finds of ancient bronzes were presented to the court and recorded as auspicious events. During the Han dynasty (206 BC– AD 220) lower ranking individuals also collected antiques.

Archivists and scribes at the dynastic courts collected historical documents and kept chronicles throughout the Zhou dynasty (*c.* 1050–249 BC) and probably earlier; the first narrative accounts of history were composed after the fourth century BC. These are accounts of history that discuss historical events with the intention of identifying precedents for good and bad politics and of correlating such events with cosmological phenomena such as portents. Scholarship on the past, however, began in earnest during the Han dynasty. Sima Qian's (*c.* 145–80 BC)

ABOVE: *Two axes, dated the thirteenth to eleventh century* BC, *made by bronze-using peoples who lived to the north and west of Shang territory.* ROYAL ONTARIO MUSEUM

OPPOSITE: *These storage vessels feature a style of geometric decoration typical of the Banshan and Machang phases (c. 3200–2500* BC*), which flourished along the upper reaches of the Huang (Yellow) River in northwest China during the Late Neolithic period.* WENWU PUBLISHING

PREVIOUS PAGES: *Today's Great Wall of China is actually the consolidation of many walls built over the centuries. Originally made of rammed earth, it was only much later that it was lined with brick.* CHINA PHOTO LIBRARY LTD

The Song imperial court published two catalogs illustrated with woodcuts detailing its rich collections of antiquities: *Kaogutu* ("Illustrations for Enquiry into Antiquity") by Lü Dalin (*c.* 1042–90), and *Bogutulu* ("Pictorial Record Widely Opening up Antiquity"), presented in 1123. These pioneering works accurately record the shapes, ornaments, size measurements, and inscriptions of a large number of bronzes and other antiques, and are all the more valuable because the objects recorded were lost soon afterward due to war. Other Song scholars produced the first specialized studies of inscriptions based in part on these two catalogs.

Although collecting and connoisseurship continued to flourish during subsequent centuries, scholarly catalogs of bronzes and inscriptions did not appear again until the Qing dynasty (1644–1911). Scholars also rigorously studied other categories of ancient objects, such as jades. Qing scholars developed sophisticated methods of critical analysis of literature and used material, non-textual evidence such as musical instruments and weapons, in explaining passages in the classics.

In general, traditional antiquarians concentrated on the study of individual artifacts and took little interest in aspects of ancient culture outside the realm of text-based scholarship. Despite great differences in both approach and goals vis-à-vis modern field archaeology, the present-day impact of antiquarian scholarship remains considerable. For instance, archaeologists still follow — with only minor modifications — the classification of bronzes worked out during Song times and based on the ancient ritual texts.

Shiji ("Records of the Historian") became the first of the "Official Histories," which each successive dynasty continued to compile.

About two centuries after Sima Qian, Xu Shen (*c.* AD 58–147) compiled the dictionary *Shuowen jiezi* ("Discussing the Graphs and Explaining the Characters"), which served later generations as an indispensable key to the early stages of Chinese writing. This work marks the beginning of Chinese epigraphy (the study and interpretation of inscriptions), a discipline that has remained intricately connected with archaeology.

TRADITIONAL ANTIQUARIANISM

Scholarly preoccupation with material objects from the past became one of the sanctioned activities of Confucian literati during the Song dynasty (AD 960–1279). Idealization by later generations of the age of Confucius may explain the strong Song interest in ritual bronzes from the Zhou dynasty, during which Confucius had lived; inscriptions on stone from later periods were also avidly studied.

THE ADVENT OF MODERN ARCHAEOLOGY

The experience accumulated in centuries of epigraphic research was put to the test when, around the turn of the twentieth century, inscribed oracle bones were discovered near Anyang, traditionally regarded as the site of the last capital of the Shang dynasty. A number of studies and catalogs were published, including one by Wang Guowei (1877–1927) proving the essential correctness of the

Shang royal genealogy as given by the Han historian Sima Qian.

This vindication of traditional historiography in the light of a body of indubitably authentic sources was heartening in a time when a new, iconoclastic school of historians led by Gu Jiegang (1893–1979), the self-styled *yigupai* ("Doubters of Antiquity"), had started to doubt the authenticity and historical accuracy of the classical texts. Frustrated with China's political weakness, intellectuals including the *yigupai* critically reevaluated the entirety of the Chinese cultural tradition during the May Fourth movement of 1919. They called for new standards of proof for historical arguments — mere mention in ancient texts was no longer good enough — and realized the value of excavations as a means to open up new perspectives on ancient Chinese history.

It was at this time that the first Chinese scholars trained in modern field archaeology, Li Ji (1896–1979) and Liang Siyong (1904–54), returned to China from their studies at Harvard University. From 1928 onward, they took charge of archaeological research sponsored by the Nationalist government through the Institute of History and Philology (*Lishi Yuyan Yanjiusuo*) of the newly founded Academia Sinica (*Zhongyang Yanjiuyuan*). That year, archaeologists began large-scale excavations of the palaces and tombs of

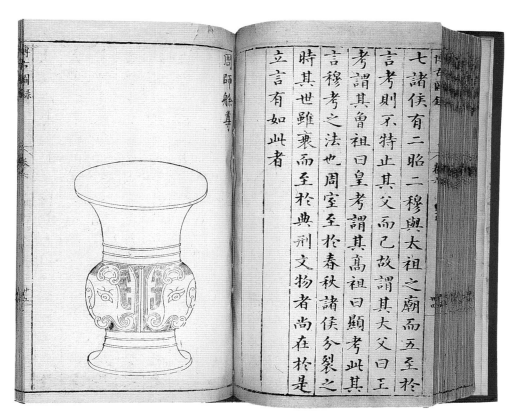

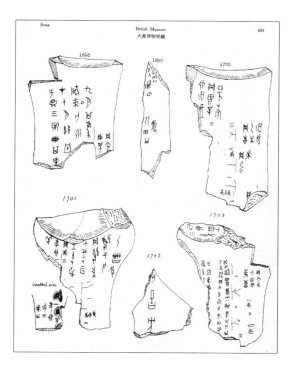

the Shang kings at Anyang, and these continued until the outbreak of the Sino-Japanese War in 1937. Anyang became the training ground for the first generation of Chinese archaeologists.

EARLY DEVELOPMENTS IN PREHISTORIC ARCHAEOLOGY

In China, compared to other cradles of ancient civilizations, archaeological fieldwork undertaken by foreign scholars under the auspices of Imperialist powers such as England, France, Russia, Germany, and Japan has played a minor role, except for border areas. Expeditions from several European countries operated in Chinese Central Asia during the decade or so before World War I, and Japanese archaeologists did pathbreaking work in the northeast of China and in Taiwan before 1945. But except for some activity by Japanese scholars in occupied areas of China during World War II, all serious fieldwork in the core areas of Chinese dynastic civilization has been undertaken under Chinese auspices.

The only foreigner to make a major contribution to field archaeology within China Proper was the Swedish geologist Johan Gunnar Andersson (1874–1960), who became the founder of prehistoric

ABOVE: A spread from the Bogutulu *("Pictorial Record Widely Opening up Antiquity"), a catalog of the Song dynasty court's collection of antiquities illustrated with woodcuts and published in 1123.*
BRITISH LIBRARY, LONDON

LEFT: A page from the catalog, published in 1935, of inscribed oracle bones collected early this century by Samuel Couling and Frank Herring Chalfant. The catalog lists 670 mammal bone pieces, 1,016 turtle plastron fragments, and one antler piece which, although acquired from antique dealers in Wei Xian, Shandong, had probably come from Yinxu, the site of the last capital of the Shang dynasty near Anyang, in Henan province.
BRITISH LIBRARY, LONDON

archaeology in China. In 1920, while in the employ of the Chinese Geological Survey, Andersson stumbled across fossils of *homo erectus* at the cave of Zhoukoudian, southwest of Beijing. For the longterm research at Zhoukoudian, Andersson and the Chinese pioneer scholar Pei Wenzhong (1904–82) secured the cooperation of leading scholars from all over the world. Unfortunately, these fossils, the remains of "Peking Man," were lost during World War II.

Andersson was also the first to identify Neolithic sites in various parts of northern China. Following his 1923 excavations at the site of Yangshao in Henan, which gave its name to the principal Neolithic culture of the region, Andersson conducted explorations in the northwestern provinces. Other archaeologists have criticized Andersson's excavation methods for their crudeness (he used geological rather than archaeological dating methods and had little interest in the cultural context of the objects he

found), and subsequent research has largely overturned his conclusions with regard to the dating and Western derivation of the archaeological cultures he had discovered.

In 1934, the Academia Sinica published the first full-scale archaeological report on a prehistoric site in China: Chengziyai in Shandong, where the late Neolithic Longshan culture was first identified during excavations in 1930 and 1931. Researchers gradually realized that Neolithic cultures in different parts of northern China differed from one another. Sundry discoveries of prehistoric materials, such as stone and metal tools and ceramics, in southern China before World War II compounded this impression of early cultural diversity; but the time was not yet ripe for a comprehensive assessment.

FROM WORLD WAR II TO THE CULTURAL REVOLUTION

After the Nationalist defeat in 1949, the Institute of History and Philology was moved to Taiwan, where Li Ji and his colleagues proceeded to publish the Anyang materials. Since the mid-seventies the institute has also engaged in field research in Taiwan. Methods and theories in Taiwanese archaeology have been heavily influenced by current trends in the United States ever since a joint field project in 1964–66 that was led by the Chinese-born American archaeologist K. C. Chang (born 1931) in association with the National Taiwan University.

On the Chinese mainland, the Communist takeover brought about a thorough reorganization of academic activity. Under fairly generous government sponsorship, archaeology in China underwent tremendous expansion.

The Institute of Archaeology (*Kaogu Yanjiusuo*), part of the new Academy of Sciences (since 1977, of the Academy of Social Sciences), was founded in 1950 to supervise and coordinate archaeological research in the country, and the teaching of archaeology was established at major universities (first at Beijing University in 1952). While the State Bureau of Cultural Relics (placed under the Ministry of Culture) created a nationwide system for protecting archaeological sites and extant monuments, the Institute of Archaeology erected permanent field stations at some particularly important sites: Anyang (where excavations resumed in 1950), the ancient capitals near Xi'an and Luoyang, and the early Bronze Age site of Erlitou.

The rapid pace of construction of roads, factories, and houses all over the country led to the discovery and massive destruction of innumerable archaeological sites, imposing urgent practical demands on the archaeological research agenda. Perhaps wisely, the Institute of Archaeology, headed from 1962–82 by the British-trained Xia Nai (1910–85), concentrated its research efforts on a relatively small number of sites, most of them located in the core

ABOVE: Painted terracotta ping *water vessel of the Yangshao culture.* WENWU PUBLISHING

ABOVE LEFT: Anyang during the fifteenth season of excavation. COURTESY OF THE INSTITUTE OF HISTORY AND PHILOLOGY, ACADEMIA SINICA

FAR LEFT: Portrait of Johann Gunnar Andersson (1874–1960), the Swedish geologist who came across fossils of homo erectus at Zhoukoudian, southwest of Beijing. MUSEUM OF FAR EASTERN ANTIQUITIES, STOCKHOLM, SWEDEN

LEFT: Portrait of Xia Nai (1920–85), the British-trained archaeologist who headed the Chinese Institute of Archaeology from 1962 to 1982. CHINA PICTORIAL PHOTO SERVICE

area of the early dynasties along the Huang (Yellow) River. The initial aim was to establish an archaeological chronology from Neolithic through early imperial times that could serve as the standard for the entire country. Tombs and urban sites from later dynasties were also excavated, extending the scope of archaeology from prehistory to the seventeenth century AD.

During those years, archaeologists spent most of their time ordering and classifying the data with a view to defining the basic geographical and temporal units; as a result, a comprehensive perspective on cultural developments gradually emerged for most parts of China.

A uniform method of typological analysis (classification and dating of objects by physical features and building chronological series on the basis of changes of these features) was established in a number of "model archaeological reports" that were published during the fifties with the intention to set standards for future publications. Adapted by Su Bingqi (born 1909) from the principles propounded in 1903 by the Swedish archaeologist Oscar Montelius, this method continues to be widely used in archaeological research everywhere in China today, in spite of some recent dissatisfaction with its arbitrariness and subjectivity.

As regards the interpretation of the archaeological finds, both the government and archaeologists expected that excavated materials would demonstrate the conformity of Chinese history to the Marxist scheme of social development (primitive society, followed by slave holding society then by feudal society) as applied to China by Guo Moruo (1892–1978), the new regime's

Historical and archaeological research are concerned, respectively, with the textual and the material remains of the past as they exist in the present. In both historical and archaeological research, clarity as to the fundamental questions of who, where, when, and what must precede any discussion of more general ideas and theories. Answering "when" questions is particularly crucial, though it is sometimes difficult given the inevitably fragmentary records available. The twofold task of chronology consists in tracing the accurate sequence of events (relative chronology), and in establishing, as accurately as possible, the actual dates for these events (absolute chronology). In applying their different methodologies to China, historians and archaeologists have worked out parallel chronologies that, though based on different kinds of reasoning, should, ultimately, be mutually reinforcing. Historical chronology is concerned mostly with historical events and personalities, whereas archaeological chronology is based on changes in the appearance of material objects and features.

HISTORICAL CHRONOLOGY

When the great Han historian Sima Qian (c. 145–80 BC) made the first attempt to establish a general chronology of early Chinese history, he found that the chronicles at his disposal diverged irreconcilably before a year in the Western Zhou dynasty corresponding to 841 BC. Although Sima Qian and other historians after him made many attempts to reconstruct the history of earlier periods, the exact reign dates of the Shang and early Western Zhou kings remain under dispute. Recent research, based on Zhou bronze inscriptions and the *Bamboo Annals*, an early chronicle not available to Sima Qian, has narrowed down the date of the end of the Shang to somewhere between 1050 and 1045 BC, over 70 years later than the 1122 BC date that had long been accepted by traditional historians. While research has thrown some light on events during the final two centuries or so of the Shang, the beginnings of that dynasty are still shrouded in darkness.

For periods before the Shang, a reliable historical chronology has not yet been established. Archaeology has so far failed to determine conclusively the historical existence of the Xia, traditionally regarded as the first Chinese dynasty; for the moment, the Xia is regarded as, at best,

THE PROBLEMS OF CHRONOLOGY

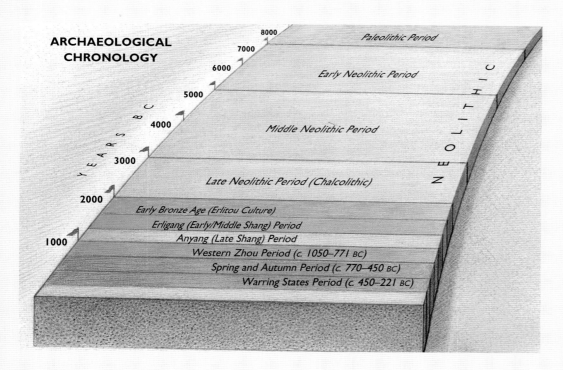

ARCHAEOLOGICAL CHRONOLOGY

YEARS BC

8000
7000
6000
5000
4000
3000
2000
1000

Paleolithic Period

Early Neolithic Period

Middle Neolithic Period

Late Neolithic Period (Chalcolithic)

Early Bronze Age (Erlitou Culture)

Erligang (Early/Middle Shang) Period

Anyang (Late Shang) Period

Western Zhou Period (c. 1050–771 BC)

Spring and Autumn Period (c. 770–450 BC)

Warring States Period (c. 450–221 BC)

NEOLITHIC

hallmarks of the Neolithic (New Stone Age) reflect themselves archaeologically in the presence of village sites, ceramics, and ground-stone tools. The advent of metal use during the Bronze Age is associated with archaeological indications of significant differences between rich and poor, urban settlement, elaborate religious activities, and warfare. However, this is only a rough scheme. Progress in archaeological research has shown that there is rarely if ever a clear dividing line between successive ages, and there may be millennia-long transition periods. Significant differences exist, moreover, between different geographical areas.

The term Iron Age, the final stage of the European prehistoric sequence, is rarely used in Chinese archaeology; for China already entered the light of history during the Bronze Age, which overlaps with the time of the early royal dynasties. From the Shang dynasty onward, it is therefore useful to reconcile archaeological and historical chronologies; Bronze Age material evidence is conventionally assigned to archaeological periods that run roughly parallel to the main historical periods. Due to the availability of tight archaeological sequences in which each stage is well defined by objects, as well as inscribed materials, even more accurate dating is often possible within these periods.

Later archaeological remains are dated by dynastic designations corresponding to those of the historical chronology of imperial China. Long dynasties, such as the Han and Tang, may additionally be subdivided in archaeological periods that are usually defined as corresponding with a number of imperial reigns.

semilegendary. The reign dates assigned to the mythical "Three August Rulers" (*Sanhuang*) and the "Five Thearchs" (*Wudi*) preceding the Xia in Sima Qian's historiographical scheme are patently fictional and useless to archaeology.

Scrupulous record-keeping by historians during later times of Chinese history makes the outlines of historical chronology of China after 841 BC relatively unproblematical. (See pages 46–47.) The Eastern Zhou dynasty (771–249 BC) was subdivided in two main segments, the Spring and Autumn and the Warring States, whose exact dates are subject to differences of opinion, making for some awkward gaps in the sequence. After the foundation of the Chinese empire under the Qin dynasty (221–207 BC), the succession of imperial dynasties continued unbroken until 1911; the only complications are introduced by the periodic division of the country among several dynastic regimes.

ARCHAEOLOGICAL CHRONOLOGY

The date of excavated objects can rarely be pinpointed to a specific year. Archaeologists therefore assign their evidence to periods that are defined by material and stylistic changes. The radiocarbon (C–14) method, which has been widely used in China since the 1950s, can indicate approximate absolute time ranges. Depending on the state of knowledge, the length of archaeological periods may vary from several centuries or even millennia to a span of little more than a decade.

Since the beginnings of the study of prehistory in the nineteenth century, archaeological data have been fitted into a generalized scheme based on the evolution of material culture. Though generated in a European context, such a scheme can be applied to Chinese realities without much difficulty. The Paleolithic (Old Stone Age) runs all the way from the earliest humans to the beginnings of settled life; in the archaeological record, the hunter–gatherer life-style during this long period is characterized mainly by chipped-stone tools. Settled life and agriculture, the main

LEFT: Li Ji (seated on the upper left corner of the wooden box) working in the field at Anyang, where he was responsible for training the first generation of home-taught Chinese archaeologists.

COURTESY OF THE INSTITUTE OF HISTORY AND PHILOLOGY, ACADEMIA SINICA

HISTORICAL CHRONOLOGY

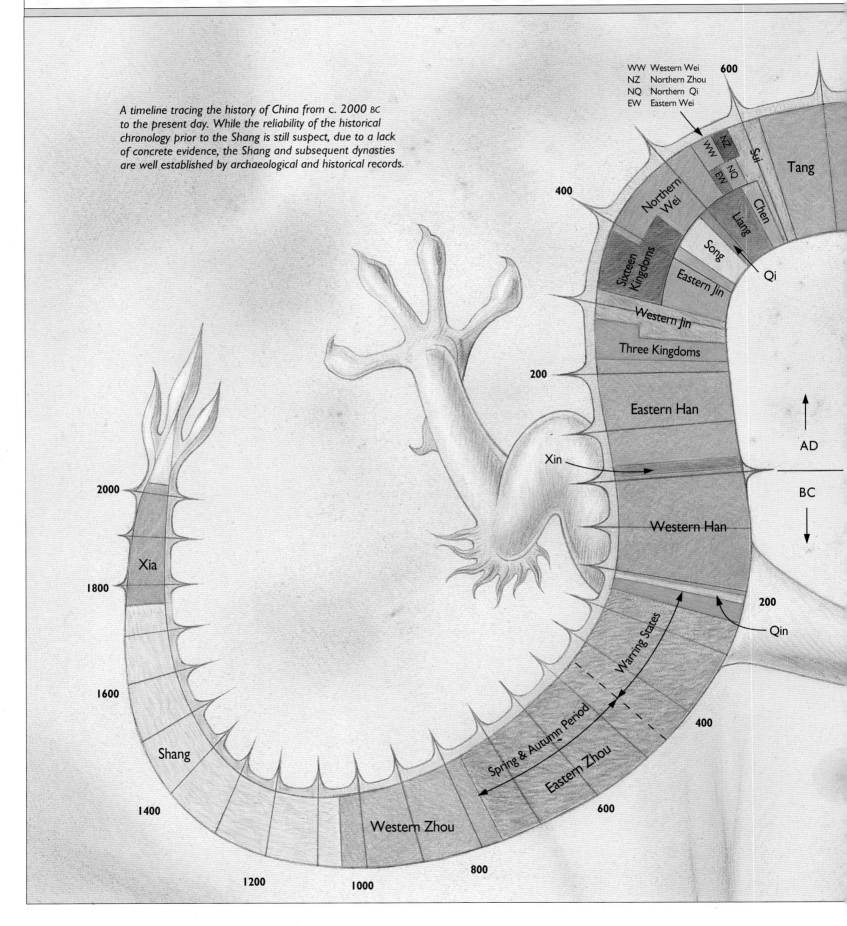

A timeline tracing the history of China from c. 2000 BC
to the present day. While the reliability of the historical
chronology prior to the Shang is still suspect, due to a lack
of concrete evidence, the Shang and subsequent dynasties
are well established by archaeological and historical records.

WW Western Wei
NZ Northern Zhou
NQ Northern Qi
EW Eastern Wei

600

400

200

AD

BC

Tang

Sui

Chen

Liang

Qi

Song

Northern Wei

Eastern Jin

Sixteen Kingdoms

Western Jin

Three Kingdoms

Eastern Han

Xin

Western Han

WW

NZ

EW

NQ

Qin

200

Warring States

400

Spring & Autumn Period

Eastern Zhou

600

800

Western Zhou

1000

1200

1400

Shang

1600

Xia

1800

2000

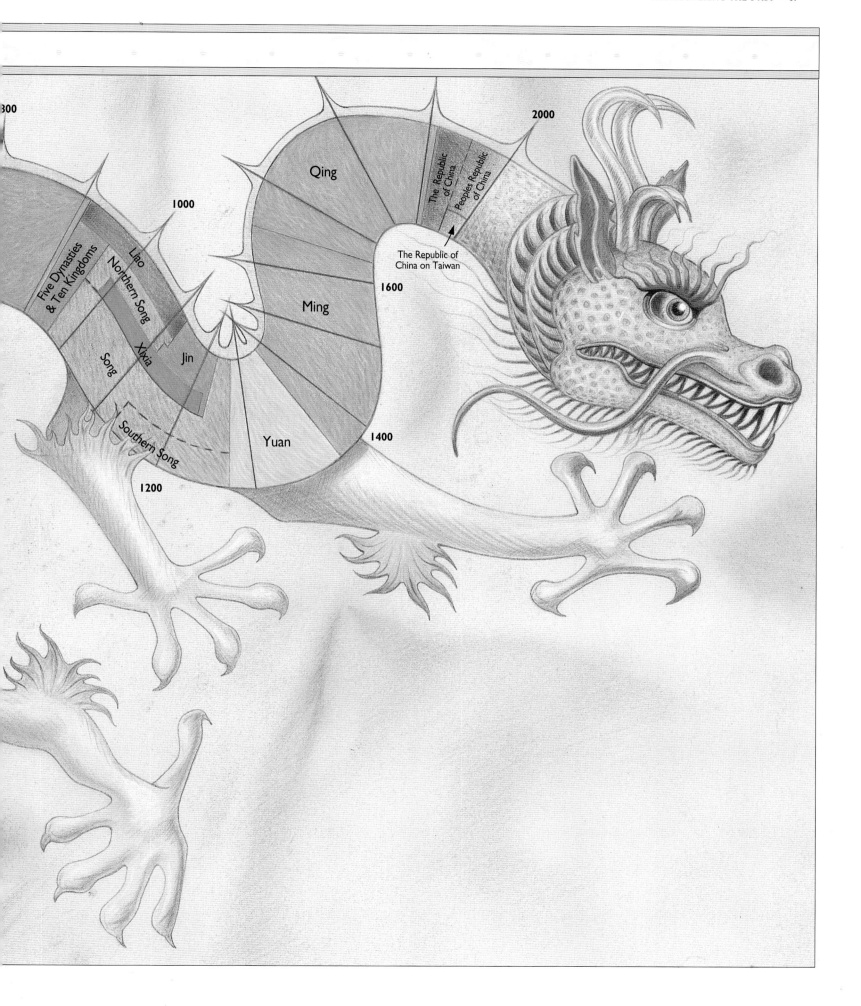

300

2000

1000

Qing

The Republic of China

Peoples Republic of China

The Republic of China on Taiwan

Five Dynasties & Ten Kingdoms

Liao

Northern Song

1600

Ming

Xixia

Jin

Song

Yuan

1400

Southern Song

1200

Minister of Culture. In spite of earnest efforts, especially in the area of prehistory, the search for such archaeological proof has so far yielded results that are ambiguous at best.

FROM THE CULTURAL REVOLUTION TO THE NINETIES

The Cultural Revolution (1966–76) disrupted the progress of Chinese archaeology: museums and research institutions were closed; all preoccupation with traditional culture was declared bourgeois and became a dangerous thing to pursue; the government allocated no resources to the recovery and preservation of archaeological relics; and many ancient buildings and sites were wantonly destroyed by Red Guards. Archaeological journals were, however, allowed to resume publication as early as 1972, years before the normalization of academic life in the country, perhaps because of a new policy of using

archaeological exhibitions to create goodwill in Western countries. The focus of fieldwork came to be directed to the procurement of objects with "exhibition value," a development that was spurred by some particularly spectacular discoveries during the late sixties and seventies. With the growth of tourism, many archaeological sites and museums have been turned into attractions for foreign visitors.

In the course of the administrative decentralization brought about by the economic reforms of the eighties, significant power has been granted to newly founded provincial Institutes of Cultural Relics and Archaeology. This reorganization has led to a fundamental change in archaeology. Previously, under the Maoist regime, archaeological data from everywhere in the country had to be accommodated into a unilinear sequence, similar to that of the most traditional historiography. With the shift in emphasis to the provinces, ancient China has come to be envisaged as a multitude of interlinked but separate regional cultural traditions, each of which had played a distinct role in the genesis of Chinese civilization.

Consequently, in the eighties, scholars have increasingly directed their attention to regional phenomena that had previously been either unknown or regarded as peripheral, such as the spectacular Neolithic cultures of the

LEFT: *One of the large tombs in the vicinity of the Shang capital at Anyang. Tomb number 1 at Wuguancun, excavated in 1950, is remarkable for the number of human victims, who were buried in orderly rows on the second-level ledge surrounding the central coffin chamber.* MACQUITTY COLLECTION/SHANGHAI MUSEUM

BELOW LEFT: *These Tang dynasty, cast-iron oxen were discovered on the edge of the Huang (Yellow) River in Yongji County, Shanxi province after rain washed away a large section of the bank. The waterlogged mud, where they had slowly sunk since their creation between AD 713 and 742, was responsible for their near perfect preservation. When excavations began, archaeologists found six iron pillars which were originally bridge stanchions on the river bank.* AUSTRAL/CAMERA PRESS

BELOW: *Human-headed storage vessel from the Shilingxia phase of the Majiayao culture (around 3000 BC), which flourished along the upper reaches of the Huang (Yellow) River during the Late Neolithic period.* CHINA PICTORIAL PHOTO SERVICE

northeastern and southeastern coastal areas and the regional Bronze Age cultures of Sichuan and the lower Yangzi area. With each province vying to demonstrate its own historical importance, a new, regional kind of centralism has arisen, in which a province arbitrarily defines its own uniform culture under which all archaeological finds are subsumed. Nevertheless, the regional system does far better justice than earlier modes of interpretation to the enormous quantity of new data and allows for a more fine-tuned reconstruction of ancient cultural history.

THE CURRENT OUTLOOK

The recent relaxation of government controls has unfortunately led to the resumption, since *c.* 1987, of illicit looting of archaeological sites at a scale unprecedented at any time of Chinese history. The impact on archaeological fieldwork has been, and continues to be, devastating. The sense of crisis is compounded by drastically diminished government support for archaeology, which in some areas has led to the virtual cessation of fieldwork.

In this situation, Chinese archaeologists, long isolated from the outside world by strict government policy, have started to look to the outside world for help. In what is obviously an attempt to open up new sources of funding, the long-standing regulation barring foreign archaeologists from any fieldwork in China was rescinded in 1991. Chinese archaeologists trained since the Cultural Revolution are taking an increasing interest in modern Western archaeological methods and theories. If joint field projects become a reality, as appears likely, we may hope for significant intellectual cross-fertilization and growth of the field in Western countries, where Chinese archaeology has so far been vastly understudied.

THE BEGINNINGS OF SETTLED LIFE

Christopher Fung

MANY OF THE DISTINCTIVE FEATURES OF modern Chinese civilization first appeared during the prehistoric period before written records began, and developed over thousands of years of cultural change. Archaeologists studying this period have divided it into two large periods; the Paleolithic (literally, the Old Stone Age), which spans the period 1.7 million to 10,000 years ago, and the Neolithic (literally, the New Stone Age) 10,000 to 4,000 years ago. The Paleolithic period covers human evolution up to and including the appearance of modern human beings (*Homo sapiens sapiens*). By the end of the Paleolithic, humans had migrated into all major parts of the globe and had become highly specialized hunters and gatherers. During the following Neolithic period, human groups in China became sedentary villagers, adopted an agricultural lifestyle, and began making pottery. By the end of the Neolithic period, some people were living in highly stratified societies ruled by powerful leaders. By convention, the Neolithic period ends with the introduction of bronze vessels for use in rituals around 2000 BC.

In order to understand China's vast and complex civilization archaeologists are trying to resolve such issues as where the Chinese people came from, when agriculture and village life first began, and

how and why the first kingdoms and complex art developed. Many of these issues are still the subject of intense debate, fueled by dramatic new archaeological finds each year.

For the whole of the prehistoric period, the area covered by what is now modern China was made up of distinct regions each with its own separate identity. Within these regions were many archaeological cultures, groups of ancient communities that archaeologists have identified through similarities in such things as pottery, houses, and the style of burials. Archaeological cultures are generally named after one particular site, either the first site where archaeologists recognized that particular culture, or a particularly famous site. Interaction between different cultures and regions over several thousand years was an important factor in the eventual appearance of the first Chinese states.

AGRICULTURE

The adoption of food production and the appearance of sedentary villages around 7000 BC were important developments in Chinese prehistory. The rural villages that are still a dominant part of the modern Chinese landscape are the direct descendants of these first farming

ABOVE: Polished stone and jade ceremonial axeheads and disks from the Neolithic period, c. 10,000 to 4,000 years ago. ROYAL ONTARIO MUSEUM

OPPOSITE: Statue head from the Goddess Temple at the Hongshan culture archaeological site of Niuheliang, Liaoning province. WENWU PUBLISHING

communities. Prior to the advent of food production, human groups in China were nomadic hunters and gatherers who used microlithic (that is, small chipped stone) tools and moved across the land methodically exploiting different plant and animal resources.

The first evidence for pottery making, which in ancient societies is usually associated with agriculture of some sort, comes from rock shelters in southern China, such as Zengpiyan and Dalongzhang in Guangxi, and Xianrendong in Jiangxi, that date to 10,000–7000 BC. Although these sites contain pottery, most of the animal remains found were of wild animals such as deer, boar, small mammals such as monkeys and rabbits, fish, mollusks, turtles, and crabs, and possibly domestic pigs and cultivated root crops. The actual transition from hunting and gathering to farming probably took place during this period, for which unfortunately few archaeological sites have been discovered. Investigating the exact nature of this transformation will be one of the major tasks facing Chinese archaeology in the future.

By 7000–5000 BC, the first clearly agricultural villages had appeared in north China. Villages such as Laoguantai, Cishan, and Peiligang had several hundred inhabitants who grew crops such as millet, and vegetables such as hemp, oil cabbage, and Chinese cabbage. The villagers ground up plant foods on distinctive footed grinding slabs, and harvested the millet with large sawlike sickles. They also kept domesticated chickens, pigs, and dogs.

In south China during this time, the plants and animals that people domesticated were slightly different and included rice, water chestnuts, pigs, water buffalo, and chickens. The people at Hemudu, an unusually well preserved village in Zhejiang dating from 5500–4000 BC, lived in wooden houses built on stilts above the marshy waters near Hangzhou Bay. Artifacts, such as bone awls, wooden handles, and agricultural hoes, that survived inadvertent burial in the wet mud indicate that the people of Hemudu were skilled woodworkers and bone carvers. The world's earliest known lacquer ware, a red lacquered bowl, was also recovered from this site. Bone weaving tools and wooden artifacts found at Hemudu suggest that many of the most beautiful works of ancient Chinese craftspeople may well have been created in perishable materials such as cloth and wood. It is likely that other groups living in China at this time also practiced similar arts, but due to the generally poor preservation of organic remains at archaeological sites, in most cases these important artworks have not survived.

All of the domestic plants and animals found in these early Neolithic sites had already undergone dramatic evolutionary changes in size and shape, indicating that they were true domesticates rather than species that had been hunted or collected from the wild. This implies that agriculture

PALEOLITHIC SITES IN CHINA

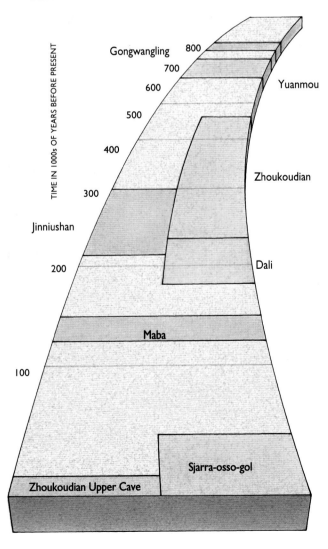

BELOW: Timeline for the Chinese Paleolithic period showing approximate ages for the various sites mentioned in the text.

TIME IN 1000s OF YEARS BEFORE PRESENT

Gongwangling 800
700
600
500
400
300
200
100

Yuanmou
Zhoukoudian
Dali

Jinniushan

Maba

Sjarra-osso-gol

Zhoukoudian Upper Cave

had already been practiced for a significant period before the occupations at these early villages.

However, the presence of food-production systems did not mean that people necessarily stopped hunting and gathering. All Neolithic communities, and even the highly sophisticated agricultural societies of the Bronze Age, continued to hunt wild animals and collect wild plants to supplement their own food production. People living in some areas of China, especially in the northern steppe regions, continued to subsist primarily from hunting and gathering.

Agriculture made settled village life possible. With permanent houses, and stored supplies of grain and other kinds of food, people could stay indefinitely in one area. The possibility of surplus food and goods also paved the way for the second important development in Chinese prehistory, the advent of complex societies.

THE DEVELOPMENT OF COMPLEX SOCIETIES

During the period 5000–1900 BC some of the early village-based communities developed into societies with well-defined rich and poor classes, where ordinary

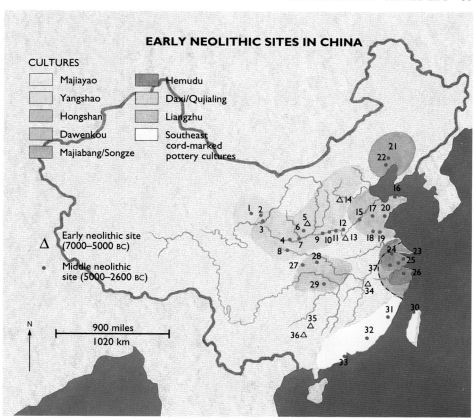

EARLY NEOLITHIC SITES IN CHINA

CULTURES

Majiayao · Hemudu · Yangshao · Daxi/Qujialing · Hongshan · Liangzhu · Dawenkou · Southeast cord-marked pottery cultures · Majiabang/Songze

△ Early neolithic site (7000–5000 BC)

• Middle neolithic site (5000–2600 BC)

ABOVE: Early Neolithic sites: 1. Machang; 2. Banshan; 3. Majiayao; 4. Banpo; 5. Laoguantai; 6. Yuanjunmiao; 7. Jiangzhai; 8. Lijiacun; 9. Miaodigou; 10. Yangshao; 11. Wangwan; 12. Dahecun; 13. Peiligang; 14. Cishan; 15. Yedian; 16. Yantai; 17. Dawenkou; 18. Liulin/Dadunzi; 19. Huating; 20. Donghaiyu; 21. Hongshan; 22. Niuheliang; 23. Songze; 24. Beiyinyangying; 25. Majiabang; 26. Hemudu; 27. Daxi; 28. Guanmiaoshan; 29. Huachenggang; 30. Dapenkeng; 31. Fuguodun; 32. Chao'an; 33. Shenwan; 34. Xianrendong; 35. Zengpiyan; 36. Dalongzhang; 37. Qianshanyang.

NEOLITHIC CULTURES OF CHINA

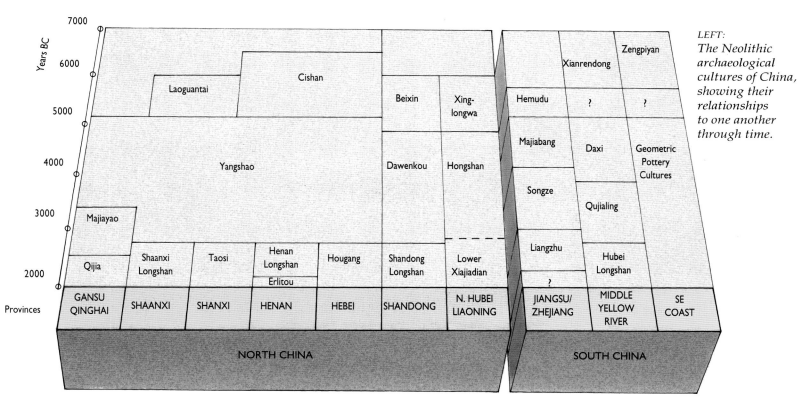

LEFT: The Neolithic archaeological cultures of China, showing their relationships to one another through time.

RIGHT: *Late Neolithic sites:*
1. Liangchengzhen; 2. Chengziyai;
3. Jiangou; 4. Hougang;
5. Wangyoufang; 6. Fanshan/
Yaoshan; 7. Liangzhu; 8. Taosi;
9. Wangwan; 10. Sanliqiao;
11. Kexingzhuang; 12. Qujia;
13. Qinglongquan; 14. Erlitou.

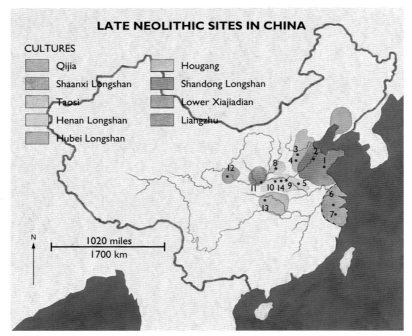

LATE NEOLITHIC SITES IN CHINA

CULTURES

Qijia
Shaanxi Longshan
Taosi
Henan Longshan
Hubei Longshan

Hougang
Shandong Longshan
Lower Xiajiadian
Liangzhu

1020 miles
1700 km

ABOVE: *Carved jade ritual object from the Liangzhu Neolithic culture. The incised depiction of a person in a feathered headdress, riding a supernatural animal, is an example of shamanistic art.*
WENWU PUBLISHING

people were ruled by a relatively small elite group.

Many of the features of complex society in China, including shamanism, jade carving, ceremonial platform structures, elaborate funerary rituals, the use of food and drinking vessels in rituals, and the emergence of elite groups, appear by about 4500 BC. From 3000–2000 BC features that were also important in the Bronze Age, such as warfare, walled towns, bronze metallurgy, divination, and

musical instruments, appeared in embryonic form. The first Bronze Age dynasty, known as the Xia, appeared in central Henan in 1900 BC. This signaled the end of the Neolithic period in north China and the beginning of the dynastic phase of Chinese history.

Early Beginnings
5000–3000 BC
For many years archaeologists believed that Chinese civilization developed in the Central Plains area and subsequently spread to the rest of the country. But as other areas have been increasingly studied, it has become clear that Chinese civilization developed through an interaction of diverse cultures and ideas, as illustrated by a comparison between two of the many north Chinese Neolithic cultures that flourished during the period 5000–3000 BC. Both the Yangshao culture of the Central Plains of Shaanxi and Henan, and the Dawenkou culture of Shandong and northern Jiangsu

RIGHT:
The evolution of Shang dynasty ritual bronze vessels from Neolithic ceramic prototypes.

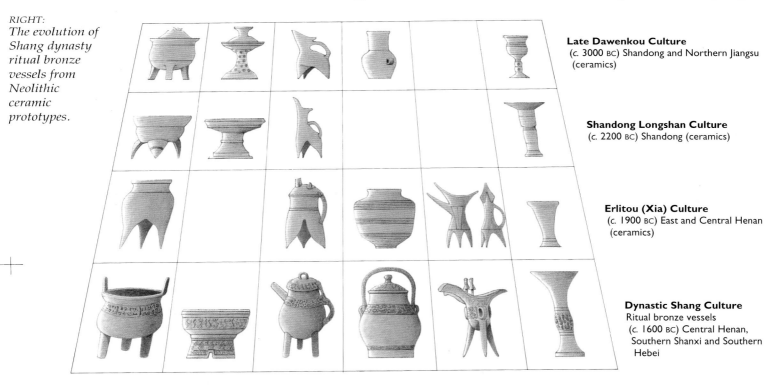

Late Dawenkou Culture
(*c.* 3000 BC) Shandong and Northern Jiangsu (ceramics)

Shandong Longshan Culture
(*c.* 2200 BC) Shandong (ceramics)

Erlitou (Xia) Culture
(*c.* 1900 BC) East and Central Henan (ceramics)

Dynastic Shang Culture
Ritual bronze vessels
(*c.* 1600 BC) Central Henan, Southern Shanxi and Southern Hebei

ding   dou   he   yu   jue   gu
           (rare in bronze)

SHAMANISM

The practice of shamanism underlies traditional Chinese notions of rulership. Shamanism is a form of religion based on the idea of a layered universe. Powerful beings (shamans) can travel from one plane of the universe to another, aided by spirit doubles, animal helpers, or ecstatic trances brought on through meditation, asceticism, dance and music, or hallucinogenic drugs or alcohol. The act of transport or transformation allows shamans to act as curers, spirit mediums, diviners, prophets, or magicians. Forms of shamanism are still practiced in Japan, Korea, and Siberia, and shamanistic beliefs continue to be an important component of many Native American cultural traditions.

Shamanism was practiced in ancient China as far back as the Neolithic period. The shell mosaics in the Yangshao grave at Xishuipo identify the occupant of the grave as a shaman. Examples of X-ray art (an important shamanistic style in which the inner bones of human and animal figures, where the soul is thought to reside, are prominently displayed instead of their outer flesh) adorn certain ceramics and floor paintings from Yangshao sites. The engraved designs on Liangzhu jades have also been interpreted as depictions of shamans riding animal helpers as described by later historical accounts of ancient shamanistic practices. Alcoholic beverages may have been used in the Dawenkou culture to induce shamanic trances. In the late Neolithic period, other aspects of shamanic practice appeared: oracle bones were used for divination in Shandong Longshan sites, and musical instruments were used at Taosi.

The earliest evidence of shamanism was not associated with material wealth, but by the end of the middle Neolithic period, shamanic images appeared on costly jade artifacts in Liangzhu culture, identifying shamanism with the elite class. This association between shamanism and political hierarchy reached its peak with the Shang and Zhou rulers of the Bronze Age whose rule was based on their claim to be the sole beings able to communicate with divine authority.

were agricultural societies made up of many small villages, and both probably had some sort of shamanistic religion. However, differences between the two cultures included ceramic styles and technology, burial rituals, and possibly also the degree of social stratification.

The large Yangshao villages were often surrounded by a ditch that could have been dug as a means of defense against wild animals or possibly human enemies. It also could have functioned as a symbolic divide between the world of the living and the world of the dead, as is suggested by the fact that Yangshao cemeteries are always found outside of the ditch. The villages themselves consisted of groups of semisubterranean round or square houses, the walls and roofs of which were constructed of wooden poles plastered with mud. Inside each house, archaeologists have found hearths for cooking and heating, and wide benches that could have been sleeping platforms.

In many Yangshao villages, such as Banpo and Jiangzhai, large houses are often surrounded by a group of smaller houses. This has led some archaeologists to speculate that the large houses were communal structures or the residences of high-status individuals. However, if there were people of high status in Yangshao culture, they did not display their wealth or position very prominently.

Yangshao burials, which were not generally elaborate, also suggest that differences in status were not great. The graves often contained a small quantity of grave goods such as pottery vessels, jewelry, and tools made of stone, bone, or ceramic, to accompany the deceased. In some cases graves held a single occupant. However, graves containing multiple burials were also common at sites such as Banpo and Yuanjunmiao. One particularly interesting burial comes from the site of Xishuipo in Henan, where the remains of

BELOW LEFT: Painted bowl from the Majiayao culture of Gansu province. The decorative designs are very similar to those found on pots of the neighboring Yangshao culture.
CHINA PICTORIAL PHOTO SERVICE

BELOW CENTER: Spouted effigy vessel of a pig or dog, found in a grave of the Dawenkou culture, in Shandong province.
WENWU PUBLISHING

BELOW RIGHT: Painted funerary jar from the Majiayao culture of Gansu and Qinghai.
ÖSTASIATISKA MUSEET/MUSEUM OF FAR EASTERN ANTIQUITIES, STOCKHOLM, SWEDEN

THE ORIGIN OF MODERN HUMANS IN CHINA

The earliest archaeological remains in China date to 1,700,000–1,500,000 years BP (before present) and consist of crudely modified stone tools found in association with the fossilized bones of extinct Pleistocene (1.6 million–10,000 years BP) animals such as elephants and mastodons, horses, hyenas, and gazelles. However, these earliest sites so far lack convincing hominid fossils.

The first clearly hominid fossils in China are remains of *Homo erectus* (known in the West as Peking Man) found at sites such as Yuanmou, Gongwangling, and Zhoukoudian. Finds at Zhoukoudian (better known in the West as the Peking Man Cave site) were particularly rich, including the antlers, bones, and teeth of many kinds of animals, numerous stone tools, and perhaps the earliest evidence for human use of fire in China.

Evidence of local evolution in China from 250,000–100,000 years BP comes from sites such as Dali, Jinniushan, and Maba, where fairly complete archaic human (the Chinese equivalent of European Neanderthals) fossil skulls

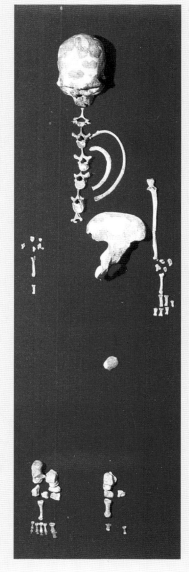

have been found. At Dali, stone tools have also been found. These include more advanced flake tools such as scrapers, points, and awls. The fossil skulls at these sites appear to be closely related to the Chinese *Homo erectus* populations found in sites like Zhoukoudian.

The relationship between these earlier remains and fossils of anatomically modern humans (*Homo sapiens sapiens*) found at sites such as Sjarra-osso-gol and the Upper Cave at Zhoukoudian is uncertain. These anatomically modern human remains are thought to be ancestral to the modern Chinese population and have been found in association with Upper Paleolithic (35,000–10,000 years BP) stone tools that were more sophisticated, such as small, bifacially flaked, highly retouched scrapers, engravers, small choppers, and points.

Some scholars believe that the anatomically modern human specimens in China are descended directly from the earlier

Homo erectus and archaic human populations. Others have argued that the physical features used to establish the link between modern humans and the older hominid populations in China are not accurate indicators of an evolutionary relationship. Most of these researchers believe that anatomically modern humans in China are descended from a population that evolved in Africa between 200,000 and 100,000 BP and then spread out into the rest of the world. The most recent studies of genetic relatedness and of hominid fossils worldwide tend to support the latter view.

With the establishment of modern human populations in China by 100,000–80,000 years BP, stone tool technologies such as the Ordosian of northern China continued the Upper Paleolithic tradition of smaller, more highly worked tools. By the Upper Paleolithic period, human groups everywhere had become skilled hunters and gatherers. From about 18,000–15,000 years BP a number of cultures made distinctive microlithic stone tools. Microliths are extremely small stone tools designed to be fitted onto wooden or antler hafts and used for a wide range of tasks, from arrow barbs to engraving tools and drill points. Some of these microlith-using cultures (probably nomadic hunters and gatherers or herders) continued into the Neolithic period, especially in the steppe regions of northern China.

LEFT: Homo erectus (Peking Man) skeleton from Jinniushan archaeological site in Liaoning province.
CHINA PICTORIAL PHOTO SERVICE

an elderly man, flanked by large mosaics of a tiger and a dragon made of river mussel shells, were discovered. These mosaics are the earliest depictions of these two highly symbolic animals in Chinese culture, and because of their prominence in this grave, it has been interpreted as the burial of an important shaman.

Yangshao potters made highly polished redware pottery bowls, jars, and vases. These vessels were often decorated in black paint with complex designs. The earliest designs often depicted human figures, animals, or fish arranged in geometric or repeating patterns. Later examples of Yangshao pottery featured

more complex geometric arrangements of abstract or curvilinear elements. Pottery with similar geometric decorations has been discovered in Yangshao's neighboring cultures, such as the Dawenkou, Daxi, and Majiayao, providing evidence for some kind of interaction among them.

Comparatively little is known about the village sites of the Dawenkou culture, but the available archaeological evidence suggests that people lived in large square houses similar to Yangshao houses. Most of the information about Dawenkou society comes from cemetery sites such as Yedian, Liulin, and the site of Dawenkou itself. Dawenkou graves include many cooking and serving vessels, such as tripod-shaped cooking vessels (*ding*), pitchers (*gui*), pedestaled serving stands or dishes (*dou*), and a range of stemmed and often lidded goblets. Vessels like these are rare or nonexistent in Yangshao sites.

This difference in ceramic vessels implies social differences between the Yangshao and Dawenkou cultures. Although both cultures used the same kinds of food plants and animal species, they had quite different cooking practices. The presence of ornate drinking and serving vessels implies that Dawenkou meals were more elaborate, at least during funeral or burial rituals. The discovery of large vatlike vessels, together with the range of drinking and pouring vessels, suggests that Dawenkou communities brewed an alcoholic

beverage that may have been consumed in ritual feasts similar to those known from the Zhou dynasty.

The ceramic technology used by Dawenkou potters was more sophisticated than that of the Yangshao. Dawenkou vessels more frequently had appendages such as spouts, legs, and ringbases, and by about 2900 BC, Dawenkou potters had developed a firing technology using higher temperatures to produce blackware and whiteware vessels that were finer and harder than the redwares and graywares commonly made in both cultures.

Both rich and poor Dawenkou burials were much more elaborate than Yangshao burials, where even graves with many occupants usually contained only four or five grave goods. Most Dawenkou graves

contained five to ten funerary items including sacrificial offerings of pig skulls or lower jaws. Some of the burials in Dawenkou cemeteries were extremely large and were made up of elaborately constructed log chambers filled with hundreds of burial goods including objects of jade, ivory, and turquoise, and blackware and whiteware ceramics. These elaborate graves may have been those of high-status Dawenkou people, while the more common, smaller graves were those of ordinary people. Dawenkou burial ritual emphasized inequality and hierarchy, while for the Yangshao it emphasized egalitarian and group ideals.

Other Neolithic cultures of this time have also provided archaeological evidence for a rich ritual life. The Hongshan culture of Liaoning produced beautiful jade carvings, and a well-built ritual structure at the site of Niuheliang contains a life-size clay figure and small female figurine fragments. The Liangzhu culture of southern coastal China also produced jade carvings, the most important of which are the ceremonial disks (*bi*), the broad-bladed axes (*yue*), and the ritual tubes (*cong*). It is still unclear exactly how these objects were used. Light engravings and low-relief carvings on jade plaques, *cong*, and *yue* depict human figures in elaborate feather headdresses riding fanged supernatural beasts, images which probably relate to early shamanism. The association of shamanic images with these costly ritual tools and objects suggests a link between shamanism and high social status.

Other evidence for increasing social stratification comes from Liangzhu sites such as Yaoshan where graves containing hundreds of jade and ceramic artifacts have been excavated. These graves are found in ritual platforms surrounded by numerous small graves with few or no grave goods. In several rich Liangzhu graves, partial human skeletons or decapitated skulls were placed beside the body of the primary occupant, suggesting human sacrificial burials.

There is evidence for increasing inter-regional interaction throughout the third millennium BC. Many cultures adopted distinctive vessels like the cooking tripod and the raised serving stand that first appeared in coastal northern China.

BELOW: Yangshao culture jar from the Neolithic village site of Banpo, near Xi'an in Shaanxi province.
RONALD SHERIDAN/ANCIENT ART & ARCHITECTURE COLLECTION

LEFT: Carved jade ring, in the shape of a dragon-like animal, from the Hongshan culture in Liaoning province.
WENWU PUBLISHING

Distinctive artifacts from other areas were also widely adopted. At the Dawenkou culture site of Huating in Jiangsu, excavators found Liangzhu ceramics, jade *cong*, *bi*, and awls in graves alongside typical Dawenkou artifacts.

Later Developments 3000–2000 BC

During the period 2600–2000 BC, many of the separate Neolithic cultures in China became progressively more similar to one another. The Longshan cultures of the Central Plains and coastal northern China are good examples of this process. All of these cultures had local versions of vessels such as cooking tripods and raised serving stands that had originated on the eastern coast. Most also had social hierarchies. Regional differences remained, however, and some areas retained distinctive elements from earlier cultures. For example, people of the Shandong Longshan culture improved upon the ceramic expertise of the Dawenkou potters to produce extremely delicate eggshell-thin pottery vessels — some of which resemble Dawenkou vessels — with walls less than $1/25$ inch (1 mm) thick. Because they were difficult to produce, these vessels were most likely important high-status objects.

The most elaborate graves found in sites such as Chengzi and Taosi contained

several hundred objects. Artifacts recovered at Taosi, from high-status tombs, include elaborately painted ceramics and important ritual objects such as jade tubes, axes, and disks. These rich graves also contained musical instruments such as tall ceramic drums with crocodile skin heads, stone chimes, and copper bells, foreshadowing the important role of music in ritual during the Bronze Age.

Burned shoulder blades of sheep and cattle, which were widely used in the Longshan cultures, were the forerunners of Shang dynasty oracle bones, and they indicate that divination was an important part of ritual practice by the late Neolithic period.

During this period sites protected by large rammed-earth walls first appeared, indicating that life was becoming more violent. At Chengziyai, the wall was estimated to have been 20 feet (6 m) tall and 29 feet (9 m) thick. Many larger, heavier spearheads and arrowheads now appear at numerous archaeological sites. These new weapons probably were designed to kill people rather than

animals. The site of Jiangou in Hebei yielded even more direct evidence of increasing violence: a well shaft filled with tangled bodies has been interpreted as the last resting place of the victims of a raid.

Several small metal artifacts such as knives, awls, bells, and rings have been recovered from Taosi, and from sites of the Shandong Longshan and Qijia cultures. However, metal was not used for casting vessels until the very end of the Neolithic period in the Erlitou culture of central

Henan. Until this point, the primary vessels for ritual as well as everyday use continued to be made of pottery. The most elaborate of these ritual ceramics were produced in the northern coastal region, and probably first appeared in the Dawenkou culture. These same vessels (cooking tripods, and pouring, serving, and drinking vessels) were later cast in bronze during the Xia, Shang, and Zhou dynasties.

All of these features point to the increasing role of ritual in human affairs during this time. The development of elaborate vessels for cooking, serving, and consuming food, possibly as parts of ritual feasting and for use as grave goods; an increasingly complex kind of ritual architecture such as the burial platforms from the Liangzhu culture or the "temple" at Niuheliang; the importance of musical instruments; and the role of divination and shamanism in Neolithic China were all key ingredients in the subsequent emergence of a distinctively Chinese civilization during the Bronze Age.

ABOVE: Pottery vessels with painted geometric designs from the Dawenkou culture of Shandong and northern Jiangsu provinces. WENWU PUBLISHING

LEFT: Painted pottery vase from the Longshan culture from a grave at Taosi in Shanxi province. WENWU PUBLISHING

BELOW: Musical instruments including stone chimes, ceramic drums, and copper bells were found at the Taosi site. DEPARTMENT OF ARCHAEOLOGY/CHINESE ACADEMY OF SOCIAL SCIENCES

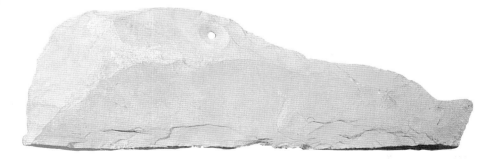

RITUAL AND POWER

Kwang-chih Chang

THE CIVILIZATIONS THAT ARE DESCRIBED in historical texts or seen in archaeological ruins are not difficult for researchers to identify: they evince magnificent wealth and mental sophistication through material monuments, literature, and great art styles. As a rule, researchers recognize a civilization when they see it. But a conceptual definition of civilization is not obvious. Western scholars tend to see civilization as a level of human attainment that lifts humans to a higher plane than that of "mere" animals and plants, and as an artificial environment that insulates us from unadulterated and hostile nature. But in ancient Chinese civilizations humans and nature were regarded as one; the Chinese were civilized precisely because they were able, or at least desirous, to be close to and harmonize with nature as a matter of conscious and deliberate choice. Civilizations are usually characterized by great urban centers, written documents, advanced bronze metallurgy, and highly stratified political states. In China these elements began to take shape during the third millennium BC and came to full maturity by the beginning of the second millennium BC.

Archaeological discoveries and studies of the past 70 years enable scholars to describe the process through which civilizations emerged in China. At the end of the Paleolithic period and the beginning of the Neolithic period population was sparse, with farming villages clustered along river valleys. Archaeologically recognized cultures varied in style from region to region; the regions were usually delineated by river systems separated by mountain ranges, hills, or bodies of water and marshes. In the course of their development, regional cultures gradually expanded, often uphill and upstream along the river valleys and the rivers' tributaries, and neighboring cultures came into contact, interacted in trade or in conflict, and came to influence each other culturally. By about 4000 BC, the archaeological picture begins to show unmistakable evidence of close contact, mutual influences, and cultural flows, making up a vast network linking the regions together to form a larger unit. This unit extends to most of the geographical area usually referred to as China Proper, and has come to be known in prehistory as the Chinese or proto-Chinese Interaction Sphere. Here was an optimal environment for civilizations to emerge.

The coexistence and incessant interaction of neighboring cultures and polities generated changes toward complexity internally within each region, and toward fierce competition externally between neighboring localities. These

ABOVE: *Painted pottery plate showing an early dragon design from a late Neolithic grave at Taosi, Shanxi province.* WENWU PUBLISHING

OPPOSITE: *Detail of a ritual white-jade* cong *carved with human and animal masks, from the late Neolithic Liangzhu culture.* Cong *are thought to have been shamanic symbols or tools.* WENWU PUBLISHING

changes enabled communities to acquire, distribute, and concentrate various scarce resources (such as metallic ores, jades, and clay that were used for art and crafts) within the framework of a new hierarchical social order. The most important instrument that was used to accomplish these undertakings was political power in the hands of the elite. All the archaeological manifestations of civilization — urban centers with defensive enclosures, writing, bronze metallurgy, and a state form of society — were components of this instrument.

The emergence of civilizations in China was closely associated with the use, by political leaders and shamans, of various symbols, especially ritual symbols, of political power for the purpose of acquiring, retaining, and increasing such power. At least, that is what archaeology has been able to demonstrate over the years, for many ritual symbols are archaeologically recoverable.

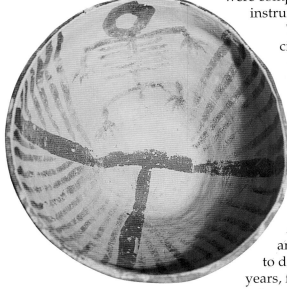

EARLIER NEOLITHIC SHAMANISM

The symbols that were instrumental in the emergence of civilizations are *all*, in fact, ritual symbols. Symbols adorn ritual

garments and paraphernalia to imbue them with power, and by their presence provide the only clues to the workings of the rituals in political or any other terms. The earliest symbols that have been identified archaeologically in China in significant numbers are found in the decorative art of the pottery of the Yangshao culture of north China and the Majiabang and Hemudu cultures in south China. The Yangshao symbols, for example, include dancing figures in

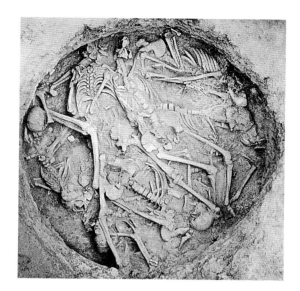

scenes that are interpreted as mortuary ceremonies; figures of animals (frogs) with human heads; human figures showing the skeleton within the body; bisexualism in human figures; and dragon and tiger images formed from mollusk shells placed alongside a human body in a burial. These symbols are consistent with a system of shamanistic beliefs and rituals that feature a concept of the heavenly and the earthly worlds, with shamanic figures able to penetrate the barrier between heaven and earth, and animal helpers assisting in the shamanic tasks of journeying and communication. On the available evidence, Yangshao shamanism is the earliest example of this religious and ritual system in China — but shamanism probably goes back to the Paleolithic period here as elsewhere. The

Yangshao village communities were models of egalitarian society (see Chapter 4). In Yangshao villages and cemeteries, houses and tombs were clustered in well-delineated groups, suggesting that society was organized in unilinear kin groups that regulated the behavior of their members. (For example, members of a unilinear — either patrilineal or matrilineal — group are usually forbidden to intermarry.) The archaeological finds disclose a picture of self-contained farming villages, with shamanistic activities performed by specialists — who seem to be scattered among the members of the community — for such routine purposes as rebirth from death, curing diseases by summoning back the soul, and warding off evil spirits.

THE LONGSHAN CULTURES AND THE MONOPOLY OF RITUAL ART

Archaeologically speaking, by approximately 3000 BC the societies in many of the regions in the Chinese Interaction Sphere showed firm evidence of stratification, violence, specialization, and hierarchical complexity. At their ruined sites there are traces of raids and battles. Many settlements were enclosed by earthen walls strong enough for

LEFT: A well filled with bodies in Handan, Hebei province, is evidence of the violent deaths suffered by many in the Longshan period.
DEPARTMENT OF ARCHAEOLOGY/CHINESE ACADEMY OF SOCIAL SCIENCES

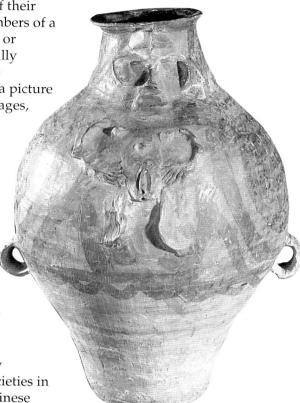

ABOVE: The bisexual human figure on this pottery vessel from Liuwan, Qinghai province, is a shamanic symbol typical of the Yangshao culture. WENWU PUBLISHING

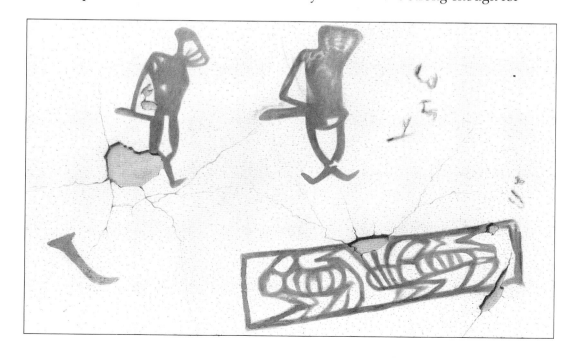

LEFT: This artist's impression of a floor painting at the Yangshao culture site at Dadiwan, Gansu province, possibly depicts a mortuary ritual performed by shamanic figures. The bodies in the boxes are depicted in the "X-ray" or skeletal style.

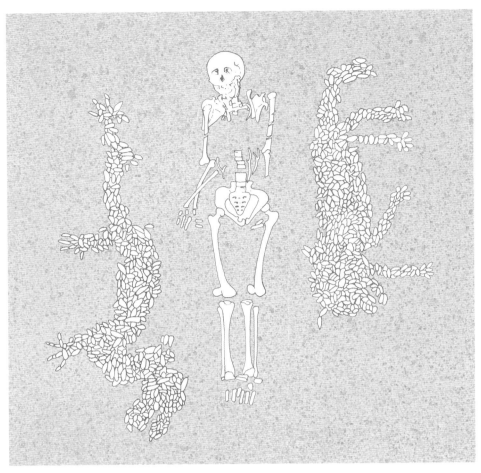

ABOVE: *Burial of a shaman, his head facing south, accompanied by his animal helpers, the dragon (left) and tiger (right), both made of mollusk shells. Discovered at the Yangshao culture site of Xishuipo in Puyang, north Henan province.*

the foundations.) In many regions pottery vessels bearing as yet undeciphered inscriptions have been found. Many pottery vessels are extremely delicately made and finely polished, presumably produced by specialized craftworkers for use at ceremonies. These cultures, showing comparable levels of societal development, are known as the Longshan cultures of their various regions, for example, the Henan Longshan culture, the Shandong Longshan culture, and the Liangzhu culture of the Lake Taihu region.

Longshan cemeteries furnish the most vivid evidence of the societal hierarchy at this time and also the best evidence to explain it. At some cemeteries individual graves vary sharply in size, scale of construction, and amount and quality of furnishings. At the Longshan cemetery at Taosi, in southern Shanxi, for example, out of more than 1,000 graves, nine are classified as "large," containing wooden chambers, whole sets of musical instruments, and dozens of beautifully painted pottery vessels; 80 are called "middle," moderately furnished; and more than 600 are "small," furnished with a pot or two, if at all. Moreover, the cemetery is divided into sections, and within each section there are large, middle, and small graves. This distribution pattern suggests a kinship system in which people live in lineages; the status of members within the lineages,

defensive use. There are cases where humans were killed as offerings at religious rites. (Chinese archaeologists consider that human skeletons and burials of infants in urns that have been found around house foundations were victims of rituals performed for the construction of

RIGHT: *Plan of Longshan culture cemetery at the site of Chengzi, Zhucheng Xian, Shandong province. The cemetery seems to have distinct clusters of several rich graves surrounded by less rich graves (based on the quanity and quality of grave goods they contain), suggesting possible lineage division and stratification within lineages — the three dotted lines emphasize the apparent tripartite separation of the grave groupings. (The black markings represent class 1 graves, the richest; through to white graves, the poorest.)*

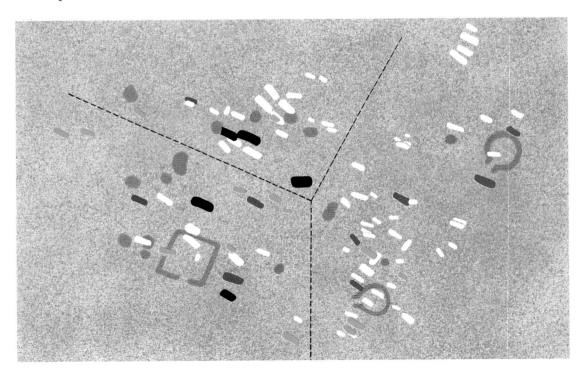

and of the different lineages themselves are dependent upon their proximity to the main line of descent from founding ancestor to current lineage head, probably through male primogeniture (as suggested by all texts relating to early China). Apparently the Longshan people were organized, according to early historical records, as ancient Chinese people were, into segmentary lineages, and their political status, both within lineages and between them, was predetermined in a hierarchical fashion. This kind of kinship group is sometimes referred to as the conical clan, and is often prevalent among societies that tend to branch off and send the branch segments to colonize new territories, where they establish new settlements and new polities. Possibly, the unilinear kinship groups of the Yangshao times developed into colonizing, segmentary lineages as the regional cultures expanded into new territories.

ABOVE: Fine red-and-black painted pottery is the trademark of the Yangshao culture of Henan, Shaanxi, and Gansu provinces.
CHINA PICTORIAL PHOTO SERVICE

Under the Longshan system of societal organization, the various regions of the Chinese Interaction Sphere were populated by a vast number of settlements or towns with earthen enclosures, which were organized into many peer polities. These polities had to contend for land to till, forests in which to hunt and to gather foods and materials, waters to fish, and other resources. Their political and ritual status may have been hierarchical by virtue of their genealogical descent, but there is ample archaeological evidence that the interrelationship of these peer polities was above all characterized by conflict and competition. In the fourth-century-BC text *Zuozhuan*, an ancient Chinese court official is quoted as saying that "the major affairs of the state are ritual and war." Beginning in the Longshan period, both weapons and ritual instruments became objects of exclusive possession or monopoly in the hands of the ruling class. Apparently the leaders who assembled more weapons and more ritual instruments were the more powerful and had the greater access to the scarce resources.

The power of weapons in a competitive world is self-evident, but the effect of the monopoly of ritual objects upon the accumulation of political power is of even greater importance in archaeology because of the abundance of ritual remains from Chinese antiquity. After all, the use of paraphernalia art in rituals is supposed to enable the user to gain access to the deities and the ancestors. The monopoly of ritual art means exclusive access by the successful leaders to the divine world and the wisdom in it. In another fourth-century-BC text, *Guoyu*, there is a myth about the separation of heaven from earth. In remote antiquity, it says, the world was in peace and there were shamans in the households serving to communicate with heaven. At the time of Supreme Leader Duan Xu, the world turned into chaos, and the traffic of communications between heaven and earth became so heavy that Duan Xu had to act to sever heaven from earth. He ordered Grand Shaman Chong to take charge of heaven and Grand Shaman Li to take charge of earth. Thenceforth, all communications to heaven

LEFT: Jade halberd blade from a middle-Shang period tomb at Panlongcheng, Hubei province. Based on a common type of bronze weapon of the Shang dynasty, this specimen was worked from a single piece of stone and measures more than 3 feet (1 m) long. When discovered, however, it had been broken into several pieces, perhaps deliberately to "kill" the blade before interment.
METROPOLITAN MUSEUM OF ART/ HUBEI PROVINCIAL MUSEUM

THE LIANGZHU JADE CONG

The *cong* of the Longshan cultures are especially abundant in the Liangzhu culture of the Lake Taihu region. *Cong* are ritual jade forms that have long puzzled Chinese antiquarians. In cross-section they are square on the outside and circular on the inside. They are tube-shaped with hollow cores, and range in length from about 1 inch (2.5 cm) to about 1 foot (30 cm). They are often decorated with fantastic animal designs. Since the 1970s many hundreds of these jade *cong* have been excavated from Liangzhu burials. The *bi* rings and *cong* tubes sometimes appeared to have been strung onto a long loop of rope that was placed on top of the body, suggesting that they were strung together and worn or carried by shamans. A bronze figurine of a human who appears to be holding a pair of *cong*, found in a Bronze Age pit at Sanxingdui in Sichuan, has led archaeologists to speculate that *cong* were held by shamans during rituals. *Cong* are currently seen as shamanic symbols or tools, the circular shape symbolizing heaven, the square shape symbolizing earth; the hollow tube is the *axis mundi* connecting the different worlds and the animal decorations portray the shaman's helpers. In short, the *cong* encapsulates the principal elements of the shamanistic cosmology.

ABOVE: *Detail on the jade cong showing a human figure with a fantastic animal.* WENWU. PUBLISHING

RIGHT: *White jade cong carved with human and animal masks from the Fanshan or Liangzhu culture of the Lake Taihu area.* WENWU. PUBLISHING

had to go first through Li and Chong.

This myth well describes the Longshan period: heaven was no longer so near the earth, and ritual art was no longer a part of everyday life — it became the private preserve of the elite and the leaders, and it was they who controlled access to heaven, to wisdom, and hence to the ideological basis for political power. The large graves in the cemetery at Taosi were furnished with musical instruments and beautiful pottery vessels, and the sacrificial altars and the burials at the sites of Liangzhu cultures were filled with jade *bi* rings and *cong* tubes; all of these were ritual objects or ritual paraphernalia art. The possessors of these instruments and art objects were the Chongs and the Lis, who were guarding the path to heaven and who thus alone were entitled to supreme political power.

RIGHT: *Bronze ceremonial water vessel of the late Shang dynasty.*
ASIAN ART MUSEUM OF SAN FRANCISCO, THE AVERY BRUNDAGE COLLECTION/B60 B1001

THE THREE DYNASTIES: THE CHINESE BRONZE AGE AND THE BLOSSOMING OF CHINESE CIVILIZATION

If the Longshan period witnessed the initial separation of heaven from earth, an event that gave the ruling elite of society exclusive access to the sacred world of divinity and thus the right to political leadership; the next period, from approximately 2000 BC to 500 BC, saw the full blossoming of Chinese civilization as marked by a writing system, an advanced bronze metallurgy, urban centers comprising palaces, temples, and workshops of specialized industries, and highly stratified states. It was a period filled with many hundreds or thousands of polities, but in traditional history it is represented by only three of the most powerful dynastic states, Xia, Shang, and Zhou.

The societies of Xia, Shang, and Zhou were highly stratified, ruled at the apex by probably endogamous (marrying within the clan) royal lineages. Younger brothers and nephews of the king were sometimes sent off to establish junior statelets to colonize the vast and sparsely populated territories between existing states and to serve as satellite polities to support and to guard the cities of their kings. Bronze Age China was a vast sea of many thousands or tens of thousands of towns and villages, organized into many hundreds or tens of hundreds of networks that the ancient Chinese called *guo* (states or kingdoms). There were kingdoms founded by members of different clans, and they were theoretically coequals. Other kingdoms founded by members of the same clan who belonged to different

LEFT: Inscription inside the bowl of the bronze rhinoceros (below).
THE AVERY BRUNDAGE COLLECTION/ASIAN ART MUSEUM OF SAN FRANCISCO, 60B1+

BELOW: Bronze rhinoceros used as a wine receptacle for rituals in the late Shang period.
THE AVERY BRUNDAGE COLLECTION/ASIAN ART MUSEUM OF SAN FRANCISCO, 60B1+

transport of the ingots, and the casting of the vessels with elaborate decorative designs by means of the intricate section-mold or piece-mold technique.

These complex bronze-making procedures were more labor intensive and required more complex management and more abundant capital than the production of the Longshan jades. Thus, the bronze vessels, with their decorations of animal helpers, also served, as had the jades, as paraphernalia art whose monopoly gave their possessors exclusive access to royal or noble status.

The political importance of the bronzes is well expressed by the legend of the Nine Bronze Tripods. It says that Yu, founder of the Xia dynasty, cast the Nine Tripods, which became the symbols of political legitimacy. When the Xia dynasty

lineages of unequal status were, amongst themselves, inherently hierarchical. The interrelationship of these various polities, theoretically characterized by a fixed hierarchy based on kinship rules, was in fact rife with intense competition. Polities rose and ebbed in status and power, and allegiances shifted back and forth.

The politically all-important ritual symbols of the Bronze Age were the bronze ritual vessels (food and drink vessels generally believed to have been used during rituals) that replaced the jades of the Longshan period in both practical function and symbolic importance. The manufacture of the bronze vessels involved the acquisition of copper and tin or lead ores from remote deposits, their smelting into ingots, the

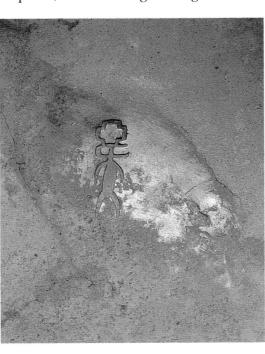

THE SHAMAN AND HIS ALTER EGO

The bronze vessel shown here is one of a pair reportedly unearthed from a Shang-dynasty site in Hunan province before World War II. It shows a human figure with its arms around a *taotie*, or fantastic animal, placing his head beneath — and almost inside — the open mouth of the *taotie*. Archaeologists have traditionally referred to this bronze vessel — a *you,* or wine container — as the "*you* with a tiger cub devouring a man." In the current context of the shamanistic interpretation of Shang religion, it seems that this vessel in fact shows a shaman and his alter ego. The open mouth of the animal is known to signify, in many ancient and modern cultures with a cosmology similar to ancient China's, the divide between the living world and the underworld. This vessel can be seen as an equivalent, both in cosmological meaning and in political function, of the Liangzhu jade *cong,* but it is obviously a much more complex object. While the *cong* is a simple shape made of one piece of jade, the casting of the elaborately decorated bronze *you* involved many complicated steps.

PHOTOGRAPH: "SEN-OKU HAKKO KAN"
(SUMITOMO COLLECTION)

fell, the Nine Tripods were transferred to the Shang. The Shang in their turn lost these symbols of legitimate power, along with their political mandate, to the succeeding Zhou dynasty. The revealing feature of Chinese bronze metallurgy lies in the use of its products: the metal was seldom, if ever, used for agricultural production or irrigation; instead, during the Bronze Age the bronze was fashioned into objects that served "the major affairs of the state," namely ritual and war. Ritual and war, as the twin instruments of political power, were the keys to the emergence of civilization in ancient China.

LEFT: Early twentieth-century photograph of a shaman in full regalia, in north China.
PEABODY MUSEUM, HARVARD UNIVERSITY/OWEN LATTIMORE FOUNDATION

SACRED CHARACTERS

David N. Keightley

THE ORIGINS OF WRITING IN CHINA are not yet fully understood. Various attempts have been made to read primitive scratches and designs on Neolithic pots, dating as far back as the fifth millennium BC, as numbers or clan symbols. Certain pictures of birds or of natural phenomena like the sun and the moon engraved on jades and pots from the fourth and third millennia BC may have served as totemic emblems that were vocalized by their readers, thus acting as early logographs (that is, as symbols that depicted words) rather than pictographs (symbols that depicted objects). However, none of this early evidence can yet qualify as writing, for the Chinese Neolithic cultures, with one or two enigmatic exceptions, have not yet produced sentences of such markings. This is hardly surprising since the existence of writing implies a society sufficiently complex to need such records. Such complexity only appears with the Chinese Bronze Age in the second millennium BC.

The earliest known extant body of Chinese writing — the oracle-bone inscriptions of the late Shang dynasty (c. 1200–1045 BC) — was used to record divinations. The existence of these inscriptions does not necessarily mean that Chinese writing developed to record the kings' attempts to foretell and influence the future. However, these inscriptions do provide information about the intimate links between divination, religion, political power, and writing.

The oracle-bone inscriptions of the Shang dynasty (c. 1570–1045 BC) represent the earliest body of writing in East Asia. Peasants in the area of modern Anyang in the panhandle of northern Henan province, had long found fragments of so-called "dragon bones" in their fields. By the early twentieth century Chinese scholars were beginning to collect the bones and to decipher their script; they were able to identify the records as those of the Shang dynasty.

Excavations at Anyang eventually revealed a site whose historical significance rivals Troy, another ancient city thought to be legendary until its excavation. The discovery of the royal Shang graves and temple-palace foundations, together with the inscriptions on the over 150,000 oracle-bone fragments found at the site, identified it as a cult center (where rituals of worship, sacrifice, divination, and burial were performed) of the last nine Shang kings, from Wu Ding (the twenty-first king, c. 1200–1181 BC) to Di Xin (the twenty-ninth king, c. 1085–1045 BC). Anyang and its inscriptions restored to history a

ABOVE: *Highly stylized carvings of dragons and other motifs on fragmentary bone spatulas excavated at the Shang cult center. The same skills used to make these designs would also have been employed in the carving of the inscriptions on the Shang oracle bones.*
ROYAL ONTARIO MUSEUM

OPPOSITE: *This turtle plastron (enlarged), from the reign of Wu Ding, was used to divine two charges — positive and negative — about whether or not a Shang officer would strike a particular enemy. The cracks are numbered "1" to "5" on the left and right of the shell. The notation, er gao, in the bottom right quadrant of the third crack on the left, indicates that the results were auspicious.*
COURTESY OF THE INSTITUTE OF HISTORY AND PHILOLOGY, ACADEMIA SINICA

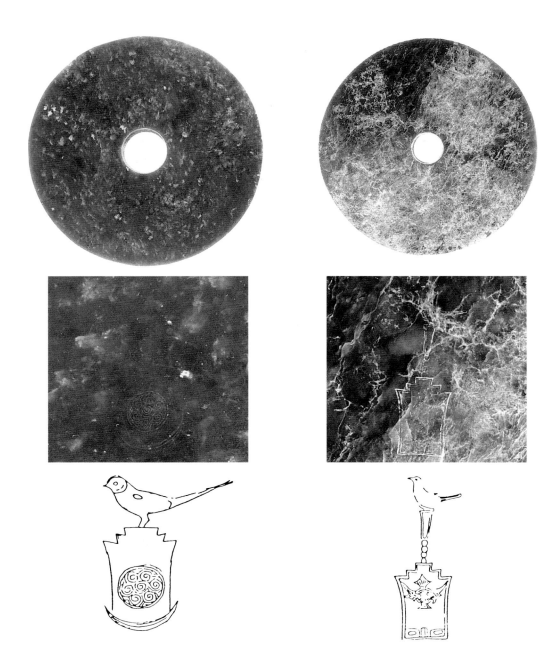

RIGHT: *Designs of birds incised on Neolithic jade* **bi** *disks. These pictures may have acted as symbols that depicted words (logographs) rather than symbols that depicted objects (pictographs). The one on the left (the disk is 12¹/₂ inches/31.8 cm in diameter) shows a bird in profile; it stands on a cartouche that contains a symbol of what may have been the sun above the moon. The one on the right (the disk is 9¹/₃ inches/23.6 cm in diameter) also shows the bird and cartouche with a symbol of the "sun bird" within it. In the third (page 73 — the disk is 9²/₃ inches/ 24.5 cm in diameter) the pictograph of the sun within the cartouche has been simplified.*

COURTESY OF THE FREER GALLERY OF ART, SMITHSONIAN INSTITUTION, WASHINGTON DC, 17.79, 17.346, 17.348

dynasty that until that point most Western scholars had regarded as legendary.

The Shang diviners practiced a form of pyromantic divination (using fire to foretell the future) that modern scholars refer to as scapulimancy (when the fire was applied to a cattle scapula) or plastromancy (when the fire was applied to a turtle plastron). Such pyromancy has been widely practiced in northern Asia and North America, where the diviners have generally placed the bone in the fire until it cracked. Finds of cracked animal bones at late Neolithic archaeological sites suggest that divinatory specialists in China were already using this method to forecast the future by the fourth millennium BC. However, in a significant indication of the human attempt to control the divine, Shang diviners were no longer placing the bone in the fire — a practice that would produce random crack patterns — but instead were placing the fire on the bone to produce cracks precisely at that point.

To facilitate the cracking of the bone, the Neolithic and early Bronze Age diviners also began the practice of boring or chiseling a series of hollows in the back of the bone: when they placed the fire in these hollows the bone, thinner at these points, would crack more easily. Such a technological advance presumably facilitated contact between the early Chinese diviners and the supernatural powers who they believed ruled their universe. The use of the preparatory hollows also encouraged the regular

as it was practiced at the Anyang cult center — known in the inscriptions as the *da yi Shang* (Great Settlement Shang) — was a highly ritualized procedure that formed one of the central institutions of the Shang kingdom. A staff of experts must have been employed to gather the cattle scapulas and turtle shells. Additional labor would have been required to clean and smooth the bones and shells and to bore the hollows in their backs: some shells might have had up to 160 hollows prepared in this way. (That many of these hollows were never actually cracked suggests the lavish and even wasteful use of manpower that the Shang kings devoted to their mantic activities.)

The names of over 120 diviners who served the Shang kings have been discovered. By the end of the Shang dynasty, however, the king himself had become virtually the only diviner of record, suggesting that the last Shang kings, Di Yi and Di Xin, were now monopolizing an activity that under Wu Ding had been shared with large numbers of other notables.

Only the king had the power to interpret the meaning of the cracks once they had been formed. The king's title of *yu yi ren* (I the one man) presumably derived part of its force from his unique position as a reader of the cracks. If, as seems likely, it was supposedly the royal ancestors who were "speaking" to the

BELOW: Drawing of an early Bronze Age scapula from the Wei River valley, showing random hollows and random bu *cracks. The drawing on the left shows where hollows had been bored to facilitate the cracking and encourage the regular* bu-*shaped cracks.*

formation of T-shaped cracks on the front surface of the bone. The shape of these cracks inspired the Shang character meaning "divination" or "to divine" (*bu*, written ⼘), that continues to be used in modern Chinese.

The hollows, burn marks, and cracks on the early divination bones were random in their placement but by the middle of the second millennium BC the Shang diviners were beginning to chisel the hollows in symmetrical patterns; the regularity of the *bu*-shaped cracks that now appeared on the front of the bone presumably reflected the increasing sense of order with which the diviners constructed their links to the supernatural.

By the time of the late Shang dynasty (*c.* 1200–1045 BC), pyromantic divination,

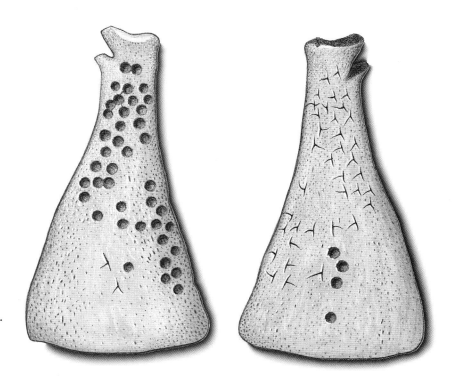

king through the cracks, it is entirely plausible that the king, as the senior living member of the royal lineage, would have been privileged in this way. Mantic power, political power, and kinship were inextricably linked in the dynastic institution.

After the king had read the cracks — usually as "auspicious" — the date, the name of the diviner, the charge, the prognostication, and the eventual result were incised into the bone or shell by special scribes. (That the Shang did incise their graphs in this way has the happy consequence that the oracle bones now serve as ideal "masters" for ink squeezes or "rubbings," which provide perfect mechanical reproductions of the ancient script.) A full inscription from the reign of Wu Ding would have been of the following form:

> [Preface] Crack making on *jimao* [day 16], Que divined
>
> [Charge] "It will rain."
>
> [Prognostication] The king read the cracks and said: "If it rains, it will be on a *ren* day."
>
> [Verification] On *renwu* [day 19], it really did rain.

Rainfall, vital for the success of millet crops upon which the Shang state depended, was in fact one of the most common topics divined.

This routine divinatory record is instructive for a number of other reasons. First, it introduces us to the system by which the Shang labeled their days. There were ten days to the Shang week and those days were named by combining (1) what, in later terminology, were called the ten "heavenly stems" — following one another in unvarying sequence, *jia, yi, bing, ding, wu, ji, geng, xin, ren,* and *gui* — with (2) the twelve "earthly branches"

A SYMMETRICAL HARVEST DIVINATION

The two inscriptions on this turtle plastron (reduced 15 percent) from the reign of Wu Ding document the king's attempt to assure himself and his supporters through the magic of the divinatory ritual that the Shang would receive a harvest in the months ahead.

The inscription on the right side of the shell, whose positive charge expressed what the king hoped would happen, reads as follows (starting at the top of the longer column on the right): "Crack making on *bingchen* [day 53]. Que divined 'We will receive millet harvest.'" This was symmetrically balanced by the negative, and undesired, charge on the left (longer column on the left), "Crack making on *bingchen*, Que divined: 'We may not receive millet harvest.' [Divined in] the fourth moon."

Both charges were written in columns that, running "against" the direction of the symmetrically formed *bu* cracks, had to be read from the center of the plastron toward its edge. The concern with symmetry was so strong that the engravers even reversed the graph used to write the name of the diviner, Que, so that the fourth graph in the longer column on the left was a mirror image of the fourth graph in the longer column on the right. The use of such complementary positive and negative charges, reinforced by the balanced placement of the cracks and the graphs, evidently expressed a profound meta-physical truth about the Shang conception of the world. After the diviners had created the stress cracks in the shell, the engravers numbered the cracks: the numbers 1, 2, 3, 4, and 5 can be seen in the upper left quadrant of the *bu*-shaped cracks on the right, and in the upper right quadrant of the *bu*-shaped cracks on the left.

The king's prognostication, "Auspicious; we will receive this harvest," was inscribed on the back of the plastron. His reading of the cracks is confirmed by the auspicious notation, *er gao*, literally "two reports" (but whose meaning is unclear), in the bottom right quadrant of the fourth crack on the left. Something about that particular crack — or about the set of ten cracks as a whole — had persuaded the diviners and the king that his hopes for a harvest would be realized.

PHOTOGRAPH COURTESY OF THE INSTITUTE OF HISTORY AND PHILOLOGY, ACADEMIA SINICA

丙 bing
辰 chen
卜 crack-making
殼 Que
貞 divined
我 we
弗 not
其 may

受 receive
黍 millet
年 harvest
四 fourth
月 moon

丙 bing
辰 chen
卜 crack-making
殼 Que
貞 divined
我 we
受 receive

受 millet
黍 harvest

二 two
告 reports

(another later term), which again followed their own unvarying sequence, *zi, chou, yin, mao,* and so on. This combination of the sequences of ten and twelve resulted in a cycle of 60 days. For example, *jia* (stem 1) was coupled with *zi* (branch 1) to form the date *jiazi* (day 1), *yi* (stem 2) was linked with *chou* (branch 2) to form *yichou* (day 2), and so on. The stems were also used to name the dead kings and to identify the days on which they were to receive cult. Accordingly, the recording of the day of divination — *jimao* in the case above — had a significant religious function.

Second, the inscription introduces the diviner Que. He was one of the most active and enduring of the diviners, serving during the latter part of Wu Ding's reign, in the reign of his successor, Zu Geng, and early in the reign of the next king, Zu Jia.

Third, the inscription documents the king's prowess as a reader of the cracks. He prognosticated that, "If it rains, it will be on a *ren* day," and the verification records precisely that: "On *renwu,* it really did rain." Rarely if ever are there cases in which the verification flatly contradicts

the king's forecasts. This indicates the degree to which the inscriptions carved on bone and shell were intended to strengthen the king's position. Fourth, it is worth stressing that the divination charges were generally not couched as questions. The king did not ask "Will it rain?" The diviner's charge proposed that "It will rain," and the diviner then proceeded to test that charge by cracking the bone or shell. "Proposed" is probably too weak a word to represent the force of the divinatory charges that were evidently endowed with a strong element of prayer or conjuration. In this case, the king wanted it to rain and he accordingly made a strong statement of his wishes. In fact, many Shang divination charges, like the routine formulas "going and returning there will be no disasters" or "In the next ten days there will be no disasters," can be partly understood as magical incantations.

Fifth, it was frequently the case in the inscriptions of the Wu Ding period that a charge like "It will rain," which was couched in the positive mode, was balanced by a countercharge, which was couched in the negative mode. In this

RIGHT: *A massive, four-legged cauldron, inscribed with the title of one of the royal consorts; it was excavated from an unlooted grave at the Anyang site, in 1976. The wealth that the Shang lavished on the care of the dead is suggested by the presence of more that 440 bronzes and 590 jades in this grave pit.*
METROPOLITAN MUSEUM OF ART/
INSTITUTE OF ARCHAEOLOGY, BEIJING

A CLASSIC ORACLE BONE

博 seized
二 two
邑 settlements
工 Gong
方 fang
亦 likewise
侵 invaded
我 our
西 western
鄙 border
田 fields

自 from
西 west
沚 Zhi
馘 Guo
告 reported
曰 saying
土 Tu
方 fang
征 attacked
于 in
我 our
東 eastern
鄙 borders

其 may
有 be
來 bringing
嬉 alarming news
乞 come
至 to
五 fifth
日 day
丁 ding
酉 you
允 really
有 was
來 bringing
嬉 alarming news

癸 gui
巳 si
卜 crack-making
殼 Que
貞 divined
旬 ten-days
亡 not be
禍 disasters
王 king
占 read cracks
曰 said
有 will be
咎 calamities

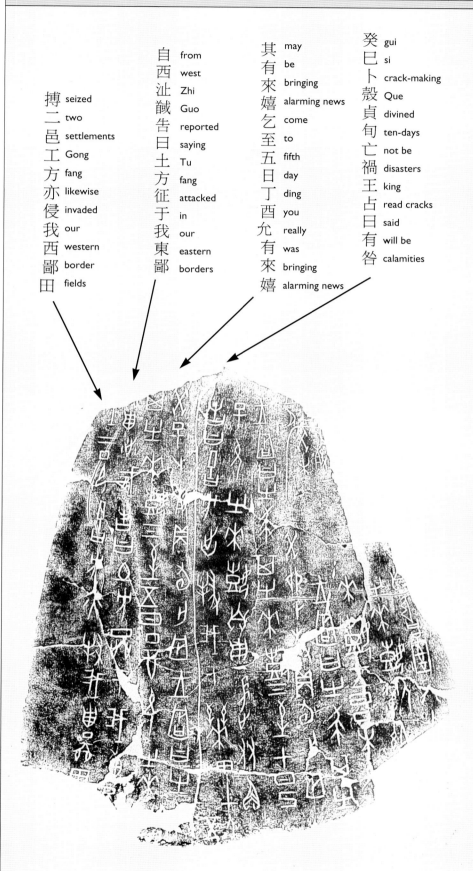

The front and back (not shown) of this large, handsomely engraved cattle scapula (reduced 45 percent) record a series of divinations (with the records sometimes separated by boundary lines) that the Shang king Wu Ding (c. 1200–1181 BC) performed over at least 30 days in fifth and sixth months of the Shang calendar. The writing is in the large, bold style of the Wu Ding period. Each divination was carried out on the last day, the *gui* day, of the ten-day week. Each of the charges was a conjuration against disasters in the week to come. The king foresaw disasters for every week and in each case he was proved right by the events that transpired, thus confirming his prowess as a diviner.

The inscription on the front left of the bone (starting from the top of the first column to the left of the boundary line, and reading down and to the left) runs as follows (modern characters and approximate English translations are given above the bone):

[Preface] Crack making on *Guisi* [day 40], Que divined

[Charge] "In the next ten days there will be no disasters."

[Prognostication] There will be calamities: there may be someone bringing alarming news.

[Verification] When it came to the fifth day, *dingyou* [day 34], there really was someone bringing alarming news from the west. Zhi Guo [a Shang general] reported and said: "The Tufang [an enemy statelet] have attacked in our eastern borders and have seized two settlements. The Gongfang [another enemy statelet] likewise invaded the fields of our western borders."

Each of the inscriptions on this bone for which there is a verification observes the same formula: (1) the wish divined on the last day of the week that there will be no calamities; (2) the identical prognostication of alarming news; (3) the detailed verification of that prognostication. Taken as a whole, the charges on this scapula were evidently divined in a time of troubles for the Shang. The inscriptions tell us that Wu Ding received news of enemy attacks on days 6, 28, 34, and 44; he was confronted with other trouble in the nights of days 38 and 39.

Not only was the calligraphy of these inscriptions uniformly bold, but the graphs themselves had been filled with bright red pigment, thus beautifying, and perhaps energizing the magic in, the inscriptions themselves. Such attention to aesthetic detail suggests that the inscriptions may have been intended for display to an unknown audience. Perhaps such bones were shown to the king's dependants at court to demonstrate his infallibilities as leader. Perhaps the audience also included the royal ancestors, who may have been regarded as the source of the lucky and unlucky cracks (not preserved on the part of the scapula that remains here) and who may have been pleased by this evidence of communication between ancestors and their descendants.

PHOTOGRAPH FROM HEJI 6057 (FRONT)

ABOVE: *A series of hunting inscriptions, incised into a cattle scapula (reduced 300 percent). The small size of the script and the regularity of the "page design" indicate that these divinations — which were mainly incantations to ensure that the king would suffer "no disasters" when he hunted on particular days, at particular places — were performed late in the Shang dynasty.* HEJI, 37362

RIGHT: *The inscriptions on this scapula fragment (reduced 35 percent) concerned the offering of animal victims to the Huan River and to various royal ancestors. As frequently happened, the bone, at some point in the last 3,000 years, fractured along the vertical lines of the divinatory* bu *cracks, so that the bottom right portion has been lost.*

COURTESY OF THE INSTITUTE OF HISTORY AND PHILOLOGY, ACADEMIA SINICA

case, the negative charge, carved into the plastron so as to balance the positive charge, was: "Crack making on *jimao*, Que divined: 'It may not rain.'" The use of the "may" indicates that this was the weaker charge. But the routine use of such positive–negative charge pairs suggests that the diviners saw the world as metaphysically balanced in a kind of proto–yin–yang opposition. Wu Ding's diviners did not employ this positive-negative treatment for all subjects, but they frequently used it when the topic being divined was, like rainfall, not under Shang control: in short, they used it when attempting to address the uncertainties of the natural world and the powers that ruled it.

Wu Ding and his diviners addressed themselves to topics like rainfall, harvests, sickness, childbirth, dreams, and enemy attacks that, in the modern world, would be the concern of secular specialists like meteorologists, agronomists, doctors, obstetricians, psychologists, and generals. To the Shang, the world was not differentiated in this way; the religious and the secular were indivisible. A divination like "Divined: 'There is a sick tooth: it is not Father Yi [the twentieth king, Wu Ding's father] who is harming us,'" reveals the extent to which the Shang elites felt themselves immersed in a web of ancestral influences. In fact, illness was frequently attributed to the recently dead. If, as in other comparable societies, the king suspected that his illness was due to witchcraft by the living, one can imagine that the diviners' attempts to identify the ancestor who might be causing the harm could have important political consequences in the Shang court. For example, a king who thought, as a result of cracking the bones, that his uncle was plaguing him might well have visited his wrath on the uncle's children. Divination was central to the kinship politics of the dynastic state.

By the end of the Shang dynasty, however, the scope of royal divination had been greatly reduced. The late kings no longer divined about such topics as harvest, sickness, childbirth, or dreams, but limited their divinatory charges to topics like the ritual cycle and the royal hunts. The charges were now invariably couched in terms of what the king desired;

none of the charges admitted the possibility of an undesirable outcome such as "It may not rain." The king's prognostications were uniformly auspicious. And the handwriting of the inscriptions was greatly reduced in size. Divination, in short, appears to have become routinized, less dangerous, less important.

Many factors may explain this evolution in divinatory practice, but one reason for the decline in importance of late Shang pyromancy may well have been the increasing popularity of a different and simpler form of divination that was eventually to result in the system of hexagrams that we associate with the *Yijing* ("The Book of Changes"), a collection of divinatory aphorisms that was probably codified toward the end of the Western Zhou dynasty (*c.* 1045–771 BC). It is plausible to assume that certain topics vanished from the pyromantic record of Shang because they were being

handled by the new divinatory system. Tradition has associated this system with the Zhou dynasty, whose founder killed the last Shang king at the battle of Muye, a battle whose outcome may have further validated the Zhou system of divination over that of the Shang!

There is some evidence, in fact, that the Shang diviners had been combining pyromancy with another form of divination that employed the manipulation of numbers. Precisely how the Shang diviners employed these numbers is not yet clear but the presence of such number piles may help explain the way in which Shang pyromancy changed over time.

A small but significant quantity of the number clumps has been found on oracle bones excavated in the Wei River valley, some 300 miles (500 km) to the west of the Shang cult center at Anyang, an area known as the homeland of the Zhou. As Chinese scholars have noted, if one represents the individual numbers by drawing an unbroken line for an odd number and a broken line for an even number, then a clump of six numbers can be easily translated into a hexagram of six lines. It was precisely such hexagrams that formed the core of the Zhou system of divination by counting off piles of counting rods or plant stalks. That very few inscribed oracle bones have been found after the fall of the Shang dynasty suggests that pyromancy lost its attractiveness as the Zhou

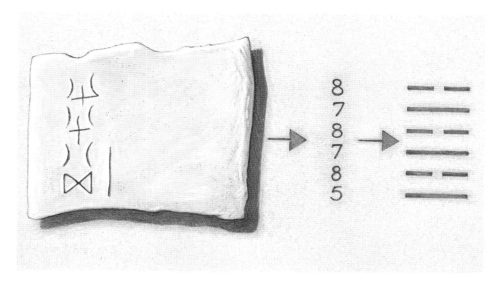

conquerors moved into the Anyang area.

The *Yijing* was to become the first of the Chinese classics. Its approach to divination was fundamentally different from the far more mundane approach and records of the Shang diviners. Where the Shang turned to the bone cracks to consult the ancestral spirits or other powers about particular problems of government and personal life, the Zhou increasingly used the hexagrams to stimulate reflections upon the nature of life and action in general. For example, the text associated with hexagram 63 starts "Nine at the beginning means: He brakes his wheels. He gets his tail in the water. No calamities ..." Although the divinatory vocabulary (like "calamities") found in the *Yijing* was often similar to that used by the Shang diviners, the whole approach to the world and the future was radically different.

Pyromancy (but without the inscribing of the divination charges on bone or shell) continued to be employed in later times but it was the Zhou divination manual, the *Yijing*, that came to dominate the divinatory concerns of the later dynasties and the Confucian elites who supported them. The *Yijing* was beloved of Confucius — who is said to have worn his own copy out — and it continued to be consulted by Chinese statesmen right down to the nineteenth century. The deeply traditional desire to develop a system that enables elites to forecast and shape the future may even help to explain the popularity of Marxism, with its claims to a scientific understanding of both the past and the future, in the political culture of modern China.

ABOVE: A drawing of a pile of numbers carved onto an oracle bone, found in the Wei River valley. If the odd numbers represent unbroken lines and the even numbers represent broken lines, then these number piles, which were usually composed of six numbers, can be taken as the antecedents of the six lines — broken and unbroken — that formed the hexagrams of the later divinatory text, the Yijing *("Book of Changes"). The numbers presumably recorded some sorts of numerical calculations that supplemented the divining of the charges on the oracle bones.*

LEFT: Photograph of the back of a turtle plastron used in divination, showing the large number of hollows (160 in this case) that had been bored into the turtle to prepare it for pyromantic cracking.

COURTESY OF THE INSTITUTE OF HISTORY AND PHILOLOGY, ACADEMIA SINICA

THE EARLY LITERARY TRADITIONS

Grace S. Fong

CHINESE LITERATURE, IN THE FORM OF poetry, and historical and philosophical writings, emerged during the first millennium BC. The literary canon that evolved over the next thousand years was rich and varied, but a selection of key works suffices to convey something of its depth and character. The "Book of Songs" (*Shijing*), while a Confucian classic, is also regarded as the fount of Chinese lyricism; the "Songs of the South" (*Chuci*), embodying a tradition of poetry with shamanistic roots, is attributed to Qu Yuan, the first individual poet of China; the writings of Zhuangzi, one of the founders of Daoist philosophy, are imaginative and witty beyond mere intellectual discourse; and the "Records of the Historian" (*Shiji*) by Sima Qian, besides creating the historiographical model that all subsequent histories followed, is also a great literary achievement. These works are central to the constitution and conception of the literary legacy of early China.

Most contemporary Chinese consider poetry (*shi*) to be the exemplary literary form in traditional China. In no other culture has poetry played such a continuous and important role in social and intellectual life as it has among educated Chinese. Throughout most of Chinese history until the beginning of the twentieth century, lyric poetry was considered the foremost tool of self-expression and communication for the elite, and every occasion, from parting to birthday celebration, was an opportunity for versification. Furthermore, the composition of poetry became a requirement in the civil service examination, a development unique in the history of the world. In short, poetry was deemed a required art of cultivated Chinese from the time of Confucius.

The origins of this long poetic tradition are in a corpus of early folk and court ritual songs. The "Book of Songs" was compiled around the seventh century BC from materials dating back several centuries, and acquired the status of a core text in education and diplomacy during the Spring and Autumn period. Traditionally Confucius was believed to be responsible for selecting, editing, and compiling the recension of the 305 songs. In the "Analects" (*Lunyu*), the recorded sayings of Confucius, the master makes several references to the edifying importance of the "Book of Songs," such as: "With the 'Book of Songs' one can inspire, observe others, be sociable, and criticize. At home one serves one's father with it, abroad one serves one's ruler." The connection with Confucius conferred on this group of largely anonymous songs an

ABOVE: A page from the biography of Qu Yuan, the great poet from the southern state of Chu who provided the popular model of the rhapsodic magical journey which influenced many later poets.
CHINA PICTORIAL PHOTO SERVICE

OPPOSITE: Confucius (551–479 BC), philosopher and author of, or inspiration for, the Five Classics which constitute the summation of the Confucian school of cosmology, ethics, and government.
CHINA PICTORIAL PHOTO SERVICE

ABOVE: Literary Gathering, by Han Huang, shows the ritualized life of the literati in a society in which the composition of poetry was an essential element in the civil service examinations.

THE PALACE MUSEUM, BEIJING

aura of canonicity. During the Han dynasty it was designated as one of the Confucian classics. Since then it has not only been dutifully studied but has generated layers of scholarly commentary materials through the centuries.

The content of the songs, with discernible roots in both folk and court cultures, reflects a largely pre-Confucian agrarian society. These songs were originally performed at court. In simple meter and refrain, the folk songs celebrate the joys or complain about the hardships of life among the common people. Images of nature bespeak an agricultural environment and life cycle. The courtly songs tell of legends of mythical dynastic founders as well as ceremonial banquets and various rituals in the life of the noble classes. One striking feature of the "Book of Songs" is the prominence of love and courtship songs. Many are bold and daring in expression, set often in a woman's voice:

If you love me and think of me,
I will lift up my skirt and wade the Zhen.
If you don't think of me,
Would there be no other man?
What craziest of crazy lads!
If you love me and think of me,
I will lift up my skirt and wade the Wei.
If you do not think of me,
Would there be no other gentleman?
What craziest of crazy lads!

In contrast to the forceful directness of the woman's song, the fewer male-voiced love songs tend to take the form of monologues in which the lyric speaker seems to be talking to himself rather than addressing his lover:

The quiet girl is beautiful
She will wait for me by the wall corner
I love her but do not see her
Scratching my head I pace back and forth.
The girl is pretty
She gave me a red flute
The red flute shines brightly
I am pleased with your beauty.
She sent me a young shoot from the pastures
It is really beautiful and rare.
It is not that you are beautiful
You are the gift of the beautiful one.

The male speaker constructs an image of his lover in his memory. He addresses the objects that were given to him by his lover and that are symbolic extensions that substitute for the woman. This song exemplifies the tendency very early on in Chinese poetry for male-voiced songs to objectify women in contrast to the direct voicing of love and emotion in female-voiced songs.

During the gradual canonization of the "Book of Songs" in the late Warring States period, the songs were treated as embodiments of general truths or moral conditions, thus distancing them from their specificities and origins in folk culture and ritual performance. Various schools of interpretation, including the Han and the Mao, often attributed the authorship of the songs to historical individuals or subjects of states and read the songs for their moral or political content. For example, orthodox Confucian commentary interprets the above two songs as criticism of the immorality and disorderliness of the times, presumably because the conduct portrayed was not acceptable according to Confucian propriety.

While the "Book of Songs" originated mostly in the Huang (Yellow) River plain in the north, the cradle of ancient Chinese civilization, the "Songs of the South" represents a very different regional culture — the state of Chu, flanking the Yangzi River, roughly the present-day

provinces of Hubei and Hunan. The mythological world of this poetry, reflected in the rich imagery and religious motifs, is complex and fantastic. There are songs summoning departed souls to guide them in their journey after life, songs of amorous shamans and shamanesses courting their elusive deities, and songs of journeys and flights through the spirit world. In comparison to the earthy simplicity of the "Book of Songs," this is a world of magic and imagination.

Although the current anthology was compiled during the Han, the oldest songs in the collection date from the fourth century BC. The most famous piece, "Encountering Sorrow," is a long poem attributed to Qu Yuan (340?–278 BC), a loyal minister of Chu alienated from his lord King Huai. According to traditional belief he was slandered by those jealous of him and banished from court, wrote "Encountering Sorrow" in protest during his exile, and then committed suicide by drowning himself in the Miluo River, a tributary of the Xiang River in Hunan. Qu Yuan has become a cultural symbol of patriotism. He was the archetype of the unappreciated yet loyal statesman upon whom later scholar–officials, who were also the poets, modeled themselves. In south China, the popular dragon-boat festival held on the fifth day of the fifth lunar month commemorates his spirit.

"Encountering Sorrow" is an allegorical narrative with strong autobiographical overtones. In telling of his estrangement, Qu Yuan casts himself in the feminine role of a rejected royal consort, and his subsequent search for fulfilment is allegorized in terms of celestial journeys in quest of unions with goddesses. These fantastic elements derive from shamanistic traditions of the region, where shamans and shamanesses worshiped and invoked female and male deities respectively as evidenced by the "Nine Songs" in the anthology, some of the most beautiful erotic love verses in the Chinese tradition. In the "Goddess of the Xiang River," the wistful longing for the goddess, the reaching out but not attaining, the continued effort, the hope, the unrequited desire, and the ultimate failure of the quest are formulated in lyrical movements punctuated by floral imagery. Qu Yuan is believed to

ABOVE: *Portrait of Qu Yuan (340?–278 BC), a loyal subject and kinsman of King Huai of Chu. His verse was inspired by the chants of the shamans (Priest-doctors) who were the chief celebrants in ecstatic and exorcistic rites practiced in southern regions of China.*
CHINA PICTORIAL PHOTO SERVICE

LEFT: *Silk funerary banner from a Han-period grave at Mawangdui, near Changsha, Hunan province. It bears scenes illustrating some of the religious beliefs of the Chu culture. This southern kingdom was situated along the Yangzi River with its capital near Lake Dongting.*
WENWU PUBLISHING

have refined the language of these regional shaman songs into polished poetic renderings.

Though Chinese poetry was still to evolve varieties of meters and genres in subsequent centuries before it attained full flowering in the Tang and Song dynasties, the "Book of Songs" and the "Songs of the South" maintained their status as canonic texts in the history of imperial China and had tremendous influence on the conception and meaning of poetry in Chinese culture.

The second half of the first millennium BC was the golden age of classical Chinese philosophy. Due to the increasing social and political change and instability in the Spring and Autumn and Warring States periods, many educated Chinese tried to come up with solutions to political, social, and ethical problems. This was a period of intellectual ferment when a "hundred schools" of thought blossomed. From Confucius and Mencius, to Laozi and Hanfeizi, great thinkers of the well-known schools of Chinese philosophy, such as Confucianism, Daoism, and Legalism, transmitted their teachings which were often recorded by followers. Each school or thinker had particular emphases and offered different views and solutions. For example, the Confucians focused on the ethical role and responsibilities of ruler and subject within society, while the Daoists emphasized the freedom of the individual that transcends social norms and conventions, and the Legalists placed supreme importance on governing people by the enforcement of law. Some of these writings are impressive in their logical argument, others in analogical reasoning. Of all the works of the philosophers from this period, the *Zhuangzi* has been most read and enjoyed for its literary qualities as much as for its philosophical content.

Not much is known about the life of

Zhuangzi, or Master Zhuang, except that his personal name was Zhou, that he lived in the fourth century BC and was thus a contemporary of the Confucian thinker Mencius. He was a native of a place called Meng in present-day Henan province. The work that bears his name has 30 chapters: the first seven chapters are regarded by scholars as being most likely the original writings of Zhuangzi; the rest are regarded as being mixed with writings by later followers. Laozi and Zhuangzi are said to be the two founders of Daoism. This school of thought advocated freedom and naturalness through communion with the Dao (the Way) by spontaneously and unconsciously according with the natural processes, rather than being contaminated by the artificial values of human existence and institutions, as illustrated in the following anecdote:

Once when Zhuangzi was fishing in the Pu River, the king of Chu sent two officials to go and announce to him: "I would like to trouble you with the administration of my realm."

Zhuangzi held on to the fishing pole and, without turning his head, said, "I have heard that there is a sacred tortoise in Chu that has been dead for 3,000 years. The king keeps it wrapped in cloth and boxed, and stores it in the ancestral temple. Now would this tortoise rather be dead and have its bones left behind and honored? Or would it rather be alive and dragging its tail in the mud?"

"It would rather be alive and dragging its tail in the mud," said the two officials.

Zhuangzi said, "Go away! I'll drag my tail in the mud!"

"THE GODDESS OF THE XIANG RIVER"

The goddess comes not, she holds back shyly.
Who keeps her delaying within the island,
Lady of the lovely eyes and the winning smile?
Skimming the water in my cassia boat,
I bid the Yuan and Xiang still their waves
And the Great River make its stream flow
  softly,
I look for the goddess, but she does not
  come yet.
Of whom does she think as she plays her
  reed-pipes?

North I go, drawn by my flying dragon,
Steering my course to the Dong-ting lake:
My sail is of fig-leaves, melilotus my rigging,
An iris my flag-pole, my banner of orchids.
Gazing at the distant Cen-yang mooring,

I waft my magic across the Great River.
I waft my magic, but it does not reach her.
The lady is sad, and sighs for me;
And *my* tears run down over cheek and chin:
I am choked with longing for my lady.

My cassia oars and orchid sweep
Chip all in vain at ice and snow.
I am gathering wild figs in the water!
I am looking for lotuses in the tree-tops!
The wooing is useless if hearts are divided;
The love that is not deep is quickly broken.

The stream runs fast through the stony
  shallows,
And my flying dragon wings swiftly about it.
The pain is more lasting if loving is faithless:

She broke her tryst; she told me she had
  not time.
In the morning I race by the bank of the river;
At evening I halt at this north island.
The birds are roosting on the roof-top;
The water laps at the foot of the hall.
I throw my thumb-ring into the river.
I leave my girdle-gem in the bay of the Li.
Pollia I've plucked in the scent-laden islet
To give to the lady in the depths below.
Time once gone cannot be recovered:
I wish I could play here a little longer.

"The Goddess of the Xiang River" is a shaman song wooing a female river deity in the amorous language characteristic of the "Nine Songs" section of the "Songs of the South," attributed to Qu Yuan.

The *Zhuangzi* is most distinguished by its wit and originality. In addition to discursive exposition, it often demonstrates points with parables and paradoxes in which Zhuangzi himself frequently appears as protagonist. It turns conventional logic and habits of thought and behavior on their heads and pokes fun at morals and values dear to society. Confucius and the Confucians, with their emphasis on social order, harmony, and outward forms of propriety, are often the objects of ridicule. In the following anecdote, the logician Huizi is caricatured for his hair splitting, and epistemological concerns are returned to their basis in empirical experience:

Zhuangzi and Huizi were strolling along the dam of the Hao River when Zhuangzi said, "See how the minnows come out and dart around where they please! That's what fish really enjoy!"

Huizi said, "You are not a fish — how do you know what fish enjoy?"

Zhuangzi said, "You are not I, so how do you know I don't know what fish enjoy?"

Huizi said, "I'm not you, so I certainly don't know what you know. On the other hand, you're certainly not a fish — so that still proves you don't know what fish enjoy!"

Zhuangzi said, "Let's go back to your original question, please. You asked me how I know what fish enjoy — so you

already knew I knew it when you asked the question. I know it by standing here beside the Hao."

Zhuangzi's writing had a strong and enduring effect on Chinese culture. His philosophy offered an alternative perspective on life; the love and celebration of nature, that is so much a part of later Chinese poetry, is a manifestation of the Daoist influence in Chinese literature.

Alongside poetry and philosophy, history was also a significant genre in early Chinese literature. Veneration and interpretation of the past, and gleaning from it didactic models and patterns of ethical and political conduct have been an important aspect of Chinese civilization

FAR LEFT: Portrait of Laozi, the Daoist sage who is credited with having written Dao de jing *("The Way and Power Classic").*
NATIONAL PALACE MUSEUM, TAIBEI, TAIWAN, REPUBLIC OF CHINA

LEFT: Portrait of Zhuangzi, Daoist philosopher who lived during the fourth century BC *and is attributed with authorship of a work that bears his name.*
NATIONAL PALACE MUSEUM, TAIBEI, TAIWAN, REPUBLIC OF CHINA

ABOVE: Ma Hezhi, Odes of Chen, *twelfth-century illustration of the "Book of Songs."* BRITISH MUSEUM, LONDON

from ancient times. Tradition has it that the post of court historiographer existed as early as the Shang and Zhou dynasties. Historical writings from this period tend to cover a relatively limited period and are characterized by an anecdotal style or by the presence of speeches and pronouncements with little narrative context. For example, the "Spring and Autumn Annals" (*Chunqiu*), believed to have been compiled and edited by Confucius and numbered as one of the Five Confucian Classics, is only a bare chronicle of events of the state of Lu (Confucius's native state) from 722–468 BC. Its commentary, the *Zuo zhuan*, considered by scholars to be China's oldest narrative history, while swift and vivid in style and providing more details, consists of short episodes broken up to fit the chronology of events in the "Spring and Autumn Annals," and thus lacks any unity of conception.

With the unification of the states under the Qin empire in 221 BC, China began its 2,000-year imperial age. The Qin conquest, through the use of Legalist measures and suppression of other schools of thought and government, brought about a brief rupture in the transmission of tradition that its successor, the Han dynasty, quickly acted to salvage and remedy. The Han spawned a great

era of scholastic and bibliographical enterprises in its attempts to retrieve the past and recreate tradition. Many of these projects were sponsored by the princely courts or were imperially commissioned; others were undertaken by individuals on their own initiative in an age that actively encouraged learning and the production of knowledge.

The first great historian of China, Sima Qian (145?–90? BC), was active during the reign of Emperor Wu, one of the most powerful and able rulers in Chinese history. Sima Qian succeeded his father to the post of Grand Historian–Astrologer

at court and completed the monumental historiographical project that they had begun together, the "Records of the Historian." It is an ambitious work that attempts to write the history of China from earliest antiquity to the time of Emperor Wu. Not one of the early historical writings can equal it in scope and organization, innovative conception and style. The form and organization of the "Records of the Historian" provided the model for all later dynastic histories and it has also been enjoyed as literature by generations of Chinese readers up to the present.

The "Records of the Historian" consists of 130 chapters divided into five large sections: "Basic Annals," "Chronological Tables," "Treatises," "Hereditary Houses," and "Biographies." The materials and chapters within each of the five sections are arranged chronologically. The "Biographies" section comprises 70 chapters and is by far the largest section in the work. It is also the most innovative in form and the most read and admired as both history and literature. For the first time in historical writing, the life and actions of an individual serve as the unifying focus for the development of theme and narrative. Although these chapters are not biographies in the sense of a detailed recounting of the life of a person that we expect to find in the modern form, his dramatized realizations of ancient historical personages, some of whom have been immortalized because of their

representation in this work, demonstrate Sima Qian's skill. In his "Biographies" he not only included outstanding individuals in the highest ranks of society, such as statesmen and generals, but he also gave a place to unusual men, such as the assassin– retainers, and with rare exceptions women other than (in)famous consorts, whose exemplary achievements or onerous deeds deserved recognition or judgment.

Until Sima Qian's time, the Chinese did not have a theory of literature that distinguished certain forms of writing as purely literary: there was no conception of writing as an end in itself, for aesthetic enjoyment without being in some way practical or informative. This developed during the early Han period with the growing popularity of a new genre, the rhapsody or rhymeprose (*fu*), with its elaborate ornamented rhetoric and structure and sensuous appeal. In his remarks on the biography of the rhapsodist Sima Xiangru, Sima Qian indicates the first critical distinction between expressive-didactic and affective-aesthetic functions and types of literature, specifically poetry. Chinese literary criticism was to develop much more sophisticated and complex theories of literary genres and their functions. In later periods, the four works mentioned here were recognized as a significant part of the early literary tradition and they have in turn influenced the development of literature, theory, and criticism in traditional China.

ABOVE: Portrait of Sima Qian (145?–90? BC), the great Han dynasty historian who served as court historian-astrologer to Emperor Wu.
BRITISH LIBRARY, LONDON

BELOW: A late eleventh- or early twelfth-century handscroll, Northern Qi Scholars Collating Classic Texts.
COURTESY DENMAN WALDO ROSS COLLECTION/ MUSEUM OF FINE ARTS, BOSTON

THE DEVELOPMENT OF CHINESE LITERATURE

SHANG (c. 1750–1045 BC)

ORACLE BONE INSCRIPTIONS

SPRING AND AUTUMN (771–c. 450 BC)

CONFUCIAN CLASSICS

Analects
Confucius (557—479 BC)

Shijing ("Book of Songs")
(four-character verse)

WARRING STATES (c. 450–221 BC)

PHILOSOPHICAL PROSE

Mozi (?479—390? BC)
Zhuangzi (?369—286? BC)
Mencius (?370—290? BC)
Lord Shang (died 338 BC)
Xunzi (?310—213? BC)
Han Feizi (died 233 BC)

CHUCI

Qu Yuan (?340—278 BC)
Song Yu (3rd century BC)

HISTORICAL NARRATIVE

Zuo Zhuan
Zuo Qiuming (5th—4th centuries BC)

HAN (206 BC–220 AD)

Fu
Sima Xiangru (179—117 BC)

MUSIC BUREAU POETRY

HISTORICAL PROSE

Records of the Historian
Sima Qian (145—86? BC)

History of the Former Han Dynasty
Ban Gu (32—92 BC)

THREE KINGDOMS (221–264)

SHI POETRY (FIVE-CHARACTER VERSE)

Cao Zhi (192—232)
Ruan Ji (210—263)
Xi Kang (223—262)

SIX DYNASTIES (317–588)

SUPERNATURAL TALES

SHI POETRY
Tao Yuanming (Tao Qian) (365—427)
Xie Lingyun (385—433)

DISCOVERY OF THE FOUR TONES
Shen Yue (441—513)

New Songs from a Jade Terrace
(an anthology of love poetry)
Xu Ling, compiler (c. 545)

TANG (618–906)

**SHI POETRY
(REGULATED VERSE AND OLD
STYLE; FIVE-CHARACTER AND
SEVEN-CHARACTER POETRY)**

Wang Wei (699—759)

Li Bo (701—762)
Du Fu (712—770)
Bo Juyi (772—846)
Li He (790—816)
Li Shangyin (812—858)

CI (LYRIC) POETRY (IRREGULAR LINE)
Wen Tingyun (?813—870)
Wei Zhuang (?834—910)

NEOCLASSICAL PROSE (GUWEN MOVEMENT)
Han Yu (768—824)
Liu Zongyuan (773—819)

LITERARY TALES (CHUAN QI)
Bo Xingjian (died 826)

BUDDHIST STORIES (BIANWEN)

*LEFT: A Shang-dynasty oracle bone.
The inscriptions on oracle bones represent the
earliest body of writing in East Asia.*
COURTESY OF THE INSTITUTE OF HISTORY AND PHILOLOGY, ACADEMIA SINICA

*BELOW: A five-character quatrain by Wang Wei
(eighth century) who is famous for his nature
poetry.* CALLIGRAPHY BY HE WAN GUAN

FIVE DYNASTIES (907–960)

CI (SONG LYRIC) POETRY

Li Yu (937—978)

Among the Flowers Anthology

SONG (960–1279)

CI (SONG LYRIC) POETRY

Liu Yong (?990–1050?)
Su Shi (Su Dongpo) (1037—1101)
Zhou Bangyan (1057—1121)
Li Qingzhao (1081—1143)
Lu You (125—1207)
Xin Qiji (1140—1207)

NEOCLASSICAL PROSE, HISTORICAL NARRATIVE, AND FU

Su Shi (1037—1107)

VERNACULAR STORIES (HUABEN)

VARIETY PLAYS (ZAJU)

SOUTHERN DRAMA (NANXI)

YUAN (1234–1368)

DRAMA (ZAJU)

Wang Shifu (13th century)
Guan Hanqing (13th century)
Ma Zhiyuan (13th century)
Bo Po (1226—1285)
Gao Wenxiu (13th century)

SANQU (LYRICS) POETRY

Guan Hanqing
Ma Zhiyuan
Zhang Kejiu (?1265—?1345)
Qiao Ji (1280—1345)
Liu Zhi (13th—14th centuries)

MING (1368–1644)
CHINESE RESTORATION

VERNACULAR FICTION

Romance of the Three Kingdoms
Luo Guanzhong (14th century)

Journey to the West

Wu Chengen (?1500—1582)

The Golden Lotus
anonymous
Feng Menglong (1574—1646) (author and editor of vernacular short stories)
Ling Mengchu (1580—1644) (author and editor of vernacular short stories)

DRAMA (KUNQU)

Gao Ming (14th century)
Tang Xianzu (1550—1616)
Shen Jing (1553—1610)

QING (1644–1911)

FICTION

The Scholars
Wu Jingzi (1701—1754)

The Story of the Stone (Dream of the Red chamber)
Cao Xueqin (?1724—1764)

The Carnal Prayer Mat
Li Yu (1611—1680?)

DRAMA

Li Yu, playwright (1611—1680?)
Hong Sheng, playwright (?1646—1764)
Kong Shangren, playwright (1648—1718)

PEKING OPERA

REPUBLIC (1912–)

VERNACULAR (BAIHUA MOVEMENT)

Hu Shi (1891—1962)

MODERN POETRY

Xu Zhimo (1895—1931)
Wen Yiduo (1899—1946)

FICTION

Lu Xun (1881—1936)

DRAMA

RIGHT: "Spring Arrives," by the Tang poet Du Fu, written in seven-character regulated style with tonal and grammatical parallelism in the middle two couplets. CALLIGRAPHY BY HE WAN GUAN

PHILOSOPHERS AND STATESMEN

Robin D. S. Yates

THE ZHOU DYNASTY (1045?–256 BC) THAT conquered the Shang toward the end of the second millennium BC was the longest in the whole course of Chinese history, lasting close to a thousand years. The founding fathers, Kings Wen and Wu, and his brother the Duke of Zhou, regent to his nephew, the young King Cheng, were believed to have created a utopia to which all later rulers aspired. Certain canonical texts, such as *Yijing* (the "Book of Changes") and some basic political institutions were attributed to the genius or the inspiration of these early paragons of virtue. Forever after, Chinese looked back to this age with deep nostalgia. Confucius (551– 479 BC) himself is said to have remarked in despair that for a long time he had not dreamed of the Duke of Zhou, on whom he modeled his behavior, believing that he had been a failure in his efforts to reform the society of his own times.

Traditional historians attributed to the Zhou a new system of governance and a new political ideology that profoundly affected future conceptions of the relation between heaven and humanity and the nature of kingship. The Zhou claimed that their success in seizing control of the whole world (as they believed they had) resulted from the fact that they had remained sober and moral while the Shang were utterly dissolute and immoral, wallowing in lakes of intoxicating liquor and indulging their passion for sexual excess. The supreme god Tian (Heaven) therefore gave the Zhou the mandate to rule, which they would maintain so long as their kings continued to behave in a ritually correct manner. But the mandate to rule was not constant: Tian could always remove it from the Zhou and give it to another more morally worthy of the task. While the Zhou ruler held the mandate, he was the Son of Tian and was given the monopoly to mediate between Tian and earth and maintain the harmony of the cosmos, but once he lost it, he was no more than any other commoner. As the Zhou were a relatively small group from northwest China, they were forced to parcel out the vast lands they had conquered from the Shang to their relatives and allies to govern: thus was instituted a feudal system with innumerable small states dotting the landscape, all owing allegiance to the Zhou overlords. Essentially, the land was ruled by a series of interrelated aristocratic lineages, each based on a walled town that was generally oriented to the cardinal directions, in which the temples to the ancestors, the altars of soil and grain, and the palaces of the elite were the most

ABOVE: *Carved ritual jade from the Western Zhou period.*
NATIONAL PALACE MUSEUM, TAIBEI, TAIWAN, REPUBLIC OF CHINA

OPPOSITE: *King Wu of the Zhou led the conquest of the Shang dynasty in about 1045 BC. This late-imperial hanging scroll depicts this paragon of moral virtue as a Confucian scholar.*
NATIONAL PALACE MUSEUM, TAIBEI, TAIWAN, REPUBLIC OF CHINA

RIGHT: Text of the Yijing *(the "Book of Changes") found as a silk manuscript in a grave at Mawangdui, near Changsha in Hunan province.*
CHINA PICTORIAL PHOTO SERVICE

BELOW RIGHT: Human figures carved from jade during mid-Western Zhou period.
BRITISH MUSEUM, LONDON

BELOW: Small cast-bronze harness plaque decorated with a human face, dating from the Shang or Western Zhou period. BRITISH MUSEUM, LONDON

conquest. One exceptional find is a bronze vessel cast just one week after the decisive battle with the Shang. The Zhou were notably different in that they were far more conscious of history than their predecessors: they engraved long inscriptions inside the vessels they used in the sacrifices to their ancestors, often describing the circumstances under which the vessels were manufactured. These naturally provide invaluable historical information.

The great watershed in the Zhou dynasty occurred in 770 BC. The Rong peoples joined disaffected Zhou vassals and sacked the dynastic capital, forcing the Zhou from their homeland to the west of the Tong Pass in modern Shaanxi province, and making it necessary for them to reestablish themselves as the Eastern Zhou in the vicinity of modern Luoyang in Henan province, just south of the Huang (Yellow) River in the heart of the Central Plains. From this time of catastrophic failure, the Zhou kings functioned merely as ritual heads of a moribund dynasty, for they were unable to prevent their erstwhile subordinate vassals from fighting each other and increasing their territories at the expense of smaller, weaker city states. Eventually, only seven powerful states remained to fight to unify the entire country, and it was the Qin who at last succeeded in 221 BC and founded the empire.

Traditionally divided into the Spring and Autumn (722–481 BC) and the appropriately named Warring States (464–222 BC) periods, the centuries of the Eastern Zhou saw immense social,

important buildings. Those who provided services for the dominant groups, such as bronzesmiths, jade and bone workers, and potters, were clustered nearby, either inside or outside the walls, depending on local custom and topography. Beyond the walls, in the hinterland, the rural peoples continued to live much as their Neolithic ancestors had done, but virtually nothing is known of their habits and beliefs.

The reality of this Western Zhou utopia is still very unclear, although recent archaeological excavations have revealed the foundations of one early Zhou house and oracle bones dating from the time prior to the

economic, military, and political changes. In the incessant wars, waged with increasingly sophisticated weapons such as the crossbow, and bronze and then iron swords, and with larger armies composed of more infantry and fewer chariots eventually supplemented by cavalry, most of the early aristocratic lineages were eliminated and a new, more complex, type of society developed. Rulers relied no longer on the assistance of their kin and fellow aristocrats but on advisors drawn from a new group of technocrats called the *shi* or knights. Trained in the arts of administration and war learned from written texts or transmitted to them orally by itinerant teachers, these knights staffed the bureaucracies of the regional state systems. As salaried employees, they owed their success to their own personal merit and competence and their loyalty to the rulers who hired them.

Confucius, a native of the tiny state of Lu, is the best known of this new group.

LEFT: Bronze ritual food vessel, the Kang Hou gui, *dating to the early Western Zhou period. The interior surface of the vessel bears a lengthy inscription that commemorates two important historical events: Zhou attacks on rebellious descendants of Shang in Henan, and the sending of the Marquis of Kang (Kang Hou) to govern the territory of Wei (in present-day Henan province). It is likely that the vessel was cast by a relative of the marquis.*
BRITISH MUSEUM, LONDON

The first Chinese educator, he accepted students from all ranks of society, and trained them in the six arts: ritual, music, archery, chariot driving, writing, and mathematics. He believed that to save society it was necessary to create a moral community led by superior men (women were not included: they were to stay home and be obedient to either father, husband, or son) and so advocated self-cultivation as the primary task of the intellectual, and maintained that personal fulfillment could only be achieved through a process of creative interaction between the self and others. Therefore filial piety, the expression of the proper relations that should adhere between an individual and the members of his family, most particularly his parents, was an archetypal virtue and was to be extended outward from this nexus to the rest of society. Thus the family unit became the template on which the whole of society was to be modeled and the individual could never be uprooted from the contingencies of his relations. Never claiming to be a sage or an innovator himself, rather a mere transmitter of the wisdom and culture of the Zhou past, Confucius expressed his philosophical beliefs

LEFT: The Zhou cast lengthy inscriptions in their bronze ritual vessels for sacrifices to ancestors or to commemorate other political or ritual events.
CHINA PICTORIAL PHOTO SERVICE

unsystematically in dialogue with his students, friends, and rulers. His observations and those of his students are preserved in the collection known as *Lunyu* (the "Analects") which show the master to be a brilliant conversationalist, a keen observer of his fellow men — though one not above making mistakes — and a truly humane man. Humaneness was, indeed, the ethical ideal to which he believed all should aspire and the most concise explanation he gave for the practice of this virtue was "not to do to others what you would not want them to do to you."

Confucius's ideas were not accepted in his own day and were only adopted as official state ideology, greatly transformed, in the Han dynasty many centuries later. First, Mozi (possibly a student of Confucius who lived in the mid-fifth century BC) challenged the basis of his philosophy, arguing that his emphasis on the family led to selfishness and, taken to its ultimate conclusion, to interstate warfare. Mozi believed that universal love was far preferable and that one should treat the children of others as one would one's own. Further, people would not practice ethical behavior merely because they knew it was right, they needed external sanctions to force them to act correctly for the benefit of society as a whole. Mozi therefore elaborated a series of tenets to

fill the gap he saw in Confucius's exposition. Belief in the reality of ghosts and spirits and the power of the will of Tian would ensure that people would perform properly, for they would be afraid of supernatural punishment, while society would be best organized if worthy people were in positions of authority and all subordinates were required to obey those immediately above them in the hierarchy.

Later on in the Warring States period, many other philosophers proposed their own solutions to the ills of contemporary society generated by the rapid changes that were taking place, although most of their writings have now unfortunately been lost. The Daoist text *Laozi* (Laozi was reputed to be a founding father of Daoism, but it is doubtful that he was a real person) urged the ruler to keep the population ignorant and supply them only with what would satisfy their basic physical appetites. The ruler should model himself on the Dao — the unique, indivisible, indescribable, immaterial metaphysical force or energy that was the source of all material substance — and rule passively through the practice of *wuwei*, or nonpurposive nonaction, in such a way that no one would realize how he was monopolizing and manipulating control of the state. This highly elliptic text, composed mostly in abstruse poetry that allows for multiple interpretation, has been one of the great favorites of the entire Chinese philosophical corpus and has been translated into other languages more often than any other work. Other Daoists, such as Zhuangzi (c. 369– 286 BC) (see Chapter 7), rejected involvement in the dangerous maelstrom of contemporary politics and urged withdrawal into the natural world and the spontaneous acceptance of change, no matter what happened.

Seeking to regain the philosophical initiative for the Confucians, Mencius

LEFT: *Part of the Daoist text,* Laozi, *written on silk which was found in the Han dynasty tombs at Mawangdui, near Changsha in Hunan province.* WENWU PUBLISHING

BELOW: *During the Zhou period, tomb objects called* mingqi, *models of things enjoyed by the deceased, were interred with the body. This bronze figure from the Eastern Zhou was possibly a lamp bearer.* ROYAL ONTARIO MUSEUM

were morally justified in removing a ruler who demonstrated a lack of a sense of propriety. Xunzi, more tough minded than his predecessor, argued instead for the application of education and a system of external rules to mold humans to behave in such a way that "kingly government" would prevail in the world.

In the unsettled conditions of the Warring States period, when rulers were enjoying immense wealth and luxury generated by interregional trade that was facilitated by the development of currency in the form of cloth and bronze coinage, and plied by a new class of merchants, appeals for moral government fell on deaf ears. The practical statesmen who followed Legalism received the greatest attention by contemporary rulers. These statesmen gained their greatest success in the state of Qin and their efforts enabled Qin eventually to unite the entire country. The Qin were responsible for the political, social, and economic transformations of this crucial stage in Chinese history.

Starting in the late fifth century BC, Qin began to adopt from their eastern neighbors certain economic practices, such as taxation of grain crops and the expansion of the size of its measure of land from 100 to 240 square paces, and customs such as the ritual initiation into manhood by capping the head and buckling on a sword, and banning human sacrifice at funerals of the elite, and aggressively sought assistance from willing and interested intellectuals and statesmen to help advise their ruler and shape new policies. The most famous of these was Gongsun Yang of Wei, also known as Wei Yang, later enfeoffed for his services to Qin as Lord Shang or Shang Yang, who answered Duke Xiao's call for

(371–289 BC) and Xunzi (298–238 BC) reaffirmed their master's original vision of humane government. Mencius centered his discourse on the notion that all humans had the potential to behave ethically and could activate their original dispositions for the good if they merely consciously willed them. Cultivation of the four initial conditions — commiseration for others, shame, modesty, and the sense of right and wrong — would lead to the virtues of humanity, rightness, ritual, and wisdom. Those who did cultivate themselves, and worked with their minds, had the right to rule others; those who just labored physically were no better than animals and were to be ruled. This argument led to the remarkable conclusion that the people

LEFT: *A large set of 65 cast-bronze bells suspended from a lacquered wooden frame, excavated from the fifth-century-BC tomb of Marquis Yi of the state of Zeng, in north-central Hubei province. The same grave also contained numerous other musical instruments, which played an important role in rituals during the Chinese Bronze Age.* WENWU PUBLISHING

talent in 359 BC. As a Legalist, Shang Yang's philosophy of practical statecraft was not intended to improve the self-cultivation of the educated elite, at the enhancement of ritual propriety and decorous behavior, as were the teachings of Confucianism and Daoism. It had only one aim: to strengthen the ruler and the state and the subordination of all others, be they members of the ruler's own family, of allied aristocratic lineages, or the common people at large. To achieve this end, and with a fundamentally instrumentalist and pessimistic view of human nature, Lord Shang advocated the introduction of a system based purely on

RIGHT: Rectangular bronze basin (fang jian) inlaid with gold and turquoise from the third century BC was found at Shan Xian in Henan province.
METROPOLITAN MUSEUM OF ART/ HENAN PROVINCIAL MUSEUM

rewards and punishments. Punishments were to be swift, severe, and numerous, whereas rewards were to be few and not excessively generous, and only given out by the ruler. Law was to rule supreme; no one, not even the crown prince, was to be above the law, as the Confucians argued for the elite as a whole ("law does not apply to the elite; ritual is not relevant for the common people"). Coupled with this emphasis on law was Lord Shang's belief that only two things mattered for the

state: agriculture and war. Secondary occupations like trade were despised and subject to intense government supervision. Grain provided for the basic needs of the people, while the army protected the state and allowed it to expand its boundaries. And individuals were to receive rank based solely on their own personal merit: they could not inherit it from their forebears.

The practical application of these policies had profound implications for the whole course of Chinese and East Asian history down to the present century. They led to the destruction of the feudalism that had existed in China during the previous thousand years and the creation of a rigidly hierarchical social system determined by the state. The Qin initiated a system of rational bureaucratic administration that has spread throughout the world and continues to flourish exuberantly today.

Rank was to be determined objectively by practical achievement: this was measured by the cutting off of heads of enemy soldiers in battle. One head was rewarded by one degree of rank; two heads, by two ranks; and officers were similarly rewarded by the number of heads their subordinates cut off as a unit. The entire society was ordered into a single hierarchy that stretched from the common people all the way up to the ruler, and through the ruler to the cosmos. Therefore, social order was conceived of as the basis for cosmic order. The initial seventeen ranks of Qin were expanded by the time of the empire to 20, and commoners of the former feudal system could only reach rank eight. The advantages of rank were numerous: it could be surrendered to the government in exchange for the manumission of a relative from slavery; with rank, one received less severe punishment for crimes; in daily life, rank was also important, for those who were graded were given certain responsibilities for organizing their comrades on social

RIGHT: Reconstructed wooden-shafted iron axes, spades, and hoes of Qin and Han design. Iron began to be cast into implements in the sixth century BC, by the time of the First Emperor, artisans had developed the skill to cast iron swords up to 3 feet (1 m) long. Production during the Han state was on an immense scale, far surpassing the output of the Roman empire, with tens of thousands of tons of cast iron being manufactured each year.

TIME LINE FOR THE EASTERN ZHOU DYNASTY

770 BC Beginning of the Eastern Zhou: the Zhou royal house forced to move its capital east to Luoyang, Henan province.

722 The beginning of *Spring and Autumn Annals*; the beginning of the Spring and Autumn period.

685–643 Rule of Duke Huan of Qi, the first hegemon; his main adviser is Guan Zhong, after whom an important collection of early philosophical treatises, the *Guanzi*, is named.

655 Jin conquers the small states of Guo and Yu, although the ruling houses are related to each other.

641 Song defeats the state of Zeng and puts Zeng's ruler to death in a blood sacrifice to Song's ancestors.

636 After a long exile, Chonger succeeds to the throne of Jin as Duke Wen.

632 Duke Wen of Jin inflicts a massive defeat on Chu at the Battle of Chengpu; as a reward, he is recognized as the second hegemon by the Zhou king.

594 Lu institutes first tax based on the amount of land held.

552 First bestowal of rank for achievement in battle (by the ruler of Qi).

551 Birth of Confucius.

514–496 Reign of King Helu of Wu who employed the famous military theorist, Sun Wu (Sunzi).

505–502 Dominance of Yang Hu in the state of Lu.

485 Wu Zixu, famous counselor to the King of Wu, Goujian, ordered to commit suicide: as he dies, he predicts the eventual destruction of Wu.

481 Chen Chengzi kills the Duke of Qi; from this time the Chen family monopolizes control of the Qi state; Chen's grandson later usurps the throne of Qi.

479 Death of Confucius.

473 Destruction of Wu by Yue.

464 Last year covered by the *Zuo Zhuan* ("Zuo Commentary") on the *Spring and Autumn Annals*.

453 The Han, Wei, and Zhao lineages unite and destroy the Zhi lineage in Jin and seize all its territory.

447 Chu destroys the state of Cai.

409 Qin orders its adult officials to start wearing swords.

403 Heads of the Han, Wei, and Zhao lineages invested as marquises, officially sanctioning the division of the territory of the ancient state of Jin.

c. 384 Wu Qi, the military strategist, travels to Chu.

c. 382 Wu Qi appointed *lingyin* (chancellor) of Chu and initiates a reform program along Legalist lines. Shortly after, the king of Chu dies and the aristocratic lineages attack Wu Qi, arrest him, and have him ripped apart by four horse-drawn chariots.

375 Destruction of the state of Zheng by Han, which proceeds to move its capital to "New Zheng."

c. 365–290 Life of the Daoist philosopher Zhuangzi.

361–337 Wei moves its capital to Daliang, where later Mencius is to meet King Hui.

355–337 Shen Buhai, the Legalist-administrator, chancellor of Han.

355 Chu destroys Yue.

352 Wei Yang appointed chancellor of Qin; he institutes many Legalist reforms in Qin and is later enfeoffed as Lord Shang.

338 Death of Duke Xiao of Qin, and execution of Wei Yang, Lord Shang, his supporter and chancellor.

c. 371–289 Life of the Confucian philosopher Mencius.

c. 334 King Hui of Liang (Wei) uses the philosopher-logician Hui Shi, the friend of Zhuangzi, as his chancellor.

325 Huiwen jun of Qin calls himself King.

316 Sima Cuo conquers and pacifies Shu (Sichuan) for Qin.

307 King Wuling of Zhao orders his cavalry to wear northern nomadic Hu dress.

c. 298–238 Life of the Confucian philosopher Xunzi (Hsün-tzu).

278 Qin captures and sacks the Chu capital; Chu is forced to move its capital to Chen.

256 Qin destroys the Eastern Zhou; Chu destroys the state of Lu.

ABOVE: Bronze (the bronze has corroded green) wine vessel (fang hu) inlaid with malachite, excavated from a Warring States period (fourth century BC) tomb at Shan Xian in Henan province.

METROPOLITAN MUSEUM OF ART/HISTORICAL MUSEUM, BEIJING

and ritual occasions. Rank also entitled the bearer to receive a house and land, together with slaves to help till the soil. Indeed, from early Warring States times the use of iron agricultural tools became more and more common and it appears that the wealth of the Qin and other states, such as its main rival the Chu, was based to a considerable extent on the greater agricultural surpluses that iron implements helped generate.

The government initiated a system of household registers in which were recorded for all the members of the population names and details of birth, marriage, and death, location of residence,

and crimes committed. This enabled the government to keep track of the vital statistics of the entire population and force them to fulfill certain obligations to the state, corvée labor duty and military service being the most onerous.

Government bureaucrats were held responsible for the performance of duties by members of their units, in addition, the government took over responsiblility for the punishment of even the smallest transgressions between family members and instituted an exceedingly detailed and repressive legal code. Punishments were meted out in the form of hard labor and physical mutilation: labor could last from one to perhaps six years, and mutilation was graded from shaving of the facial whiskers, to shaving of the head, branding the forehead, cutting off the nose, cutting off the left foot, and castration. For the worst crimes, banishment to farthest reaches of the state, enslavement, and various types of cruel execution, such as being cut in two at the waist, or being torn apart by means of ropes attached to horse-drawn chariots, were prescribed. A father, for example, could petition the government to have his son executed for lack of filial piety, or a slave owner could ask it to cut off the foot of a slave who refused to work properly in his owner's fields.

Further, a system of mutual responsibility was instituted for both populace and officials. The people were organized into units of five households and required to denounce the crimes of their fellow members. If they failed to do so, they were held equally responsible for the crime and similarly punished. Family members could even be enslaved for heinous crimes committed by other members. Government bureaucrats were held responsible for the performance of the duties in their unit, and the fines for inadequate performance grew heavier the higher up the management hierarchy one went. The active involvement of the Qin state in many sectors of the economy, including handicrafts such as bronze and iron foundries, and the production of lacquer and silk, which was also a form of currency, enabled it to monitor the quality of goods manufactured. In fact, their quality control system was one of the first in the world.

Bureaucrats were evaluated on their performance every year and had to send in detailed reports to the capital in the tenth month, the end of the Qin fiscal year, specifying exactly the state of all matters and products under their jurisdiction. Promotion was based entirely on objective standards, not on moral conduct, and officials could not overstep their areas of authority. If they did, whether they did more or less than was required of them by the title of their position, they were punished by fines. These fines were heavy and calculated in sets of armor and shields, and could be paid off immediately in "cash" (round bronze coins with square holes), or worked off by laboring for the government for free at the rate of eight cash per day, six cash per day if one received rations. If you were too poor to provide your own clothing, this too was charged to your account with the state.

Unfortunately, the exchange rate between shields, armor, and cash is not known, but it is clear that all the mutilating punishments up to and including the death penalty could be worked off in this way. Some consolation could be obtained for convicts, for they could have their slaves, oxen, and horses work off these fines at specified rates, and could even use family members or hire others to do the labor for them.

On the eve of the empire Qin society had become complex, and its bureaucracy was administratively sophisticated. Most of this information is entirely new, the result of the discovery since the early 1970s of documents written on slips of bamboo and wood. Until then, historians only had the theoretical writings of the Legalists Shang Yang, Hanfeizi, and Shen Buhai to analyze; now we can observe the actual workings of the late preimperial state. By the end of the Zhou dynasty most of the elements that are characteristic of later Chinese culture had been initiated or had passed through their first transformations. The philosophical and institutional foundations had been laid: it remained for later generations to build creatively upon them.

BELOW: Reconstruction of a building in which important rituals were held, based on a ground plan found in Fengchu, Shaanxi province. Rituals would have been performed in the central raised hall. The offerings would have been prepared in the kitchens in the wing rooms at the side — these may also have been storage rooms. The guests would have walked up the left staircase, the host up the right staircase. The spirit wall in the front may have been built to prevent evil spirits from entering the building (Chinese believe evil spirits travel in straight lines), although it could have been built for privacy or to break the force of strong winds. Whatever the reason for these walls, they were a sign of high status — only the Son of Heaven, feudal lords, and the designated rulers of towns could have one for their palace, ancestral hall, or mansion.

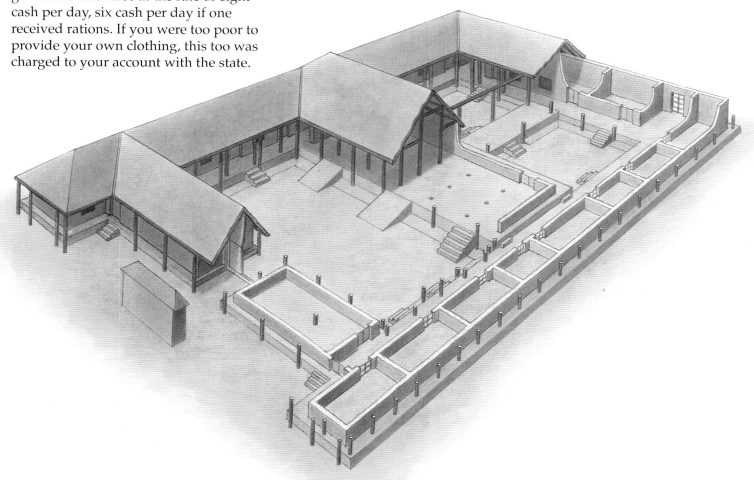

THE BIRTH OF IMPERIAL CHINA

Robin D. S. Yates

THE GREAT ACHIEVEMENT OF THE QIN dynasty (221–207 BC) was the defeat of its six rival states and the founding of the empire in 221 BC. For this they have been cursed and excoriated by Chinese scholars for the last 2,000 years: Mao Zedong was one of the very few who avidly admired them. Indeed, the name "China" comes from the Qin. Under the self proclaimed First Emperor, known as Shihuangdi, whose given name was Zheng, the Qin created a political system and the idea of empire that lasted, although with many modifications, until 1911.

The origins of the people who founded the Qin state on the northwestern border of China Proper are obscure. Some scholars maintain that they were a branch of the Yi tribes whose homeland lay in the east, in the region of modern Shandong province, and that they migrated west some time during the Shang dynasty; others claim that they belonged to the western Rong barbarians who were frequently in conflict with the Shang; a third group of scholars theorizes that in fact they descended from the Xia tribe of north central China. They themselves claimed as ancestor Nüxiu, the granddaughter of the (mythological) Emperor Zhuanxu, who conceived a male child called Daye after consuming the egg of a swallow that had swooped toward her

when she was spinning cloth. Whatever the truth, Qin first emerges as a fully fledged historical entity when the chief of the Qin lineage was enfeoffed as Duke Xiang by the Zhou king as recompense for the Qin's assistance in guarding his western flank at the time when the Rong peoples had defeated the Zhou in 770 BC.

In the centuries that followed the founding of the Eastern Zhou, the Qin were on the periphery of Chinese cultural developments and were virtually irrelevant to the great political changes that were taking place in the central, eastern, and southern regions. Very little is known of their history, except the bare-bones list of successive rulers and certain notable events, such as victories or defeats, when these impinged on the interests of the states of the Chinese heartland. In recent years, this meager record has been supplemented by the discovery of the capital, Yong, south of the modern city of Fengxiang, and archaeologists, by excavating temple and palace complexes, and a series of important graves, have been able to determine that the Qin followed the ritual practices of their more advanced cousins to the east. But the materials recovered cannot match the treasures of comparable date found elsewhere.

The Qin seem to have spent their time consolidating their western and northern

ABOVE: *A Qin bronze architectural component with an intertwined serpent design, originally fitted onto the end of a beam in a house or palace. It is one of 64 pieces found in a hoard in Yaojiagang, Fengxiang, 1973–75.*
CHAPMAN LEE/CHINA TOURISM PHOTO LIBRARY

OPPOSITE: *A column of the grey pottery army which was discovered guarding the entrance to the tomb of the First Emperor, Shihuangdi, at Lintong in Shaanxi province.*
CHINA PHOTO LIBRARY LTD

borders against the many tribes, nomadic and settled, that pressed upon them, inculcating in their people a military ethic, spartan habits, and an innate respect for legitimate authority, with little taste for the more refined and aesthetic side of life. Nevertheless, the Qin gradually pushed east, coming into conflict with such powerful states as the Jin located in the loess hills of Shanxi province in north central China, expanding their agricultural base throughout the whole length of the Wei River valley, biding their time for the moment when they would change the course of Chinese and world history. In the late fourth century BC, they marched south across the Qinling range and conquered the Sichuan basin, then inhabited by the non-Han peoples of the kingdoms of Shu and Ba. With its rich mineral and human resources, this region provided a testing ground for the expansion of Qin administration: this stood them in good stead when they came to conquer the rest of China.

Until the advent of modern archaeology, and most particularly until a series of chance discoveries starting in the mid-1970s — such as the cache of Qin legal documents and almanac texts in the tomb

of a local official named Xi ("Happy"), who died in 217 BC, and the First Emperor's mausoleum — very little was known of the actual details of Qin administrative, legal, and social practice, and artistic proclivities. Scholars recognized however, that the Qin had adopted as their basic ideology the so-called Legalist political philosophy, which stressed strong authoritarian government through strict laws and harsh punishments rather than reliance on the moral virtues of the people. What has been revealed in the last 20 years or so is an extraordinarily sophisticated and complex state whose cultural level was every bit as advanced as Rome's when it founded its own empire in the Mediterranean two centuries later. One of the most famous archaeological sites in the whole world in the late twentieth century is the First Emperor's mausoleum, with its serried ranks of infantry, cavalry, and charioteers, up to 8,000 life-size pottery warriors each of whose facial features is different and seemingly individualized. Equally well known is

being united. In the more than 200 years of the Warring States period from the time of the death of Confucius in 479 BC, to 221 BC, many philosophers and statesmen had advocated unification, and many rulers had adopted policies that they thought might be conducive to *them* being the fortunate unifier, yet that did not mean that the unification itself was inevitable. Undoubtedly, the creation of the empire resulted from a combination of many diverse factors and policies, and the appearance of particular personalities in positions of power who made certain fateful decisions at particular points in the process. The increasing number of significant discoveries may help scholars determine more precisely which factors were most important in the creation of the Qin empire.

China on the verge of unification was a highly diverse subcontinent. Many peoples of different ethnic heritage stretching back into the Neolithic period lived in geographically diverse regions, spoke mutually unintelligible languages, and had different economic, political, and legal systems, and religious and philosophical traditions. Furthermore, local populations were nowhere completely integrated into administrative hierarchies of the different states, there were different conceptions of time, and different conceptions of belonging to a state. People didn't think of themselves as being "Chinese," as belonging to a single cultural tradition that was dominant or all encompassing, and to which those who wished to be socially acceptable aspired to mold their behavior. That was to develop in time out of the unification process itself. The Chinese had to learn to be Chinese; both orthodoxy and orthopraxy, how to think correctly and how to act correctly, was knowledge only "painfully acquired": we must not read back into the past what we know to be

the Great Wall of China which was considerably expanded and improved during this period. Constructed of rammed earth on the orders of Shihuangdi (and lined with brick during much later dynasties) it is said to be visible from the moon, although this belief actually derives from a vision once dreamed by the First Emperor himself. These are wonderful expressions of the human spirit, but they are also equally powerful manifestations of the coercive nature of Qin rule and its prodigious ability to mobilize hundreds of thousands, even millions, of its citizens in massive, harsh corvée labor projects.

It would be unwise to assume that the events leading up to the unification were somehow preordained or that the mere passage of time itself resulted in China

LEFT: Portrait of emperor Shihuangdi (259–210 BC), founder of the Qin dynasty and architect of the first unification of the Chinese nation.
WENWU PUBLISHING

BELOW: A section of the western end of the Great Wall, in Gansu province, showing its original rammed earth construction. Subsequent dynasties added the more familiar brick linings.
CATHERINE TREASURE/ANCIENT ART & ARCHITECTURE COLLECTION

typical of the later tradition or of the present.

How then did the Qin state transform itself from a relatively small, backward, and peripheral polity into the most powerful juggernaut that East Asia had ever seen? How was it able to crush its rivals within the space of ten years and found an imperial system that was to last 2,000? In the past, some argued that its geographical location on the northwestern edge of the Central Plains protected by the Tong Pass, was the crucial factor; others argued that Qin had access to more advanced weapons technology, specifically cheap mass-produced wrought-iron swords. But recent archaeological finds disprove this theory: virtually all the weapons found at the First Emperor's tomb, and at other Qin sites, are made of bronze. The secret of Qin's success lay elsewhere, most likely in the adoption of Legalist political theory and the sophisticated application in daily administration of its techniques of social control.

Qin created a comprehensively repressive system in which it harnessed all the human and physical resources of the state to its own expansionist ends. In many respects, the Qin resembled a giant prison camp, but one in which the rewards in the form of rank were just enough to encourage the people to work toward the state's goals. With the vision, hard work, and overwhelming ambition of the First Emperor, the Qin succeeded in creating their empire. However, by pressing its population so savagely in a series of immense labor projects — including the construction of over 200 palaces, the Great Wall, the First Emperor's mausoleum, and water engineering projects — and military campaigns to the far south into Vietnam and the far west into the Gobi Desert, in which perhaps hundreds of thousands of people died, the Qin finally forced the common people into revolt and the dynasty collapsed a bare thirteen years after its inception.

When the Qin conquered its rivals in 221 BC, it initiated a series of reforms to consolidate control and make manifest the new order. Whether or not King Zheng started his mausoleum at this time is not known, for the historical records are silent on this point, but it is significant that he called himself by a new title, *huangdi* (august *di* or emperor), signifying that he was on a par with the major deities who also bore that title. He gathered the bronze weapons of his former enemies, melting them down to make twelve giant statues to decorate his new palace, called Afang, and destroyed their city walls and other fortifications to ensure there were no strongholds left to oppose his rule. He unified the writing script, simplifying, rationalizing, and standardizing regional variants of graphs, and enforced the new system throughout China. In this reform, perhaps 25 percent of all earlier graphs

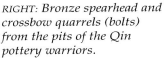

RIGHT: Bronze spearhead and crossbow quarrels (bolts) from the pits of the Qin pottery warriors.
ROBERT HARDING PICTURE LIBRARY

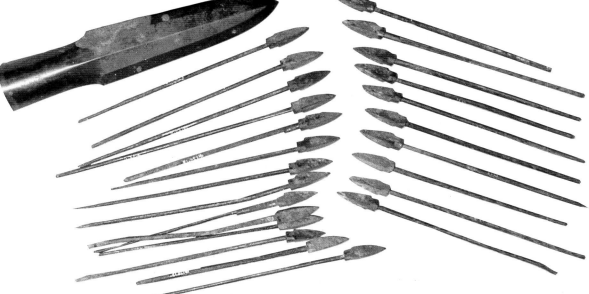

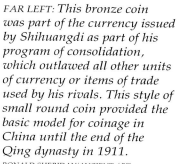

FAR LEFT: *This bronze coin was part of the currency issued by Shihuangdi as part of his program of consolidation, which outlawed all other units of currency or items of trade used by his rivals. This style of small round coin provided the basic model for coinage in China until the end of the Qing dynasty in 1911.* RONALD SHERIDAN/ANCIENT ART & ARCHITECTURE COLLECTION

LEFT: *The Chinese writing system was standardized and an even simpler form, known as "clerk's script," a precursor of modern characters, was introduced. This Qin writing brush was found in a tomb in Hubei province.* WENWU PUBLISHING

were eliminated. Further, the use of an even simpler form of writing employed by bureaucrats, called the "clerk's script," became more common and it is this script that is the direct ancestor of modern characters. He also unified the system of weights and measures, standardized the width of cart axles to ensure that a single vehicle could travel anywhere in the land without interruption, and expanded Qin bronze and gold currency, suppressing the units of his rivals, and the use of pearls, jade, tortoise and cowry shells, silver, and tin in commercial transactions. By these means, he was able to control communications throughout the land and enhance regional administrative, cultural, and economic integration.

King Zheng abolished the old feudal system of allotments of fiefs to nobles and divided the empire into units of counties and commanderies, a hierarchical system of administration in which the central government directly appointed most of the staff of local bureaux. The number of commanderies thus created is important: there were 36. The emperor believed in the cosmological theory advanced by Yin Yang and Five Phase specialists who claimed that a dynasty could only claim legitimacy if it accorded with the natural order as manifested in the continuous cycle of alternation between Yin and Yang and the successive changes of the phases: wood, fire, earth, metal, and water. These were coordinated with the directions, east, south, center, west, and north, and seasons, spring, summer, late summer, autumn, and winter, with the colors, green, red, yellow, white, and black and with the numbers. As conquerors of the Zhou, the proper Qin phase was water, its direction north, its season winter, its color black, and its number six. All ritual paraphernalia were coordinated with this scheme, even the number of braids in the hairstyles of the pottery warriors, three and six, may reflect this belief. And, perhaps, as winter was the time of the dominance of Yin when nature was "punished" and at rest, so did the Qin try to emulate or harmonize with it by

LEFT: *The First Emperor also introduced a unified system of weights and measures. This bronze bowl-shaped oval measure has a socket into which a handle could be inserted.* CHINA PICTORIAL PHOTO SERVICE

BELOW: *A reconstruction of one of the Qin palaces excavated in the capital of Xianyang. There are no details available yet about the functions of the rooms, but one can assume that the largest hall was for audiences and that the side walkways would have been patrolled by guards. No one was allowed to wear a sword in the main audience hall of the main palace, for it is recorded that the assassin, Jing Ke, nearly succeeded in killing the Qin king Zheng (before he became the First Emperor) because no one could run up the steps to the throne carrying a weapon to help the king. We do not know, however, whether this particular palace, was the palace in which the assassination attempt took place.*

expanding its punitive legal system and forcing the entire population into corvée labor service.

Major roads were constructed from the capital Xianyang north, northeast, east, and southeast, 50 double paces wide and planted with trees every 30 feet (9 m). General Meng Tian took on the task of consolidating earlier walls along the northern border to demarcate civilized space from the land of the barbarians and to enhance its defensive capability. Initially a pounded-earth wall, eventually this came to be known as the "ten thousand *li* wall" or Great Wall, whose mythic proportions far outstripped its actual military value as a single static defensive line. Most of the troops were stationed at forts in the rear; the soldiers at the wall were there for observation purposes only. And during the campaigns of expansion into Guangdong and Guangxi, the 3 mile (5 km) long Lingqu Canal was cut to join a southern tributary of the Yangzi River and a northern tributary of the Xi River, thus permitting uninterrupted travel by water between north and south China.

While the emperor's successes were enormous, he became more and more obsessed with the desire to achieve physical immortality, this at the same time as he became more and more suspicious of his courtiers, not least the result of having survived several assassination attempts. He sought elixirs from fraudulent magicians and sponsored lavish naval expeditions to find the mythical islands of the blessed in the eastern sea. Five times he progressed through his empire performing sacrifices to local divinities and erecting monuments to his own genius, and it was in 210 BC on one of these journeys in the east that he died of an unknown cause. But three years

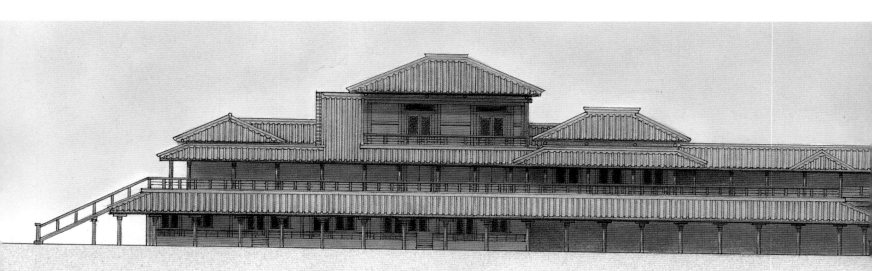

access to knowledge. He then executed 460 scholars by burying them alive for daring to criticize him. After his death, his favorite son, Huhai, engineered a coup d'état and brought his corpse back to be buried in the famous mausoleum. But this son, the Second Emperor, acted so arbitrarily and cruelly that the people soon revolted and the Qin collapsed in flames: the last line of defense for the capital were the workers engaged in constructing the mausoleum. But they were no match for the rebels and the site, left unfinished, was burned and looted.

The power and glory of the Qin can still be discerned in the pottery army that surrounds the tomb of the First Emperor, Shihuangdi. The tomb itself has yet to be opened to reveal its riches. Perhaps archaeologists will find the remains of the workers who were buried alive inside to

earlier, in 213 BC he perpetrated one of the most pernicious and hated acts in all of Chinese history. He ordered the burning of private copies of books of the philosophical enemies of the Legalists, notably those of the Confucians, such as the *Shijing* (the "Book of Songs"), and the histories of the rival states he had conquered, thereby hoping to silence criticism of his policies and to monopolize

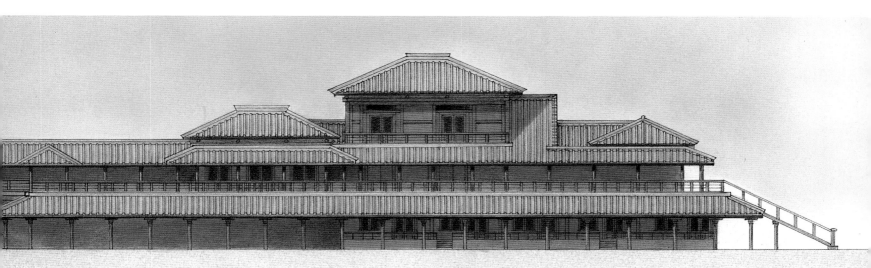

QIN TIME LINE

BC

770 King Ping of Zhou flees east; Qin is enfeoffed as a full status feudal lord; the official creation of the state of Qin.

476 Beginning of the Warring States Period.

384 Duke Xian initiates the reform movement, banning human sacrifice in funerals for the elite.

383 Qin capital moved from Yong in the west to Yueyang in the east, close to the Tong Pass.

375 Qin establishes household registers and initiates the mutual responsibility system.

359 Duke Xiao askes Gongsun Yang of Wei to "reform the laws" of Qin.

350 Capital is moved back a few tens of miles west to Xianyang.

338 Duke Xiao dies; Lord Shang rebels and is put to death.

301 Sima Cuo pacifies Shu (Sichuan).

260 General Bai Qi defeats Zhao and puts to the sword 450,000 soldiers who had surrendered.

256 Qin destroys the Zhou dynasty.

246 King Zheng, later the First Emperor, is enthroned at the age of 13 *sui* (years).

BC

230 Conquest of Han by the *Neishi* Teng.

228 Conquest of Zhao by Generals Wang Jian and Yang Duan.

227 Prince Dan of Yan orders Jing Ke to assassinate King Zheng, but the attempt fails and Jing Ke is killed.

226 In revenge, Qin attacks and seizes the Yan capital, forcing the King of Yan to flee northeast to Liaodong; General Wang Ben attacks Chu.

225 Wang Ben attacks and destroys Wei.

223 Wang Jian attacks and destroys Chu.

222 Wang Ben eliminates Yan.

221 Wang Jian conquers Qi; Qin unifies China and establishes the empire; Zheng assumes the title of "First Emperor"; division of the empire administratively into 36 commanderies; unification of the weights and measures, the writing system; width of cart axles.

219 The First Emperor's first tour of inspection of his empire; beginning of his search for the elixir of immortality.

218 Zhang Liang fails to assassinate the First Emperor.

215 General Meng Tian leads 300,000 men to attack the Xiongnu steppe nomads.

BC

214 Meng Tian is recorded as constructing the Great Wall.

213 The First Emperor issues the infamous order to "Burn the Books" on the advice of his prime minister, Li Si.

212 The First Emperor orders the burial alive of Confucian scholars; construction of the Afang Palace.

210 The First Emperor dies at Shaqiu on his fifth tour of inspection.

209 Huhai succeeds to the throne as the Second Emperor; seventh month, Chen Sheng and Wu Guang begin their rebellion against Qin oppression.

208 The eunuch Zhao Gao gains supreme influence; execution of the prime minister Li Si.

207 Death of the Second Emperor; Ziying succeeds to the throne and executes Zhao Gao.

206 11 January to 9 February: The rebels attack and burn the First Emperor's mausoleum and capture Xianyang; Ziying surrenders to them and dies shortly afterward; the Qin dynasty collapses, succeeded — after a bitter civil war — by the Han.

prevent them from revealing its secrets. While we may wonder today at the brilliant lifelike sculptures, possibly representing individual soldiers in the emperor's personal guard, but more likely symbolizing an ideal contemporary fighting force in battle array, it is well to remember the extent of the entire complex. Seven hundred thousand people were said to have labored on it, including thousands of convicts whose graves have

been found. Temples existed above ground for the worship of the emperor's departed spirit, and to the west of the mound miniature bronze chariots with all their fittings were buried to enable his soul to travel abroad. In addition, rare wild birds and beasts were interred, as were members of his harem. The Second Emperor also buried there those of his siblings and their supporters whom he murdered when he usurped the throne.

RIGHT: The burial mound, or tumulus, of Shihuangdi's tomb at Lintong, Shaanxi province, located just over half a mile (1 km) west of the buried guardian army. WENWU PUBLISHING

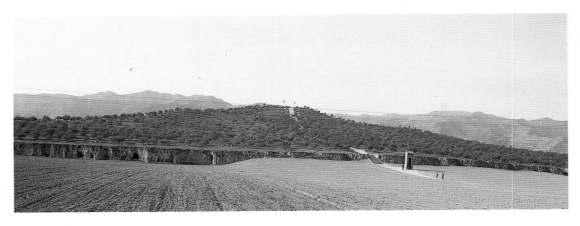

It will take many years before the entire scope of the site, surrounded by earthen walls and located within the sacred space of the Qin capital region, is revealed, but it is quite clear that it was carefully chosen for its auspiciousness; with Mount Li to the south and the Wei River to the north, the emperor could look forward to a paradisiacal life-after-death, protected by his warriors from evil spiritual forces emanating from the east, the lands of those whom he had destroyed and who might seek vengeance.

So far, the names of more than 80 master craftsmen who worked on the emperor's mausoleum have been confirmed from inscriptions incised on the backs of figures in pit number 1, the large rectangular formation. These craftsmen were drawn from members of the imperial workshops, from private operations in the Qin capital region and from other parts of China. In making the sculptures, they followed contemporary ceramic technique, building the figures from the feet up using the coiled clay method. Heads were made from molds, usually in two parts, and then individuating features of eyes, nose, and mouth were sculpted afterward, as was the hairstyle. Figures could be fired as an entire unit, or the head and body fired separately and then attached. Finally, a light glaze was applied over the entire figure which was then painted in brilliant colors. Most of the paint has been lost because of this technique, but enough remains for the archaeologists to reconstruct what they originally looked like.

LEFT: The three pits are 16½–23 feet (5–7 m) beneath the present ground level with the figures placed in corridors on an east-west axis. Wooden beams, up to 55 feet (16.75 m) long were laid across the corridors, covered with bamboo or reed matting, followed by a thick layer of a mixture of red soil, chalk, and sand; finally, topsoil was rammed down on top, completely sealing the army. Since their discovery, a museum has been constructed over the top of the site.
CHINA PICTORIAL PHOTO SERVICE

Although the pits were burned and most of the weapons stolen, the robbers left behind some items that are of great historical interest: there are crossbow mechanisms and crossbow quarrels, maces and a type of curved scimitar never seen before, together with long bronze swords that still shine brightly today. These are coated with chrome, a technique not known in the rest of the world until very recently. Finally, the remains of chariots and cavalry, who lack stirrups — they had not yet been invented — provide a remarkable insight into Qin military equipment and the formations of warriors, supply valuable evidence of contemporary military practice.

The whole complex reveals a unique and stunning glimpse of the ancient Chinese world. Although the First Emperor of Qin could not gain immortality in life, he most certainly gained it in death.

BELOW: One of two miniature inlaid-bronze chariots and charioteers found in a pit to the west of the First Emperor's tomb, perhaps intended for the use of his soul after death. The chariot was known in China as early as 1300 BC and many ornate bronze fittings have been recovered from Shang and Zhou dynasty tombs.
WENWU PUBLISHING

THE TERRACOTTA WARRIORS

RIGHT: Plan showing the burial mound or tumulus surrounded by an inner wall and much larger outer wall. Just over half a mile (1 km) to the east are the three burial pits of the underground army, clockwise from the front: pit number 1, the smallest pit, number 3, and pit number 2 which is estimated to contain some 1,400 figures and 89 chariots.

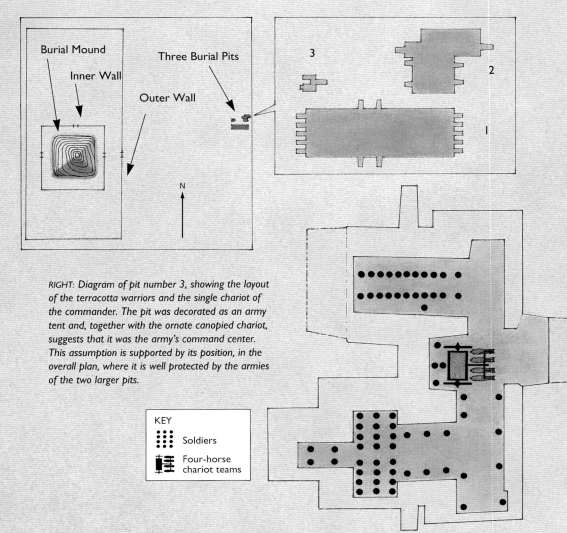

Burial Mound

Inner Wall

Three Burial Pits

Outer Wall

N

3

2

1

RIGHT: Diagram of pit number 3, showing the layout of the terracotta warriors and the single chariot of the commander. The pit was decorated as an army tent and, together with the ornate canopied chariot, suggests that it was the army's command center. This assumption is supported by its position, in the overall plan, where it is well protected by the armies of the two larger pits.

BELOW: Plan of pit number 1, showing the layout, according to Qin military prescription, of the 6,000 figures and chariots. Pit number 1 is the largest and houses the main body of the guardian army. At the head of each of the nine principal columns of four-soldiers-abreast is a four-horse chariot team. Around the outer edge on the north, south, and west sides are 518 crossbowmen to guard the sides and rear of the army.

KEY

Soldiers

Four-horse chariot teams

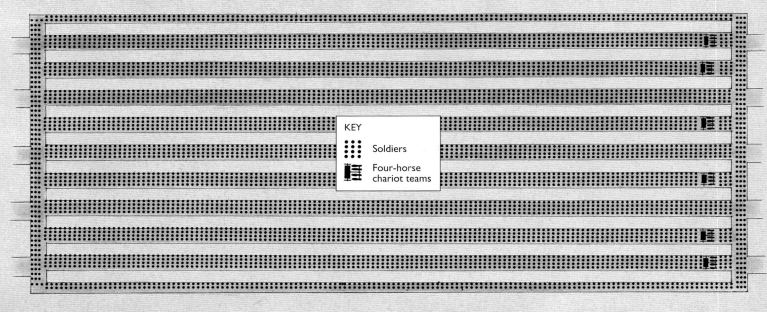

KEY

Soldiers

Four-horse chariot teams

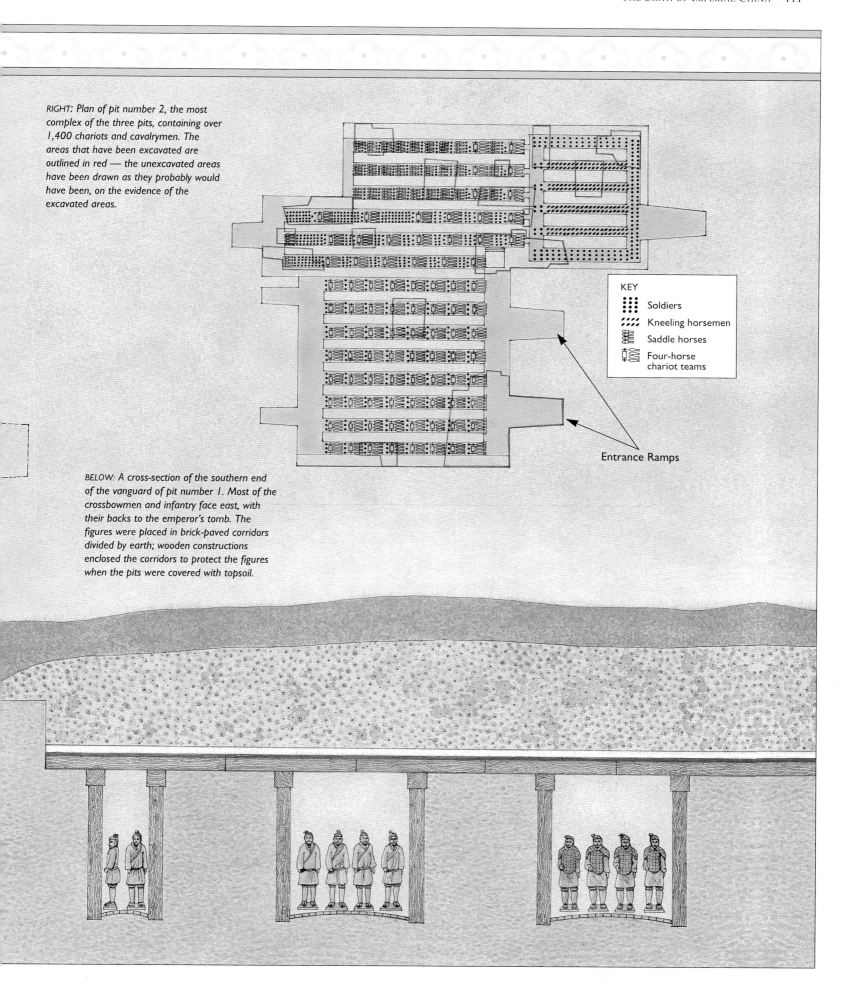

RIGHT: Plan of pit number 2, the most complex of the three pits, containing over 1,400 chariots and cavalrymen. The areas that have been excavated are outlined in red — the unexcavated areas have been drawn as they probably would have been, on the evidence of the excavated areas.

KEY

- ▦ Soldiers
- ▨ Kneeling horsemen
- ▦ Saddle horses
- ▤ Four-horse chariot teams

Entrance Ramps

BELOW: A cross-section of the southern end of the vanguard of pit number 1. Most of the crossbowmen and infantry face east, with their backs to the emperor's tomb. The figures were placed in brick-paved corridors divided by earth; wooden constructions enclosed the corridors to protect the figures when the pits were covered with topsoil.

CHINA'S GROWING STRENGTH: THE HAN DYNASTY

Michael Loewe

IT WAS DURING THE HAN DYNASTY, which, with one short interruption, lasted from 206 BC to AD 220, that much of China's cultural, political, and administrative framework was formed. The preceding 2,000 years had seen the spread of the written word and the formulation of China's earliest literature, including poetry, philosophical tracts, and historical writing. The earliest of the kingdoms, the Shang and then the Western Zhou, had given way to a large number of estates or units that had arisen under aristocratic or military leaders mainly in the northern part of the country. By the fourth century BC, these had developed into seven major kingdoms that were in turn welded into the short-lived empire of Qin (221–207 BC).

The characteristics that emerged during the Han dynasty affected China until the middle of the twentieth century. The Han emperors and their advisors demonstrated that government of the country by a single, centralized authority could be accepted as legitimate and effective. It was largely thanks to them that government of that type became regarded as the norm to which all future regimes and pretenders to power would aspire, however effective or ineffective their efforts to establish it may have been.

Acceptance of rule by a single united empire as the norm involved acceptance of certain ideas of the function, duties, and place of the emperor. During the Han period a new concept of emperor evolved. This was a ruler appointed to serve the needs of human beings and who was in duty bound to report on his stewardship to a superhuman authority, identified eventually as Tian (Heaven). The chief function of the emperor was now seen to be that of serving and propitiating such a godhead; and in doing so, that ruler formed an integral and essential part of the universal order, comprising as it did the heavens and their bodies, the earth and its products and all living creatures. In this way, the Han period saw the development of religious links with superhuman powers and the formulation of abstract ideas; these both served to assert the continuity of the imperial line and to provide it with legitimate authority to rule over the people of the earth.

The process of creating centralized government involved major, drawn-out changes with religious, intellectual, cultural, political, and social implications. The religious cults of state, in which the emperor himself took part, were now directed to forging a link between his authority and superior powers who controlled the universe; ministers of state and essayists were addressing questions

ABOVE: Ornate gilded bronze double cup, 4½ inches (11.2 cm) high, cast as a single piece, with inlaid turquoise; the central bird holds a jade ring in its mouth and its feet are planted on a mythical animal. Excavated at Mancheng, Hebei province, in the tomb of Dou Wan, a wife of King Liu Sheng of the Zhongshan kingdom during the Han dynasty. WENWU PUBLISHING

OPPOSITE: Gilt-bronze lamp, held by a female servant, from the Han tomb of Dou Wan at Mancheng, Hebei province. The lamp consists of some twelve component parts, including a sliding door to regulate the direction and quantity of light. WENWU PUBLISHING

ABOVE: *From 136 BC, certain early texts were treated as having scriptural authority and singled out for training scholars and officials. Different versions came into circulation and it became desirable to determine which would be regarded as orthodox. In AD 175 the approved texts were engraved on stone tablets, in fine calligraphic style, to act as a permanent, unalterable record. This fragment is from the* Book of Documents. *The dimensions of the original tablets are estimated to have been 5³/₄ feet (175 cm) high, 3 feet (90 cm) wide, and 4³/₄ inches (12 cm) thick.*
FROM HAN SHU JING JI CUN, BEIJING, 1957

RIGHT: *This emblem of authority, a bronze tiger, 7¹/₂ inches (19 cm) long, with gold inlay and inscription, was probably intended as a token that conveyed permission to call out troops in an emergency. It is from the tomb of the king of Nan Yue (one of the subordinate kingdoms of the empire) who died* c. *122 BC.*
WENWU PUBLISHING

of political ideas and the duties of men and women to their rulers, their neighbors, their families, and their own spiritual well-being.

CIVIL-SERVANT SCHOLARS

In the early days of the Han empire, literacy had been a rare and prized skill, to the point that many of the dominant leaders of the new regime were probably unable to handle documents of state. By the end of the dynasty there had evolved means of educating and training a sufficient number of officials and clerks to fill the ranks of a complex civil service. New standards of administrative efficiency enabled the imperial government to enforce its authority with a new and deeper intensity. In social terms, the long process whereby the value of nobility of birth was yielding to that of meritorious service and scholarly abilities had begun. The provision of a sufficiency of educated civil servants to achieve the aims of imperial government depended partly on the official patronage of learning and literature, and there followed a new

set of developments in China's cultural tradition: the advent of the civil-servant scholar, that particular creation of China's imperial society. Educated in China's philosophy, literature, and history and trained to wield their brushes as authors, poet–artists, or calligraphers, civil-servant scholars sought advancement along the path that led to the most responsible positions in both the palace and the imperial government.

ADMINISTRATION

Administration of the empire depended on a systematic structure of central, provincial, and local government, so as to ensure that imperial decisions (for example, regarding taxation, or military moves) were promulgated to the provinces and that reports coming from these outlying provinces (for example on crop failure, or banditry) kept the center fully informed of local conditions. Administration also required the organization of officials in acknowledged grades with their specified duties and with the corresponding degrees of dignity, privilege, and salary that stimulated competition. The civil servants that the administration needed had to be capable of a whole range of activities, whether that of humble clerks in the ministries or of officials dutifully waiting for audience with their emperor. They could be called upon to make technical decisions, such as how to control floods, which would affect the livelihood of tens of thousands, or the pronouncement of sentence on a single local criminal; or, when they reached the highest levels, they would be required to advise the throne on major matters of policy. In all these respects, the Han governments left a heritage to

their successors that molded China's social hierarchies, encouraged scholarship and attention to the arts, and could take an educated person to the most highly privileged and prominent places in public life.

Some officials received their appointment through favoritism or patronage, and a rudimentary form of grading had appeared in the first century BC. But by the first and second centuries AD there had been a change. For some centuries now imperial government had been taking active steps, such as the foundation of the Imperial Academy, to promote scholarly activities, and as a cumulative result of these efforts a number of different schools of learning had emerged. These were largely concerned with interpreting texts that were, by then, up to 1,000 years old and were treated with almost scriptural reverence owing to their connection with Confucius (551–479 BC). Some of the newly trained scholars acted as the tutors of those who were now striving for a place in the ranks of the civil service. To achieve this they needed to conform with the officially sponsored interpretation of those texts so as to apply them to the needs of the day. Qualification for office had come to include proficiency at doing so. Above all, a highly significant principle was now recognized, if not always implemented: appointments should rest on personal merit and not on hereditary succession,

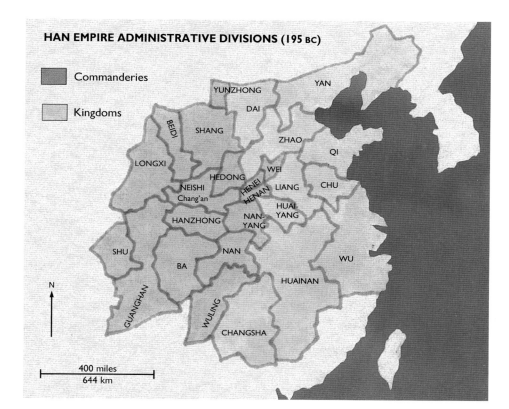

HAN EMPIRE ADMINISTRATIVE DIVISIONS (195 BC)

Commanderies

Kingdoms

YUNZHONG
YAN
DAI
BEIDI   SHANG
ZHAO
QI
LONGXI
WEI
HEDONG
NEISHI   HENEI   LIANG   CHU
Chang'an   HENAN
HUAI-
HANZHONG   NAN-   YANG
YANG
SHU   NAN
BA   WU
HUAINAN
GUANGHAN
WULING
CHANGSHA

N

400 miles
644 km

and officials were subject to dismissal if their efficiency was found wanting or if they were brought to book for corruption or oppression. The basis had thus been laid for the much more sophisticated systems of examination of the Tang, Ming, and Qing dynasties; the way also lay open for political intrigue and factionalism.

ORGANIZATION

The administration of a large empire comprising over 100 major constituent units demanded organs of government on a scale that had so far not been seen. Three, and then two senior officials stood at the head of the government to offer advice to their emperor, to determine

LEFT: Figurines of male and female attendants, in gray earthenware; buried in tombs of officials, noblemen, and members of the royal and imperial families. High-ranking people were buried with objects that suited their social status.
ROYAL ONTARIO MUSEUM

policies of state, and to give orders for their implementation. Ideally, they were also charged with the duty of remonstrance or protest, if they believed that their emperor was set on an inadvisable or even an unethical course. Some of these senior officials deliberately suggested policies designed to enrich and strengthen the empire; others preferred steps that would encourage human beings to attain higher standards of social behavior and individual quality.

At the next level, nine departmental ministers of the central government were responsible for matters such as the observance of religious cults, overall security, the trials of criminal cases, the reception of foreign visitors, and the maintenance of the palace. It was at this level that the rate of taxation was determined and it was also decided how far the government should attempt to regulate the currency, or to control and coordinate activities such as mining.

As in the organs of the central government, so in the provincial units a system of hierarchies and defined responsibilities prevailed. The hundred or so major administrative units of the empire, which included some subordinate kingdoms, varied widely in respect of area, population, terrain, and the type of product that the land could yield. Altogether they were subdivided into some 1,500 minor units, or counties, many of whose names and territorial boundaries still survive. Officials of the counties were responsible to their superiors of the higher units, known mainly as commanderies; but it was through the officials of the counties, or even those of the small hamlets of which they were composed, that the great majority of the Chinese population felt the heavy hand of imperial government. The county magistrates and their subordinates were responsible for the routine tasks of running the empire, such as registering the population; conscripting able-bodied males for statutory service in the armed forces or the labor gangs; raising revenue, largely in the form of grain, and transporting it for collection and distribution; the upkeep of waterways; the arrest of bandits or criminals; the dispensation of justice; and the implementation of the highly detailed series of statutes and ordinances that sought to regulate the daily work of the Chinese population.

AGRICULTURE

By the beginning of the Christian era, the registered inhabitants of China numbered some 60 million souls. Perhaps 90 percent of these lived in the countryside, engaged mainly in farming; and despite the establishment of organs of government in many areas south of the Yangzi River, the great majority of the registered population lived in the north. The most thickly populated regions included the fertile valleys of the Huang (Yellow) River and the Huai River, and the enclave in the southwest (modern Sichuan province) that is watered by four tributaries of the Yangzi. This area gave rise to a number of local cultural characteristics, such as terraced paddy fields, and was partly influenced by the non-Chinese tribespeople of the land known much later as Tibet. The north was often subject to major hazard from flooding of the Huang River.

Millet was the staple product of the northern part of the country, while south of the Yangzi the inhabitants grew rice. Fortunate farmers could afford to plow with an iron plowshare drawn by oxen. Others had to be content with manual labor and the less expensive tools that were made of wood, bone, or horn. Horses, which were in short supply and difficult to feed well, were available as transport for officials and express couriers, or for some of the more wealthy merchants. Grain and other products were usually transported by water, and the maintenance of canals and precautions against devastation by floods could require the work of a considerable part of the labor force that the county magistrates conscripted.

Imperial governments repeatedly insisted on the need to promote agriculture and to prevent the population forsaking the arduous work of the fields in preference for a more lucrative and rewarding way of life in industry, mining, or commerce. Envious of the fortunes made by magnates who had secured control of the salt and iron mines or organized an efficient trade in manufactured goods, Han governments established a series of commissioners who were ordered to operate these undertakings as a monopoly of the state. Set up *c.* 120 BC, these monopolies were effective from time to time, and they acted as examples to which later dynasties could point as a precedent for setting up similar controls.

BELOW: *One of a number of bronze objects (20⁹/₁₀ inches/ 53 cm), possibly used to store cowry shells — that were at one time used as currency — found in a burial site of about 108 BC, in Yunnan province, in a grave identified as that of one of the kings of Dian, a subordinate kingdom of the Han empire. The lids of the objects carried representations of a number of scenes of religious rites, daily life, or military training. The scene shown here is one of human sacrifice; other objects carry those of making textiles, rearing cattle, or horsemanship.*
LAURIE PLATT WINFREY, INC

RELIGION

Religious aspects were no less important in the heritage that the Han empire left to its successors than administrative forms, social structure, military organization, or city plans. Religious sanction was essential if the leaders of a dynasty were to claim a right to rule that was any more valid than that of its rivals. Long before the days of empire had dawned, the leaders of China's small states had been accustomed to worship a variety of deities and to perform a number of rites that were designed to bring blessings such as rain or an abundant harvest. The concept of a supreme deity, identified sometimes as Tian (Heaven), had emerged some 1,500 years before the imperial age, but it was only shortly before the start of the Christian era that the worship of Tian was established as the major element in the imperial cults. From then on Chinese emperors have portrayed themselves as stewards acting on behalf of Tian whose charge they bear. Sacrifices to Tian, initiated some 2,000 years ago, were performed at the imperial capital until the early years of the twentieth century. Han had forged the link whereby the rulers of human beings could claim to exercise their authority legitimately; for such

authority had been conferred upon them by a supreme power with whom they were in contact.

The great palaces from which the emperors gazed south to survey their flock and govern their charge could not fail to impose the idea of imperial might on the inhabitants of the city; and the processions to the religious sites, with their gaily colored robes, their music, and their armed guard, surely formed some of the few colorful moments in the lives of the great majority. The imperial mausolea, constructed for most of the emperors in the year after their accession, also acted as a material display of imperial majesty. They were multichambered edifices, each topped by a symmetrical tumulus, and they towered over the countryside as a mark of imperial glory. Nearby were the shrines and other chambers built to ensure a regular supply of the offerings that were needed to keep the souls of the dead at peace.

DEFENSE

Senior officials were also faced with the need to determine what type of relations they wished to enjoy with the non-Chinese peoples and their leaders. For

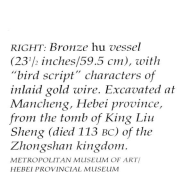

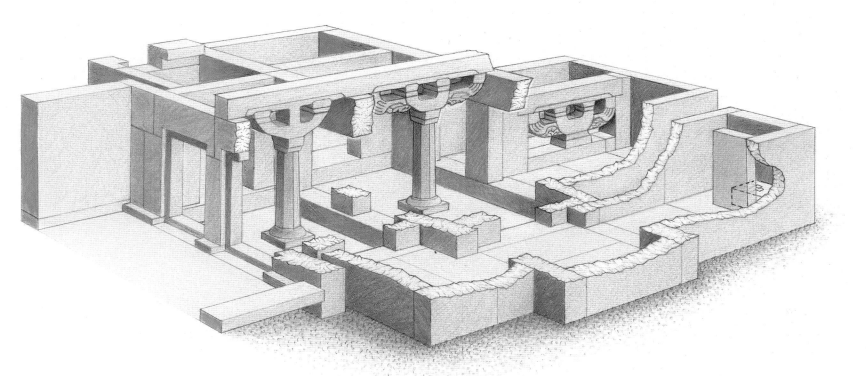

although the emperor's government claimed that the empire was self-sufficient, and that it would provide a safe homeland for all those willing to serve him with loyalty, stern realities could be somewhat different. The existence from time to time of a strong

nomadic non-Chinese confederacy in the north, backed by able leadership and mobile forces of horsemen, could pose a threat to the Chinese homeland, where these foreigners could sometimes force their way close to the capital city. Han governments were at times obliged to appease a strong adversary with expensive silks or other goods; at other times they were able to muster sufficient strength to dispatch an expedition to campaign in the cruel terrain of the central Asian deserts. The would-be permanent defense lines of the north, the first of China's "great walls" that had been built under Qin, existed to deter alien invaders, to restrain Chinese criminals and deserters from escaping justice, and to provide an armed cause-way for the passage of commercial caravans. Pioneer steps by the Qin and Han governments to build a system of walls left examples to be followed by later dynasties, principally those of Tang and Ming.

During their short-lived reign the Qin emperors had established their seat of government at Xianyang, lying close to their place of origin. The site possessed one major strategic advantage: being placed within mountain ranges that allowed access through a limited number

ABOVE: Tomb built of stone, with rich carving in low relief, dated c. AD 250, Yinan, Shandong province. This elaborate structure, which was oriented to the north, comprised front, central, and rear chambers with a series of side rooms. A number of pillars, some of which were octagonal, marked the gateways and supported the roof; it is 8¹/₃ yards (7.55 m) by 9¹/₂ yards (8.7 m). The exceptionally rich carving includes a variety of robed officials and others, whose titles are identified by captions; religious motifs that do not derive from Buddhist symbols; figures drawn from Chinese mythology; and large comfortable residences and courtyards.

LEFT: In addition to the array of thousands of terracotta figures of infantrymen and cavalry, buried around the tomb of the First Emperor of Qin (died 210 BC), in a separate pit the funerary furnishings included two bronze chariots with horse and rider, made to half life size.
WENWU PUBLISHING

BELOW: *Attempts to preserve the body after death were meant to enable one element of the soul, known as the* po, *to continue to live with the body. Supplies of food were included at the burial and subsequently brought to the tomb at regular services. For this purpose the body was accompanied by disks or other pieces made of jade, a mineral believed to possess and convey powers of eternal life. For the highest ranking members of society the body was enclosed in a suit made by sewing small rectangles of jade together, thus fitting the individual who was being buried. The example shown here was reconstructed from remains found at Mancheng, Hebei province, in the tomb of King Liu Sheng (died 113 BC) of the Zhongshan kingdom.*
WENWU PUBLISHING

of passes, the area was defensible from possible threats from the east or the south. Chang'an, which lay close by, provided the same advantage for the emperors of Former Han (reigned 202 BC–AD 9) and served as their capital city until the Later Han emperors established themselves further east, at Luoyang, (AD 25–220). Whereas Chang'an was stronger in material terms, Luoyang could claim to possess greater dignity and majesty, in so far as it had been regarded as China's cultural center during the latter days of the Zhou kings. After the Han period each of these cities was at times adopted by

subsequent dynasties, until a pronounced move to the east started in the tenth century, culminating in the adoption in the thirteenth century of the city that is now termed Beijing.

Armed Forces
The Qin and Han imperial governments needed armed forces no less than those of other empires. Their duties lay in ensuring the safety of the emperor in his capital; enforcing security from criminals; campaigning when expeditions were ordered, either to extend imperial territory or to expel an invader; or

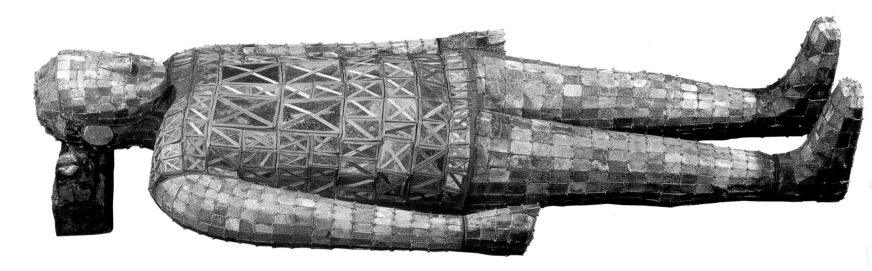

keeping watch on the static defense lines of the north and northwest. Conscripts were enrolled to serve in the ranks for two years, and were thereafter liable for recall in times of emergency until they reached 56 years of age. They drew their supplies of clothing and weapons from the government, and were likely to serve in any part of the empire where troops were required. Remnants of the written records that they left behind in the rubbish pits of the defense lines reveal that they had attained a high professional standard: their command posts, weapons, and housing were subject to regular inspections; much of their routine work was subject to careful timing, and the time taken for a task was recorded; and they maintained a regular postal service up and down the lines.

CHINA'S EXPANSION DURING THE HAN DYNASTY

Two motives explain China's expansion into central Asia: defense and trade. Faced with the threat of armed incursion from the north and the west by the Xiongnu confederacy (a tribal federation of pastoral nomads whose territory spread from Chinese Turkestan to Manchuria) from 221 BC the first Qin emperor had had the walls of the north put into order as a coordinated system of defense, but this had not proved a completely successful means of repelling enemy forces in Han times. A series of expeditions launched from c. 130 BC was more successful for a time, but while a few short victorious campaigns could remove immediate threats, there remained the likelihood that the Xiongnu could gain the support of the independent communities of central Asia. It was to win such friendship, and to deny it to the Xiongnu, that the Han governments embarked on diplomatic means of dealing with the Xiongnu threat. These included the presentation of imperial princesses as brides for the local leaders of the uncultured north.

Generous presents of the superior products of Chinese civilization, mainly in the form of silk, played no small part in such maneuvers; and it was just about this time that a few far-sighted officials realized that China could be enriched by exporting such products in return for imports of horses. By c. 100 BC a series of incidents had led to the extension of the original defense lines as far west as Dunhuang, and the inauguration of what has come to be known as the Silk Road. Traveling with some degree of safety along this route the caravans could then proceed round the Taklamakan Desert; and eventually their bales of silk would find their way to the Roman cities of the Mediterranean world. The terrain that the caravans had to traverse was savage, and it was only thanks to the friendship and support of the communities who held the oases that they could hope to get through. The route was in no sense permanent and its maintenance was not easy. In addition, to ensure protection of the northern provinces from the Xiongnu or others, Han governments had to embark on military action from time to time. However, the successful penetration by a few highly courageous generals was never able to secure lasting results, and there were times when parts of the empire fell out of Chinese control.

The new administrative units of the provinces, known as commanderies, that were established in the south c. 100 BC brought examples of a superior Chinese way of life to peoples who were not accustomed to the sedentary habits of the Chinese farmer or the benefits of Chinese civilization. Officials and colonists brought with them many elements of Chinese language to the peoples of what is now Vietnam, and such elements remain firmly embedded in that language today. They took refined methods of agriculture to the tribes of the southwest who, though they were accustomed to raising cattle, were still tilling the fields with rudimentary equipment and basic methods. The extension of the empire to the northeast led the way to the foundation of Han commanderies in Korea (108 BC), where elements of Chinese culture were similarly planted. From about the fifth century, the Korean peninsula itself acted as a bridge whereby many of the products and gifts of Chinese civilization traveled to Japan, leaving an indelible mark on the native language and way of life there. As yet there were no official contacts between the court of Luoyang and the leaders of the Japanese islands, other than the emperor's gift of a seal to a party of Japanese visitors in AD 57. The main impact that China was to make on Japan did not come until about the seventh century.

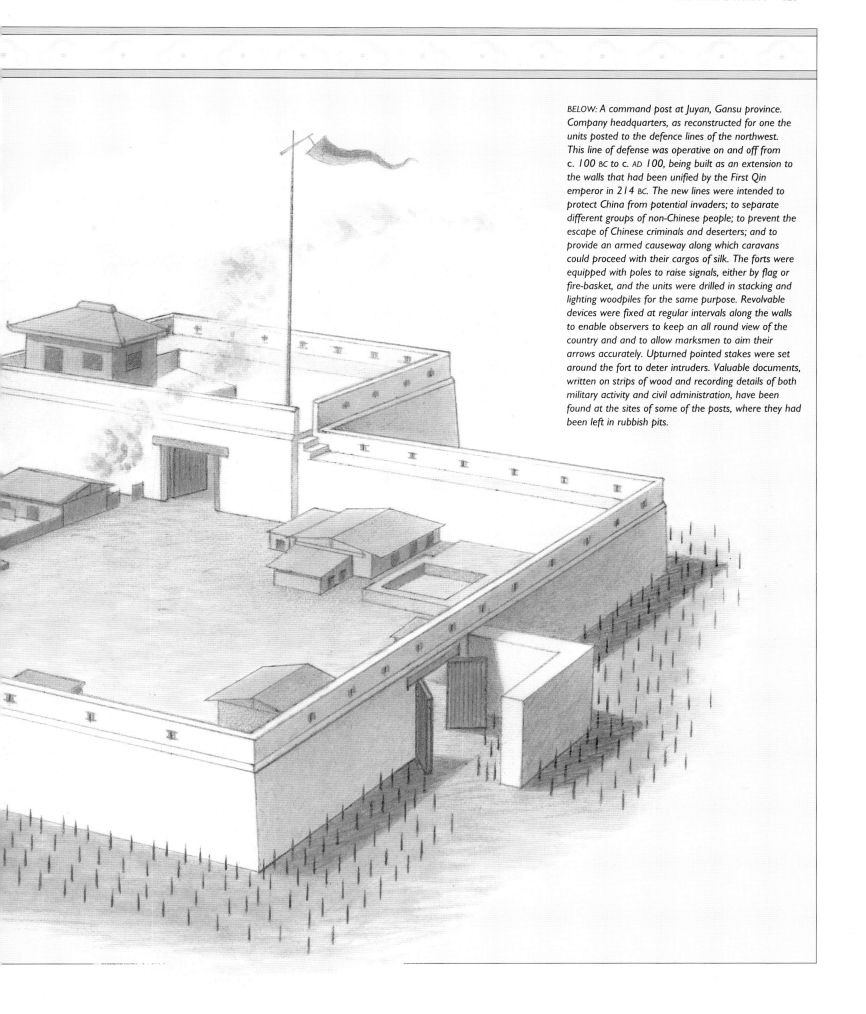

BELOW: A command post at Juyan, Gansu province. Company headquarters, as reconstructed for one the units posted to the defence lines of the northwest. This line of defense was operative on and off from c. 100 BC to c. AD 100, being built as an extension to the walls that had been unified by the First Qin emperor in 214 BC. The new lines were intended to protect China from potential invaders; to separate different groups of non-Chinese people; to prevent the escape of Chinese criminals and deserters; and to provide an armed causeway along which caravans could proceed with their cargos of silk. The forts were equipped with poles to raise signals, either by flag or fire-basket, and the units were drilled in stacking and lighting woodpiles for the same purpose. Revolvable devices were fixed at regular intervals along the walls to enable observers to keep an all round view of the country and and to allow marksmen to aim their arrows accurately. Upturned pointed stakes were set around the fort to deter intruders. Valuable documents, written on strips of wood and recording details of both military activity and civil administration, have been found at the sites of some of the posts, where they had been left in rubbish pits.

THE FLORESCENCE OF BUDDHISM

Tim Barrett

ONE OF THE LASTING CONSEQUENCES OF the expansion of trade during the Han dynasty (206 BC–AD 220) was the introduction to China of a new religion, Buddhism. Founded by the Indian prince Gautama Siddhārtha, probably in the fifth century BC, Buddhism was already well established in the lands to the northwest of India and in central Asia. The earliest reliable mention of Buddhism in China dates to AD 65, but it is possible that some non-Chinese had been practicing Buddhism in China before this. By AD 166 emperor Huan had sacrificed to Buddha.

With the founding of the Wei dynasty in AD 220, came a tough new regime singularly lacking in devotional tendencies. Wang Bi (AD 222–249), the chief philosopher of the day, used Daoist language but was greatly influenced by Confucius. He believed that all proceeded from Original Nonbeing — a cosmic *tabula rasa* — corresponding to the clean sheet of the new Wei dynasty political agenda and he aimed for mystical tranquillity rather than spiritual enthusiasm. The Wei regime had a firm grip only on north China, while the west and south supported the rival Shu and Wu dynasties whose values remained closer to those of the Han. Buddhism, for all the continued production of translations, appears to have made little impact on thinkers of

the third century AD. Early Buddhist art in China, in which images of the Buddha simply join the ranks of deities commonly represented in Chinese tomb art, suggests that for the ordinary worshiper Buddhism was seen as an exotic addition to the repertory of Chinese cults, not a radically new analysis of the human condition.

By AD 280 Shu and Wu were incorporated into the empire once more under the Sima family, who ruled from AD 265 as the Jin dynasty. In AD 304 one of the leaders of the many non-Chinese peoples rose against the Jin. The whole Chinese heartland in the basin of the Huang (Yellow) River devolved into chaos; for over a century military leaders of non-Chinese origin attempted to establish stable regimes on the wreckage of the former Jin state, but they lacked the civil skills to match their ambitions. Meanwhile the remnants of the Jin court and a mass of other Chinese refugees retreated to the former territory of Wu (in the south) to reestablish a Chinese state, the Eastern Jin, at Jiankang, present-day Nanjing.

Now Buddhism came into its own. In the north, Chinese culture no longer attracted the automatic commitment of non-Chinese rulers who were now as likely to look to Buddhist monks of foreign origin as they were to Chinese

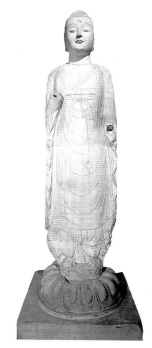

ABOVE: Temple sculpture inscribed "AD 595", depicts the Amitabha Buddha, inspiration for the Pure Land school of Buddhism which was at one stage the most popular religious movement in China.
BRITISH MUSEUM, LONDON

OPPOSITE: Interior of the Sleeping Buddha cave temple in Dazu in the mountains of Sichuan province.
FONG SIU NANG/THE IMAGE BANK

ABOVE: *Gilt bronze sculpture from the Wei dynasty shows the Bodhisattva Padmagani, one of the followers of Buddha who is able to reach nirvana but delays doing so through compassion for human suffering.* BRITISH MUSEUM, LONDON

ABOVE RIGHT: *Statues guard the Sleeping Buddha in the cave at Dazu in Sichuan province.*
FONG SIU NANG/THE IMAGE BANK

RIGHT: *Calligraphy by Wang Xizhi (AD 309–c. 365), an outstanding calligrapher whose family had in north China followed the cult of the Heavenly Master. The success of the Shangqing revelations can in part be gauged by Wang Xizhi's acceptance of them.* NATIONAL PALACE MUSEUM, TAIBEI, TAIWAN, REPUBLIC OF CHINA

scholars for advice. In the south, intellectual qualities were better appreciated: the key Mahāyāna concept of emptiness, *kong* (*śūnyatā* in Sanskrit) now seemed curiously akin to the nonbeing spoken of by Wang Bi, and much discussion was devoted to the elucidation of this Buddhist term. But a man like Zhi Dun, China's earliest known Buddhist philosopher (AD 314–366), was in retrospect too entangled in Chinese analogies to have a clear perception of basic Buddhist ideas. After all, Wang Bi's nonbeing provides an account of the origin of things, whereas the Buddhist concept of emptiness is addressed exclusively to their religious and philosophical status — the two ideas cannot be straightforwardly equated.

A reaffirmation of southern traditions

came from the gods themselves, gods of the Heaven of Supreme Purity, Shangqing, who revealed their scriptures to Yang Xi (AD 330–?), a visionary at the center of a circle of southern aristocratic devotees. But while many of the occult traditions first glimpsed in the writings of Ge Hong (AD 283–343) are endorsed by these revelations, it is clear that other forms of religion were now also a part of southern Chinese culture: the rites of the Heavenly Master (imported from the north by refugees) were assigned an inferior but significant part in the new synthesis, and some of the basic teachings of Buddhism were incorporated into Yang's scriptures also.

It was not until China entered a period of relative stability in the northwest, due to the second ruler of Later Qin, Yao Xing

XUANZANG

Xuanzang was born under the Sui dynasty in Luoyang and became a monk during the early Tang. He traveled both to Sichuan in the west and Zhaozhou in north China before, toward the age of 30, conceiving the ambition of undertaking the perilous journey to India in search of answers to the many philosophical questions left unresolved in the translations of Buddhist texts then extant. Although the emperor refused him permission to leave China, in AD 629 he seized an opportunity to slip away westward through central Asia; he was not to return for sixteen years. His route took him up through present-day Gansu and then passed to the north of the Gobi Desert. He eventually descended to India via present-day Afghanistan. In India he stayed in Kashmir, a great center of scholastic studies (including logic and grammar), before moving on to Mathurà and eventually Nālandā, a long established Buddhist university in east India. Here his studies concentrated on Yogācāra, the Buddhist philosophical system which analyzes the external world as a product of our own consciousness.

More travels within India broadened his knowledge yet further, and brought him into contact with some of the greatest rulers of the day, such as the playwright-king Harsha (AD 606–647). Finally, after accumulating 527 boxes of Buddhist scriptures and other materials, Xuanzang headed north again over the Pamirs, before returning westward, this time south of the Gobi Desert through Khotan, arriving in China in early AD 645. Fortunately the emperor was now considering the prospects for Chinese expansion into central Asia, and so was badly in need of firsthand information on the area. This Xuanzang provided, in a description of his itinerary, useful to this day as a remarkable source on the kingdoms he visited.

In return the emperor generously provided all the assistance needed to translate the Buddhist works and Xuanzang settled down to a second career as a translator. As a result of his efforts more than one-fifth of the huge corpus of surviving materials in Chinese from Indian languages appears under his name. As a native speaker of Chinese who had been forced to grapple with the complexities of Sanskrit, Xuanzang's translations are meticulous, even pedantic, allowing scholars to perceive much of the original structure of texts long since lost in their Indian versions

— though in many cases his more careful renderings did not replace in popularity translations by Kumārajīva already well established with their Chinese readership.

Where Xuanzang has proved quite remarkably popular, however, has been as a figure of folklore. The popular Chinese mind has responded much more readily to the heroism of his achievements than to the subtleties of the specific philosophical system. In the celebrated Ming novel Xiyouji ("The Journey to the West") it is his companion,

ABOVE: Xuanzang carrying scrolls. The translations he made upon his return from India increased the volume of Buddhist literature in China by about 25 percent. BRITISH MUSEUM, LONDON

the mythical Monkey King, a figure from popular religion, who commands the reader's attention, but without Xuanzang and his purely Buddhist quest there would be no story. And remarkably enough, however fantastic the novels, plays, and now even films devoted to the theme, the story itself is true.

ABOVE: *Illustration of the*
Lotus Sutra, deemed by the
Tiantai, the distinctively
Chinese school of Buddhism,
to be the supreme utterance
of Buddha. BIYITSU KENKYUYO, TOKYO

RIGHT: Lead-glazed pottery
statue of the Yama (Yanluo
Wang), *a figure of wrath*
who was a general of hell
commanding an army of
demons, often animal-headed.
ROYAL ONTARIO MUSEUM

RIGHT: Yuan Jiang's painting,
Penglai, Isle of Immortals
(1708). *Daoist immortals are*
said to live on several islands
— the earliest written reference
to these islands is in the Shiji
record for 219 BC.
INTERNATIONAL ARTS COUNCIL

arrived in Chang'an in AD 402.

This was Kumārajīva (AD 344–413), who was born in Kucha (in central Asia) and was carried off to Gansu when his homeland became part of a northern warrior's empire. The region had long been open to Buddhist influence, and in AD 368 its great contribution to the Buddhist artistic heritage had begun with the start of work on the magnificent Dunhuang cave temples.

Kumārajīva's translations are of unprecedented fluency. In particular the *Lotus Sūtra* was a revelation of the truth of Mahāyāna Buddhism in the form of a dramatic description of the Buddha's preaching. It has had an immense impact on East Asian culture.

For his fellow monks, however, the chief interest of Kumārajīva's work was his presentation of the philosophy of emptiness, as understood by Indian Buddhist thinkers, in terms that the Chinese could understand and that, thanks to the presence of disciples of Daoan in both north and south China, could now become the common property of all Chinese Buddhists. Now there was no possibility of Chinese Buddhism

(reigned AD 394–416), that China entered a new phase in its religious life. A number of monks bringing Buddhist scriptures unknown in China were able to reach Yao Xing's capital at Chang'an. There they found a Chinese monastic community ready to receive them, thanks to Daoan (AD 312–385). He was perhaps the first Chinese monk to be fully aware of the need to study Buddhism seriously as a system of thought quite independent of the Chinese tradition, whatever the incidental parallels, and had accordingly cataloged existing translations, set up guidelines for future work, and organized teams of collaborators. During Daoan's own lifetime the main works rendered into Chinese by this now-systematic method were based chiefly on the scholastic Buddhism of Kashmir, but many of the disciples whom he trained still remained in the north when a monk capable of transmitting the Mahāyāna philosophical vision to China finally

THE DUNHUANG FINDS

LEFT: *Head of a Bodhisattva, or high-ranking follower of Buddha, dated to the seventh or eighth century, was among the finds in the Dunhuang caves in Gansu province.* BRITISH MUSEUM, LONDON

RIGHT: *Avalokiteśvara — Five Dynasties. This is a typical example of the early use of printing by Buddhists in China for a "prayer sheet." It is taken from a single wood block, with the image of a Buddhist figure above and one to two hundred characters of text below.* ANCIENT ART AND ARCHITECTURE COLLECTION

The remarkable series of events which has made the study of Dunhuang an international venture may be traced back into the nineteenth century when Europeans venturing into this area discovered that it concealed the remains of long-vanished civilizations, where the dry air could preserve written materials for centuries.

In 1907, a Hungarian, M. Aurel Stein (1862–1943), who worked on behalf of the British government in India, led an expedition eastward toward Dunhuang where, in 1900, an old Chinese soldier turned Daoist priest, named Wang Yuanlu, had made his home and discovered, behind a hollow wall, bundle upon bundle of texts of an age quite unknown to him. Wang was persuaded to part with 50 bundles of Chinese and five bundles of Tibetan texts for a sum equivalent to 500 rupees. Although a half

dozen manuscripts remained (and remain) at New Delhi on Stein's return to India, by 1909 the first parcels from Dunhuang had arrived in London where an exhibition was held in 1914.

In 1907 another expedition, headed by the French orientalist Paul Pelliot (1878–1945), acquired more material which the scholar Luo Zhenyu (1866–1940), then head of agriculture at the future Beijing University, heard about and telegraphed the local Chinese authorities demanding action. As a consequence, a large portion of the remaining texts were transferred to Beijing in 1910, though the success of the operation may be judged by the numerous manuscripts which were subsequently to enter both Chinese and European private collections. By the early 1920s, the business of cataloging, photographing, and studying the manuscripts was making uneven but undeniable progress

around the world. Today the field is by no means confined to linguistic, sinological, religious, literary, and art historical studies, but embraces social and economic history, and a scattering of other historical disciplines involving medicine, astronomy, divination, music, and dance.

RIGHT: *Painting on paper, from Dunhuang, showing Siddhartha and his groom on horseback.*
The story of the Buddha's life, from his early days as the Prince Siddhārtha to his enlightenment and beyond, remained a firm favorite in China from the time of its first translation into Chinese in the late Han. At Dunhuang we find episodes of this story not only in pictorial form but also as retold dramatically in popular literature. E.T. ARCHIVE/MUSEE GUIMET, PARIS

CHAN BUDDHISM

It is no accident that Chan Buddhism, especially in its Japanese form, Zen (the Japanese word for *Chan*), should be the variety of East Asian Buddhism best known in the West. Chan has always stressed directness and immediacy, not in results (which may take years to achieve), but in perception of the truth, beyond all barriers of time and cultural distance — the belief that truth is not found in doctrinal studies but that it is beyond the written word and lies in self knowledge.

Also, the direct appeal of Chan's heroes has won them not only the respect of dedicated seekers of enlightenment but also a remarkable degree of popular affection. This is particularly true of Bodhidharma. This exacting meditation master left behind such

LEFT: Portrait of Bodhidharma, the Indian monk who settled in China about AD 520 and is credited with introducing a system of relaxation exercises as well as being regarded as one of the founders of Chan Buddhism. The painting is attributed to late Qing artist, Qi Baishi (1863–1957). BRITISH MUSEUM, LONDON

an impression that it was easy for later Chinese to believe that he had in fact conveyed to China the "separate transmission" of the Buddha's message that was transmitted directly "from mind to mind."

The emergence of "encounter" based Chan, associated with pioneering figures such as Mazu Daoyi (AD 709–788) which extended to the start of the Song dynasty, gave the Chan movement many of its most striking dicta and also its characteristic literature, termed "Recorded Sayings," which bristles with colloquialisms reflecting the living speech of the masters, quite unlike the sedate classical Chinese of most learned monks.

If the spread of Zen to the West has largely been due to Japanese writers like D.T. Suzuki (1870–1966), it is equally the case that Suzuki himself, and a large number of other contemporary Japanese, have been concerned to return to the roots of the Zen tradition through the study of Dunhuang manuscripts and other early texts.

ABOVE: White Horse Pagoda, an early Buddhist structure in Luoyang, western Henan province. ROBERT E. MUROWCHICK

RIGHT: Near life-sized lead-glazed figure of Arhat (Luohan), one of a group of eight seated clay monks discovered in 1912 in caves in Hebei province. ROYAL ONTARIO MUSEUM

developing in completely unorthodox directions, even if it was to assume characteristics all its own.

The new age in the south also brought direct contact with Indian Buddhism in the person of Faxian (away from China AD 399–412), the first Chinese to journey to the sacred places of India and return to tell the tale and to translate many texts. The clearer picture of Buddhism furnished by Kumārajīva, Faxian, and other translators seems to have also stimulated developments in Daoism: the concept of the Mahāyāna as a higher form of Buddhism appears to have allowed Lu Xiujing (AD 406–477) to compose for the first time an organized Daoist canon in three divisions, ranking the new Shangqing and Lingbao revelations above older literature. But the notion that these separate strands constituted a unified religious tradition, similar to the many different teachings ascribed to the Buddha, in itself sharpened the differences between Daoism and Buddhism, especially now that imperial

patronage was at stake. It might be argued that the true spirit of Daoism was more readily to be found in the secluded life of the poet Tao Qian (AD 365–427), a figure also claimed by Buddhism. Tao's poem about a lost utopia, the "Peach Blossom Spring" may be read as a counterpoint to a political climate in the fifth-century south that remained far from stable.

A non-Chinese group, the Toba, founded the Northern Wei dynasty in AD 386, far to the north of any former Chinese territory, and it succeeded in eliminating its competitors in the Huang River region in AD 439. Here, too, the new order brought with it new forms of religion: again, a form of officially recognized Daoism owing not a little to Buddhist example seems to have been important in reconciling the remaining Chinese in the north with the Toba regime, under the guidance of the scholar Cui Hao (AD 381–450) and the priest Kou Qianzhi (AD 365–448). But in the harsher world of north China, government support turned to persecution rather than mere polemic against Buddhism, and from AD 446–450 an attempt was made by the Toba emperor Taiwu to end Buddhism in the north and to impose a Daoist theocracy. Such a reversal, however, was more than one man could achieve and with Taiwu's death a reaction set in, bonding the Toba rulers yet more closely to Buddhism than Taiwu had been to Daoism.

In the late fifth century the impetus from the court was to transform the old tribal aristocracy of the Toba into well-regulated subjects on the Chinese model: the capital was moved from Pingcheng in the north to Luoyang, the former Han capital, in AD 494, and once more religious fervor inspired the construction of further monasteries in the city itself, and further carvings at Longmen, a new, more southerly Yungang. Yet what ultimately resulted from this transition was a rift between the Chinese-style court and the tough Toba garrisons on the northern frontiers who protected the luxury-loving courtiers from the incursions of Inner Asian warriors. In AD 523 the garrisons

LEFT: Sculptures in Buddhist cave temples at Yungang near Datong in Shanxi province show the beginnings of a style distinct from that of India and Afghanistan. The work dates from AD 460 to the sixth century though most were completed before AD 494 when the capital was shifted to Luoyang. SALLY & RICHARD GREENHILL

ABOVE: When the capital was shifted to Luoyang, south of the Huang (Yellow) River in Henan province, work began on another complex of cave temples at nearby Longmen. Among the many Buddhist sculptures are these rock carvings from c. AD 672.
ROBERT E. MUROWCHICK

LEFT: A contemporary interpretation by Nie Ou (born 1948) of Peach Blossom Spring, *a tale of a lost utopia written by the poet Dao Qian (AD 365–427).*
BRITISH MUSEUM, LONDON

revolted, and the glories of Luoyang entered upon an era of decline. The Northern Wei was split between competing generals into Eastern and Western Wei regimes, and Luoyang itself, the scene of fearful massacres and reprisals, was abandoned in AD 534.

The evidence for southern Buddhist devotion is not so striking as in the north: there are no great rock sculptures in the region of Nanjing. There certainly was statuary, but much of it was in the form of precious metals that have long since been melted down.

There are however, surviving cultural products of this age: perhaps the most influential compilation was an anthology of literary works, the *Wenxuan*, made by an imperial prince, Xiao Tong (AD 501–531). This anthology came to be seen as a normative selection of literary gems memorized by every candidate for the civil service examinations of Tang times, and constitutes a valuable source for early Chinese literature even today. Though little trace of Buddhism may be found in the *Wenxin diaolong*, we know that Liu Xie was as devout as his emperor. It seems as if the summation of the cultural heritage that was undertaken at this time kept to a clear division between the "worldly" sphere of the Chinese tradition and the "otherworldly" sphere of Buddhist learning.

The spirit of the age, however, cannot be so neatly summarized. The great Daoist leader, Tao Hongjing (AD 456–536), whose influence on Emperor Wu was to wane only as old age increased the latter's depth of devotion to Buddhism, was nothing if not a scholar of matters both sacred and secular — not only of the Daoist scriptural heritage, but also of such diverse but related topics as pharmacology, dynastic chronology, and the manufacture of swords.

During the latter half of the sixth

But whereas the Northern Qi promoted Buddhism enthusiastically, the Northern Zhou fell into the hands of a ruler (known as Emperor Wu) determined to create his own religious and political regime, whatever the opposition. Buddhist monasteries were destroyed in their hundreds, and monks and nuns were stripped of their religious credentials in their thousands.

Fortunately for Buddhism, Emperor Wu died in AD 578, and his dynasty was replaced in AD 581 by the Sui, who further eliminated the southern Chen dynasty in AD 589 so as to achieve the reunification of China for the first time in centuries. Rather than see Buddhism as a hindrance, Emperor Wen, founder of the Sui, saw it as a vital force to be harnessed in achieving the cultural integration of a China so long divided.

However, as more and more time passed from the time of the Buddha and more and more texts claimed his authority, the doctrine that Buddhism itself was bound to lose its integrity and ultimately disappear inevitably gained a firm hold on Chinese minds by the end of the sixth century. Not only had the Buddha died long ago; even when he had lived he had been very far away. The Chinese needed a Buddhism that dealt with the here and now, offering them hope in the context of their daily lives in China, not some far-off prospect of salvation of no relevance to Chinese experience. And that is precisely what developed in China from the sixth century onward.

Beginning in Song times, China evolved a distinctive and perhaps more inward-looking civilization that was more wary of foreign influences — even Chan (that found Buddhism in everything) did not succeed in resisting this shift to what we term Neo-Confucianism. But if for a while the Chinese put behind them the memory of a time when China was but a part of a great continental religious movement, the problem of the relationship between Chinese civilization and the wider world has not gone away. The period of Buddhism's flowering in China may offer insights into how it may be possible to be Chinese and yet part of the global community.

century the mood was one of regret for lost glories, and fear for the future. In Buddhist circles this mood was further heightened by developments in the north. The eastern portion of the former Toba empire became, in AD 550, the Northern Qi when the warlord supporting it took power for himself, and the same process in the west brought into being the Northern Zhou, based at the old Han capital of Chang'an, in AD 557.

LEFT: Scroll entitled Buddhist Retreat Between Two Peaks, *by Zha Shibiao (1615–98). Though early Buddhists who settled on mountains in China usually found them already occupied by followers of other cults, they were so successful in claiming such sites as their own that later writers complain that Buddhists had taken over all the most scenic places in the empire.*
INTERNATIONAL ARTS COUNCIL

ABOVE: *Thousand Buddhas Cave, Fubo Hill. The practice of creating complex cave temples, usually cut into cliffs overlooking rivers in China, may be traced through Central Asian examples back to Indian Buddhism.*
DON KLUMPP/THE IMAGE BANK

THE GOLDEN AGE OF TANG AND SONG

Patricia Ebrey

THE SIX AND A HALF CENTURIES encompassed by the Tang (AD 618–907) and Song (AD 960–1276) dynasties were a time of remarkable growth and innovation. The population doubled from 50 to 100 million, the economy grew spectacularly, and new technologies, ideas, institutions, and fashions transformed social and cultural life.

The emergence of the Tang empire in the early seventh century followed many centuries of disunion, with contending "barbarian" and Chinese kingdoms vying for supremacy. In AD 589, the Sui dynasty succeeded in defeating the southern state of Chen, reuniting north and south. During its brief reign, it succeeded in once again establishing a strong centralized government and embarked on ambitious construction campaigns to build transport canals and palace complexes. However, the Sui disintegrated barely 30 years after its emergence. From the ensuing chaos emerged the Tang and, with it, a spectacular imperial renaissance.

The first two Tang emperors (reigning as Gaozong, AD 618–626, and Taizong, AD 626–649) vigorously extended measures initiated during the Northern Dynasties (that is, the dynasties that had ruled only the north). The military establishment was kept to a minimum through use of a militia that was composed of units of self-sufficient farmer–soldiers serving periodic tours of duty in and around the capital or at the frontiers. Standard taxes in grain, labor, and cloth were assessed on each household, each of which in turn was to receive an "equal" land allotment. The upper echelon of officials was largely recruited from the aristocratic families of the Sui dynasty, but a small number were selected for their literary talents through the examination system started by the Sui.

The new Tang rulers quickly asserted their power beyond China Proper. Taizong was able to reduce the Turks to vassalage and reassert Chinese suzerainty over the Silk Road oasis kingdoms of modern Xinjiang province, creating a pan-Asian empire. As a result the capital and other major Tang cities were thronged with traders from distant lands. Foreign religions, including Islam, Judaism, Manichaeism, Zoroastrianism, and Nestorian Christianity were practiced among foreign merchants, though none spread into the Chinese population the way Buddhism had centuries earlier. Foreign influence was greater in the arts. The introduction of new instruments and new tunes from India, Iran, and central Asia brought about a major trans-formation of Chinese music. Interior furnishings were also transformed as the

ABOVE: The caravans that came from central Asia were so welcome that pottery representations of camels and their non-Han grooms were among the objects people commonly placed in tombs.
WERNER FORMAN ARCHIVE/CHRISTIAN DEYDIER, LONDON

OPPOSITE: Awaiting the Exam Results *by Chiu Ying. The examination system for selecting government officials was begun during the Sui dynasty, but reached its height during the Song era. By its end in 1276 up to 400,000 candidates sat for the prefectural examinations.*
NATIONAL PALACE MUSEUM, TAIBEI, TAIWAN, REPUBLIC OF CHINA

practice of sitting on mats on the floor gradually gave way to the foreign practice of sitting on stools and chairs.

The Tang dynasty nearly fell twice, once when an empress usurped the throne, and once when a general rebelled. Empress Wu (died AD 705) was an extraordinarily powerful personality and adroit politician. She managed first to get Gaozong to oust his empress and install her in her place, then to dominate the court during the remainder of his nominal rule, then to maintain her control during the reigns of her two sons, deposing each in turn until, in AD 690, she proclaimed herself emperor of a new dynasty. She was not deposed until she was over 80 years old and in poor health.

The second crisis occurred when An Lushan, the general, rebelled, bringing to an end the brilliant reign of Xuanzong (reigned AD 713–755). A great patron of the arts, Xuanzong in his late years left most government matters to his chief ministers and spent his time with his favorite consort, Yang Guifei. An Lushan, one of the many non-Chinese military officers employed by the Tang court, had used his position as a favorite of Yang Guifei to help him amass enormous military power along the northern and northeastern frontiers. After rebelling he quickly captured the great cities of Luoyang and Chang'an. Xuanzong had to flee, and his mutinous troops, before consenting to be led by him, forced him to have Yang Guifei killed.

Even though the rebellion was quelled by AD 763 and the Tang court reestablished in the capital, regaining full control of the

country proved impossible as large parts remained in the hands of nearly independent military governors. To bolster its revenue, the central government abandoned the equal land allotment system (thus allowing unrestricted buying and selling of land), replaced it with a twice-yearly tax on actual landholdings, and extended monopolies over salt, wine, tea, and other commodities. But reassertion of central control proved an elusive goal. By the early ninth century the eunuch palace servants gained control of the court, to the point where they and their henchmen enthroned and dethroned emperors, even murdering them with impunity. Control of the provinces continued to deteriorate, and banditry and rebellion engulfed much of south and central China after AD 860.

Over the course of the Tang dynasty, the Tibetan, Turkic, and Arab empires expanded, bringing an end to China's dominance in central Asia. Some of the warlords who briefly gained control of north China after the fall of the Tang were ethnically non-Chinese, beginning a new period of struggle for control of the region. Even though it was a Chinese general, Zhao Kuangyin (as emperor Taizu, reigned AD 960–976) who succeeded in establishing a state that lasted (the Song dynasty, 960–1276), non-Chinese rivals, such as the Tanguts and the Khitans, were not vanquished. The

ABOVE: Portrait of Emperor Taizu (reigned AD 960–976), the general who founded the Song dynasty.
NATIONAL PALACE MUSEUM, TAIBEI, TAIWAN, REPUBLIC OF CHINA

Tanguts retained parts of the northwest (the Xia state) and the Khitans retained the northeast (the Liao state). As a consequence, the early Song state had to live with the uncertainty of powerful neighbors to its north. Under peace agreements, reached in 1004 and 1044, the Song court agreed to make substantial annual payments to Liao and Xia. Early in the twelfth century the Song allied with Liao's northern neighbor, the Jurchen, to defeat the Liao. In 1127 most of north China was lost and incorporated into the Jurchen's Jin dynasty. When the Song lost north China, they established a "temporary" capital at modern Hangzhou, and maintained a vigorous social, intellectual, and economic life in south China until it (and thus the Song) fell to the Mongols in 1276.

Institutionally, the early Song government differed from the Tang above all in its emphasis on centralization. To prevent the rise of regional warlords, Emperor Taizu created a professional

LEFT: Paper money was an innovation of the late Tang dynasty. From 1024, the government issued such money itself. CHINA PICTORIAL PHOTO SERVICE

ABOVE: Detail from a Song dynasty (thirteenth-century) scroll attributed to Liang Kai showing the 24 stages of sericulture (silk making). Finished silk was a major export, traveling along the Silk Road through central Asia and eventually to Europe.
THE CLEVELAND MUSEUM OF ART, JOHN L. SEVERANCE FUND/77.5

RIGHT: Silver cups, bowls, and boxes first appeared during the Han dynasty (202 BC–AD 220) and by the Tang dynasty silversmithing reached its highest artistic levels.
WENWU PUBLISHING

BELOW: As this twelfth-century painting shows, Kaifeng was a commercial city, dominated as much by markets — open all hours — as by palaces and government offices. THE PALACE MUSEUM, BEIJING

army of career soldiers whose officers were regularly rotated. To strengthen central control of local administration, the court assigned judicial, fiscal, military, and transportation officials to supervise and coordinate overlapping sets of prefectures.

Economic growth undoubtedly lay behind much of the cultural vitality of the Tang and Song period. The reunification of the country, the opening of the Grand Canal linking north and south, and the expansion of trade with Inner Asia all stimulated the economy, which in many ways had stagnated since the Han. Economic development of the south was particularly impressive. Convenient water transportation and a milder climate made possible rapid agricultural expansion there, particularly of rice grown in flooded fields, a highly productive crop allowing dense settlement patterns. From the late Tang and continuing throughout the Song, commerce burgeoned at all levels. Port cities of Guangzhou (Canton), Quanzhou, and Fuzhou thrived as maritime trade along the coast and throughout Southeast Asia expanded greatly. The government assisted this expansion of the economy through its monetary policies.

Great cities characterized both the Tang and Song dynasties. Chang'an, the Tang capital, was a planned city laid out on a rectangular grid 5 miles by 6 miles (8 km by 9.5 km). The palace was in the north of the city, so the emperor could, in a sense, face south toward his subjects, whose homes were in the 108 wards, each enclosed by a wall. Specific blocks were set aside for markets, open only during limited hours. Home to perhaps one million people during the Tang, Chang'an was the largest city in the world at that time. A cosmopolitan city, it attracted not only craftworkers, traders, and pilgrims from much of Asia, but also literati from all over China who hoped to gain official appointments or make names for themselves as writers or artists. To feed

THE TANG MODEL IN KOREA AND JAPAN

In both Korea and Japan, Chinese culture had been an important influence for centuries. Buddhism had spread from China, carrying with it much of Chinese material culture and artistic taste. In both places learning meant learning to read and write in Chinese. However, the prestige of the Tang empire led both Korean and Japanese rulers to go much further in copying Chinese practices. The Tang dynasty — with its vast territories, magnificent capital, strong imperial institution, and fully developed bureaucratic administrative structure — inspired the ambitions of the rulers of neighboring states. To transform their own territories into great states, they emulated Tang institutions and practices.

BELOW: The Chinese Tang city of Chang'an was a walled city designed on a rectangular plan, with broad central avenues and great gates.

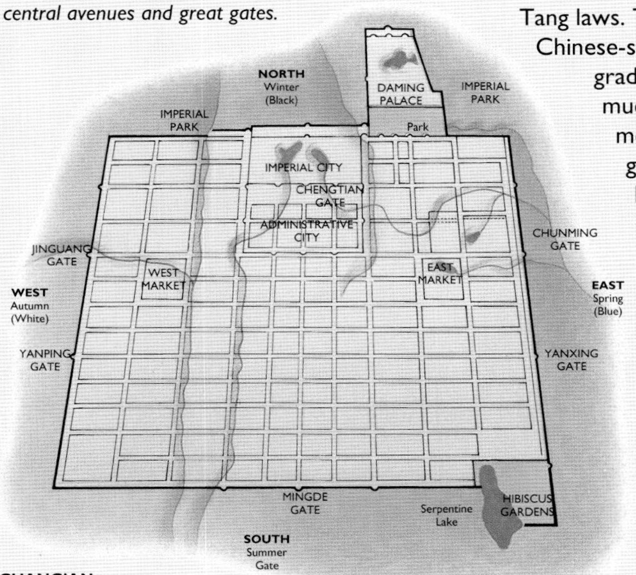

CHANG'AN

During the Tang, both Korea and Japan sent numerous embassies to Chang'an, the capital city of Tang, often accompanied by students who stayed for years studying Chinese language and culture. In AD 646 the Japanese king issued an edict abolishing the old system of private landholding and establishing a system of equal land allotments modeled on Tang laws. The Japanese also introduced a Chinese-style system of officials, with graded ranks. Indeed, Japan adopted much of the Tang law code without modification. When the government built a new capital at Nara in AD 710, it was laid out in checkerboard fashion, with the palace at the northern end, on the model of Chang'an (though without city walls, a standard feature of Chinese cities). In AD 794 when the court moved to an even larger planned capital, Heian, the model of Chang'an was again adopted. In Korea, the influenc of the Tang model was greatest after Silla unified the Korean peninsula in AD 668

HEIAN (KYOTO)

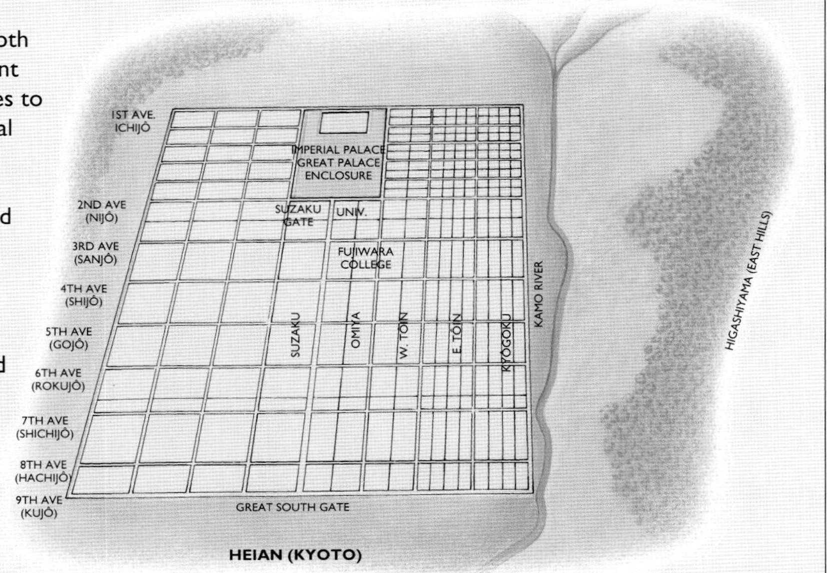

ABOVE: The original plan for Japanese Heian, shown above, was symmetrical, like the Chinese model, but smaller in scale and without walls.

with Tang help. The Silla kings copied the Tang administrative structure, down to the division of the country into counties and prefectures and the equal land allotment system. Kyongju, the Silla capital, was expanded on the model of Chang'an and grew to house 800,000 people. The National Academy was expanded in AD 682 to provide a formal Confucian education to the Korean aristocracy and in AD 788 the first government examinations were held.

Many of the similarities outsiders see today among China, Japan, and Korea in material life, social customs, and moral values can be traced back to this early stage of Japan's and Korea's development when they enthusiastically copied things Chinese.

the population of the capital, hundreds of thousands of bushels of tax grain had to be brought in from the south, making part of the journey along the Grand Canal and part overland.

Kaifeng, the capital of the Song until 1126, was situated further east, near the northern end of the Grand Canal and not far from major deposits of coal and iron. It was about as populous as Chang'an had been at its height, but was more of a commercial city. Multistory houses, directly on the streets rather than behind walls, became common. After the north

was lost, the new capital at Hangzhou quickly grew to match or even surpass Kaifeng in population and economic development.

In these Tang and Song cities, with their concentration of people and wealth, a distinctly urban style of life evolved. Numerous amenities, including a great variety of foods, entertainments, and luxury goods, were available to city residents. The division of labor reached a very high level, with many workers engaged in highly specialized enterprises. Entertainment quarters emerged where

ABOVE: *This silk scroll is worked in the most prized of weaves,* Kesi, *which is a form of tapestry. Entitled* Admonitions of the Instructress, *it depicts an interpretation of possibly the most famous of all Chinese paintings, a scroll illustrating the text of admonitions for feminine conduct at court written by Chang Hua in the third century AD. While the composition and figure style suggest a possible fourth-century original, a Tang dynasty (AD 618–907) date is generally accepted for the work.*
BRITISH MUSEUM

one could go to watch storytellers or jugglers or call on female musicians and singers (similar to the Japanese geisha). Luxury goods available in these great cities reached artistic levels rarely surpassed. Silver cups, plates, ewers, and other small objects showed the influence of Persian motifs and techniques. Fine celadon (pottery with a pale green glaze) and other forms of porcelain were produced in Tang times, but ceramic art became even more sophisticated during the Song, when many regional centers produced their own distinctive styles. Silk goods were available in all sorts of complex weaves, including light and airy openwork patterns that were in much demand in distant lands. A type of very fine tapestry weave was also perfected, allowing the depiction of flowers, animals, and almost anything that could be depicted in a painting.

The first printed books appeared in the late Tang but the impact of printing was not fully felt until the prices of books

made purchasing them an attractive alternative to copying them by hand. From mid-Tang to mid-Song the price of books dropped to perhaps one-tenth its previous level. From the tenth to the twelfth centuries, the Confucian classics and the Buddhist and Daoist canons were all published in their entirety. By the twelfth and thirteenth centuries there was an outpouring of works including: manuals for agriculture, medicine, and divination; collections of anecdotes and stories; individual authors' prose and poetry, religious tracts and treatises; and reference guides for local magistrates and candidates for the examinations.

Economic expansion and easier access to books facilitated growth in the educated class. Already in the late Tang, the aristocratic families that had been politically dominant for so long were losing their ability to make the central government their special preserve. The early Song, concerned above all to avoid domination by generals, expanded the civil service examination system and the government school system. By the middle of the dynasty about half of those holding government posts had entered the bureaucracy through success in the examinations. Competition to gain office through the examinations steadily increased during the course of the dynasty. In the early eleventh century less than 30,000 candidates took the prefectural examinations. This rose to nearly 80,000 by the end of the century and perhaps 400,000 before the dynasty's end in 1276.

RIGHT: *Woodblock print of a page from the* Diamond Sutra *printed in AD 868. The introduction of printing revolutionized the spread of ideas and contributed to fundamental changes in social structure.* BRITISH LIBRARY

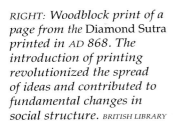

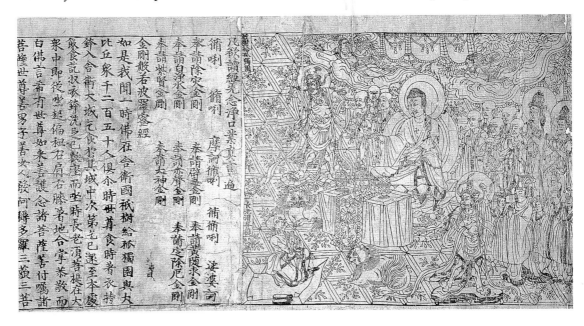

CALLIGRAPHY AND ART DURING THE SONG

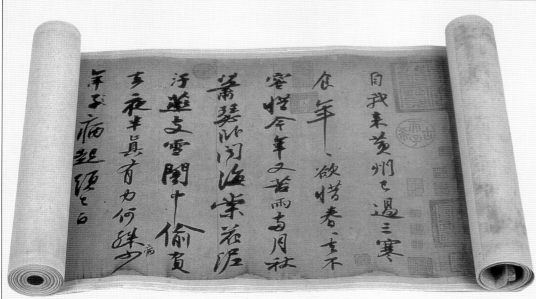

LEFT: Calligraphy by Su Shi, the Song dynasty man for all seasons. Not only was he a leading official, he was also a painter, poet, and calligrapher.
NATIONAL PALACE MUSEUM, TAIBEI, TAIWAN, REPUBLIC OF CHINA

During the Song dynasty the culture and way of life of the scholarly gentleman acquired a characteristic style that lasted for centuries. These men may have derived their income from landholding and business investments, but they identified themselves as men of letters and aspirants for office. Many cultivated artistic, literary, or antiquarian interests. Arts such as calligraphy and painting — arts that are performed with the brush of the literati — flourished in these circumstances.

The man who came closest to fulfilling the ideal of the scholar-literati-artist-official is Su Shi (1037–1101). At the center of the political life of his day, an outstanding governor of Hangzhou, an accomplished painter and calligrapher, and ranked among the greatest of poets and essayists, Su's fame was well-established in his own day and has lasted until the present. In his writings on the theory of painting, he explicitly argues that the purpose of painting was not to depict the appearance of things but to express the painter's own feelings, making it much more like poetry.

One of the most famous of the Song emperors, Huizong (reigned 1101–25), was himself a talented painter and calligrapher. Not only did he use the resources of the throne to build up the imperial painting collection (his catalog lists over 6,000 paintings), but he personally developed new styles in calligraphy and bird and flower painting.

Su Shi is known for his paintings of bamboo and Huizong for his bird and flower paintings, but another genre — landscapes — is generally recognized as the greatest glory of Song painting. Centuries before Western artists began to see natural scenery as anything more than background, Chinese artists had developed it into a great art. Mountains had long been seen as sacred places — the homes of immortals, close to the heavens. Philosophical interest in nature could also have contributed to the rise of landscape painting, including both Daoist stress on how minor the human presence is in the vastness of the cosmos, and neo-Confucian interest in the patterns or principles that underlie all phenomena, natural and social.

BELOW LEFT: White Goose and Red Polygonum is the work of Northern Song Emperor Huizong (1082–1135), remembered for government reforms but even more for his interest in Daoist religion, painting, and calligraphy.
NATIONAL PALACE MUSEUM, TAIBEI, TAIWAN, REPUBLIC OF CHINA

BELOW: Hanging silk scroll entitled Five-Colored Parakeet is also attributed to Huizong.
MARIA ANTOINETTE EVANS FUND, MUSEUM OF FINE ARTS, BOSTON

CHANGES IN WOMEN'S LIVES

Women's lives, like men's, were shaped by the cultural and economic changes of the Tang–Song period. The development and spread of printing gave more women the opportunity to learn to read and write. (One woman, Li Qingzhao, even attained fame as a poet.) Many women gained greater access to family property as a result of shifts in marriage finance toward substantial provision of dowries for daughters. Improvements in textile technology and expansion of markets for silk led some peasant families to concentrate on raising silkworms and producing silk and thus to depend more heavily on women's labor than peasant families usually did.

These changes offered women more avenues for influence both within the family and outside it. But there were other changes during this period that are generally classified as detrimental to women, particularly more rigid notions of ethically acceptable female demeanor, and footbinding.

In the Tang period, court life was occasionally dominated by powerful women like Empress Wu and Yang Guifei, and emperors seem to have liked active women — even letting palace women play polo. In the Song, notions of female modesty became more rigid, with women veiling their faces more often and riding in curtained sedan chairs when traveling through the streets. By the twelfth century, medical authorities were reporting that doctors who called on women in elite households could neither

LEFT: Standards of beauty at the Tang court favored plump women, and tomb figurines like this one reflected that taste.
LUO ZHONG MIN/CHINA TOURISM PHOTO LIBRARY

BELOW: By the Song era, standards of beauty had shifted and the delicacy suggested by a slender shape was considered desirable.
NATIONAL PALACE MUSEUM, TAIBEI, TAIWAN, REPUBLIC OF CHINA

view the woman nor question her; taking the pulse of a hand and wrist extended through the curtains was all that was allowed. These shifts in notions of modesty and beauty probably fostered the spread of the practice of binding young girls' feet to reshape them into tiny, narrow arcs. This fashion spread from the entertainment quarters in early Song to the homes of the scholarly elite by the end of the dynasty.

Philosophical currents did not undermine these trends toward a more restricted sphere for women. All of the leading Neo-Confucian teachers stressed the need for both men and women to identify with the interests of the family, which in women's case meant the family of their husbands and sons. They should have no desire to have their own property, feel no jealousy if their husbands took concubines, and remain to care for their parents-in-law and children if their husbands died. These Confucian scholars had no objections to the growing tendency toward stricter seclusion of women; to the contrary, they reiterated the need for clear separation of the men's and women's quarters in the house.

For the first time in Chinese history a large proportion of this ruling class was from central and southern China.

Educated men in Tang times were interested in a wide range of arts and learning. Poetry flourished, and the Tang produced many of China's greatest poets, including Li Bai, Du Fu, Wang Wei, Bai Juyi, Han Yu, and Li Shangyin. Buddhism continued to attract those inclined toward philosophical speculation or the search for spiritual values, especially the relatively new Chan Buddhism, a wholly Chinese form. A revival of Confucian learning began, however, with the political challenges of the late Tang and the growth of the examination system in the Song. Leaders of the Confucian revival sought ways to reconcile the vision of an ideal order they found in the classics with the rapidly changing social and political order they found around them. They argued, often bitterly, about the merits of the examination system. They sought to revitalize Confucian rites and combat Buddhist ritual practices like cremation. Personal self-cultivation became a major concern of thinkers, especially among followers of Cheng Yi (1033–1107). In the twelfth and thirteenth centuries, Confucian scholars such as Zhu Xi (1130–1200) and his followers, frustrated with the failure of the government to regain the north, took more and more interest in the ways to build a more ideal society by starting from the bottom, reforming families and local communities, establishing academies, and spreading their message through publishing.

Confucian scholars frequently disagreed about which Confucian ideas were most relevant and how to apply them to current circumstances. The most divisive episode in Song history grew from such disagreement. When Emperor Shenzong (reigned 1067–85) took the throne at age 20, he was impressed with the ideas of Wang Anshi and let him introduce a comprehensive reform program designed to make the country richer and to bring more of those riches into state coffers. Fiscal administration in particular came in for thorough revision as Wang promoted much deeper involvement of the state in economic activities. Opposition appeared almost immediately; well-respected officials such as the historian Sima Guang and poet Su Shi denounced his programs as un-Confucian. The rift between these two factions widened as Wang forced his opponents out of office. For two generations, long after the deaths of the emperor, Wang, and Sima, scholar–officials were deeply divided by the struggles between these two factions.

At the end of the Song, China was a very different society than it had been in the early Tang. It was a richer, more compact, and

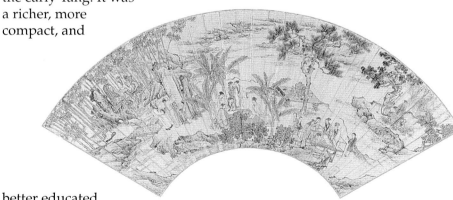

better educated society, surviving in a more hostile international environment. The region of the lower Yangzi River had become the economic and cultural center of the country. The examination system had come to dominate the lives of the elite. Drinking tea and sitting in chairs had become standard practices. And women had taken to binding their feet.

ABOVE: Composing Poetry on a Spring Outing, *attributed to the Southern Song artist Ma Yuan (active about 1190–1225), illustrates literati in their favorite activities.*
THE NELSON-ATKINS MUSEUM OF ART, KANSAS CITY, MISSOURI (PURCHASE: NELSON TRUST 63-19)

ABOVE: This sixteenth-century fan painting entitled The Elegant Gathering in the Western Garden, *attributed to Wei Zhujing, illustrates two of the advents of the Tang and Song dynasties — drinking tea and sitting in chairs.*
ASIAN ART MUSEUM OF SAN FRANCISCO, THE AVERY BRUNDAGE COLLECTION/B79 D19A

حکایت

قوریلتای بزرک جنکگرخان یومی سیدنده بایه بضب فرود ولبج جنکگرخان بوبقذر

کث وعزیت اوبجگ بیروق بازتاه یگه لمان ولرننن بربزن خان بذ کوربا جون مبارکی وفرخی ماربل که سال بوزمائدبوانق

مار رجب سنه لمین و سنمایه هجری در آمذیم دز اولد مضلهار جنکگرخان فرود مانوفی نه بایه سید ببای کردند محبیبی باعطلت

قوریلتای نبذل ساخت ودران قوریلتای لبب بزرک جنکگرخان بن بدوی مزر کردند وساری بسکنن بنث

INVADERS FROM THE NORTH

Elizabeth Endicott-West

THE MONGOLS WERE THE FIRST INNER Asian nomadic people to conquer and rule all of China. While earlier Inner Asian confederacies had dominated the Chinese–Inner Asian frontier zone and had even conquered all of north China, the Mongolian tribes of the thirteenth century, unified by Chinggis (Ghengis) Khan, were the first such group to rule of China in its entirety. The Mongols established the Yuan dynasty (1272–1368), a Chinese-style dynasty that incorporated many aspects of Mongolian and Inner Asian political and military institutions.

Patterns of Chinese–Inner Asian relations had evolved over the centuries prior to the appearance of the Mongols in the early thirteenth century. The first great nomadic empire neighboring China was that of the Xiongnu people. The Xiongnu empire (*c.* 210 BC–AD 48), centered in Mongolia, kept the Han dynasty embroiled in constant warfare for centuries, in spite of numerous attempts at peace with treaties.

After the dissolution of the Xiongnu empire, when it split into rival groups, and the fall of the Han dynasty in AD 220 after decades of internal military disorder and political fragmentation, various nomadic tribes of differing ethnic backgrounds (predominantly Turkic) formed short-lived empires or kingdoms

in north China and the Mongolian steppes. The era of Turkic dominance of the steppelands of Inner Asia was contemporaneous with the Tang dynasty (AD 618–907) in China. The first and second Turk empires (AD 552–630; AD 683–734) as well as the Uighur empire (located in Mongolia, AD 744–840) established military, diplomatic, and commercial relations with the Tang court, often on the basis of parity. The Uighurs, who in the thirteenth century became prominent advisers to the ruling Mongols of the Yuan dynasty, tipped the balance in favor of their own interests in their relations with Tang China. They were particularly adept in Tang times at exploiting the wealth of China's cities through a combination of commercial extortion and military threat. The Uighurs also used their military strength to buttress the weakening Tang state, since it was to their benefit to enjoy stable commercial relations with a unified China.

Following the collapse of the Turkic steppe empires, China endured centuries of invasion and rule by the non-nomadic, forest-dwelling tribes of Manchuria. The Liao (AD 907–1125) and Jin (1115–1234) dynasties, established respectively by the Khitans (a proto-Mongolian people) and the Jurchens (a Tungusic people), successively ruled large portions of north

ABOVE: *Although this stoneware jar is from the Ji Zhou kilns of southern China, the inspiration for its bold brown painted decoration came from the northern Ci Zhou family of kilns, indicative of the cross-culturalism of the Yuan period.* ROYAL ONTARIO MUSEUM

OPPOSITE: *The assembly of Mongolian princes at which Chinggis (Ghengis) Khan was elevated to Khan in 1206.* BIBLIOTHEQUE NATIONALE, PARIS

China. By the early thirteenth century, north China was ruled by the Jurchens; south China was under the Chinese Southern Song dynasty; and China's northwest (present day Gansu, Ningxia, and the Ordos region) was controlled by the Xixia kingdom of the Tanguts, people of Tibetan origin. The Mongols thus were presented with a politically divided and militarily weak China on the eve of their campaigns of conquest.

The life of Chinggis Khan (c. 1167–1227), as recounted by the Mongolian epic *The Secret History of the Mongols* (1228), is a story of ruthless ambition, good luck, and a personality able to inspire and retain loyalty. Chinggis was responsible for the unification of disparate, quarreling steppe tribes and their remolding into an effective conquest outfit. After being invested with the title Chinggis Khan at an assembly of Mongolian princes in 1206, the new ruler (whose given name was Temüjin) commenced his campaigns against the Tangut Xixia kingdom and the Jurchen Jin dynasty. Tangut resistance finally collapsed

shortly before the great khan's death in 1227, but the Jin dynasty held out until the reign of Chinggis's son and successor, Ögödei Khan, when in 1234 Mongolian troops captured the Jin capital. The cities of Bukhara and Samarkand in central Asia fell to Chinggis's troops in 1220, and initial forays by Mongolian troops into southern Russia in the early 1220s resulted in victories.

One central reason for the success of Chinggis Khan and his successors in their campaigns across much of Eurasia, from China and Korea in the east to Hungary, Russia, and Persia in the west, was their willingness to enlist foreign experts along the way. Without the use of Muslim and Chinese catapult operators and specialized catapult troops, the Mongols themselves would not have had the expertise to storm the cities of China. Without literate and learned Uighurs and other Turks in their service, the Mongols would not have devised an alphabet so early (in 1204) in which to record their exploits, laws, and regulations. Khitans, the former rulers of the Liao dynasty, together with Uighurs

and others guided the Mongols in setting up basic administrative and taxation systems through which to govern and control surrendered populations. Similarly, when the Mongols formally established a Chinese dynasty in 1272 replete with dynastic title (Yuan), and

adopted Chinese-style reign titles and a calendar, they were acting on the advice of Chinese literati counsellors at court.

The reign of Khubilai Khan (1260–94), grandson of Chinggis, represented the highest achievement of Mongolian rule in China proper. Khubilai surrounded himself with a multiethnic corps of advisers. The influence of his Chinese advisers was reflected in both the adoption of the dynastic title Yuan and in the construction of a new capital city, Dadu ("Great Capital") on the site of modern Beijing. Dadu superseded the original capital of the Mongols, Khara Khorum, located in the Orkhon River valley in central Mongolia. Dadu also replaced Khubilai's capital in his old appanage in Inner Mongolia; in 1263 this lesser capital was renamed Shangdu ("Upper Capital"), the Xanadu of Coleridge's poem *Kubla Khan*. The construction of the new imperial city of Dadu signified the Mongols' intention to make China their central power base.

In addition to moving the Mongols' capital into China proper, Khubilai also completed the conquest of south China in the 1270s. The governance of south China with its rich agricultural and revenue base necessitated further attempts at centralizing the burgeoning civil bureaucracy and regularizing the taxation system. Two of Khubilai's fiscal advisers, both of non-Chinese origins — the Muslim Ahmad and the Tibetan Sangha — earned longlasting opprobrium, however, for their attempts to fill the dynasty's coffers (and their own, it was rumored) by unconventional methods of revenue collection.

Khubilai's reign witnessed the end of Mongolian expansionism in East Asia. Under Khubilai, two expeditions to Japan (in 1274 and 1281) ended in complete disaster, and campaigns into Southeast Asia were turned back.

The multiethnic aspect of the Yuan dynasty is also reflected in Khubilai's continuation of Chinggis Khan's practice of religious tolerance. Most Mongols were themselves shamanist in belief, but as long as a foreign religion's clergy labored to keep its adherents loyal to the Mongolian rulers, the Mongols generally enacted tax and military exemptions for the clergy and its properties. Khubilai

LEFT: Portrait of Ögödei Khan, son of Chinggis (Ghengis) and his appointed successor, who ruled from 1227 until his death in 1241.
NATIONAL PALACE MUSEUM, TAIBEI, TAIWAN, REPUBLIC OF CHINA

BELOW LEFT: Portrait of Khubilai Khan who reigned 1260–94. A grandson of Chinggis (Ghengis), he completed the conquest of southern China and moved the capital to Dadu, the present site of Beijing.
NATIONAL PALACE MUSEUM, TAIBEI, TAIWAN, REPUBLIC OF CHINA

himself patronized the Sa-skya school of Tibetan Buddhism, more out of political expediency than deeply held convictions. The Yuan court under Khubilai and his immediate successors exercised a loose hegemony over Tibet through the cooperation of the Sa-skya clergy, whose top representative residing at the Yuan court at Dadu was granted the title of "imperial preceptor."

However, while Khubilai was attempting to centralize control over China, the rest of the Mongolian empire was succumbing to centrifugal forces embodied in the regional khanates. After Chinggis Khan's death in 1227, the empire had been parceled into four shares, as each of Chinggis's four sons received his patrimony. During the course of the thirteenth century, each of these khanates (Persia under the Il-khans, Russia under the Golden Horde khans, central Asia under the Chaghatai khans, and China and Mongolia under the Yuan dynasty) grew progressively more independent from one another. The Il-khans and the Golden Horde khans even fought a series of wars with one another, beginning in the

early 1260s, over territorial and religious issues. Even Khubilai's reign was marred by ongoing rebellions of Mongolian princes (including a rebellion by his own younger brother) in the borderlands between the Chaghatai khanate and Yuan China. It may be well to confine the notion of a Mongolian empire to the period of Chinggis Khan's own lifetime, for after his death regional considerations overwhelmed any aspiration for continent-wide unity.

China itself emerged from a century and a half of Mongolian rule with its society and culture largely intact, though certainly influenced by the presence of foreigners in China for such a long period. In Chinese history the Yuan dynasty is known as a period of drastic population decrease, a result primarily of the Mongols' campaigns of conquest in north China in the years 1215–34. To what degree the drop in population figures reflects actual deaths or rather displacement from census rolls caused by migration in the wake of warfare is impossible to resolve.

The Mongols came from a hierarchical society in which tribal, clan, and personal loyalties predominated. While at first imposing upon China their political and military systems, by Khubilai's reign (1260–94) the Mongols felt constrained to adopt some Chinese bureaucratic methods of rule over a sedentary population. To a certain extent, the

TRAVELERS IN THE MONGOLIAN EMPIRE

Among Western travelers reports on the thirteenth-century Mongols, the two accounts by John of Plano Carpini, who was sent to Mongolia in the 1240s by Pope Innocent IV, and William of Rubruck, both Franciscans, offer superb details on Mongolian customs. Friar William of Rubruck, sent in an unofficial capacity by Louis IX of France to investigate the Mongols, met with M ngke Khan (reigned 1251—59) in the Mongols capital of Khara Khorum in 1254. His report is considered to be the most comprehensive Latin source on the Mongols. Rubruck describes the doll-sized effigies, representing protective spirits, that were kept in every Mongolian family s tent. The Mongols were believers in shamanism, and their daily lives were punctuated by several taboos, such as the strict prohibition against touching the threshold when entering or leaving a tent. Rubruck s traveling companion, Bartholomew of Cremona, broke this taboo when, after bowing to M ngke Khan, he stumbled over the threshold while exiting the khan s residence; he was nearly condemned to death by M ngke s chief judge for his inauspicious error. Rubruck also provides a vivid description of fermented mare s milk, a staple of the Mongols diet:

> When one is drinking it, it stings the tongue like *râpé* wine, but after one has finished drinking it leaves on the tongue a taste of milk of almonds. It produces a very agreeable sensation inside and even intoxicates those with no strong head; it also markedly brings on urination.

Called *ayiragh* by the Mongols (or koumiss, the English word derived from Turkish via Russian), this beverage is still

LEFT: Marco Polo's father, Niccolo, and uncle, Maffeo, meeting Khubilai Khan. They first visited on a trading expedition and later returned at the Khan's request.
BIBLIOTHEQUE NATIONALE, PARIS

produced and consumed in large quantities in Mongolia today.

Marco Polo s travels in China over a 20-year period (1275—95) resulted in a very detailed and often accurate account of the Mongolian imperial court in Dadu as well as other parts of China. Traveling as a merchant with his father and uncle, and patronized by Khubilai in whose service he was employed, Marco Polo offers great insight into many aspects of the thirteenth-century Mongolian way of life. Many of Polo s most revealing passages relate to Khubilai and his court. In regard to Khubilai s lavish celebration of the lunar new year, Polo describes the splendid gifts received by the khan, among them more than 100,000 white horses. White was considered an auspicious color by the Mongols, and at the new year celebration, Khubilai and everyone else present wore white.

Marco Polo also noted the presence of some 5,000 astrologers and divination experts in the employ of Khubilai. These experts were expected to predict everything from earthquakes to rebellions, and they were regularly consulted, according to Polo, whenever court personnel ventured out on official business.

Marco Polo was amazed by the Yuan government s printing and issuing of paper money. After detailing the process of producing paper money from the bark of mulberry trees Polo describes the issuing of these paper rectangles :

> The procedure of issue is as formal and as authoritative as if they were made of pure gold or silver. On each piece of money several specially appointed officials write their names, each setting his own stamp. When it is completed in due form, the chief of the officials deputed by the khan dips in cinnabar the seal or bull assigned to him and stamps it on the top of the piece of money so that the shape of the seal in vermilion remains impressed upon it. And then the money is authentic.

This was indeed a marvel to the eyes of a thirteenth-century visitor from Europe.

The extraordinary journeys of the Nestorian monk Rabban Sauma (c. 1225—94), though less well known than the travels of Marco Polo, were recorded in the monk s diaries. The diaries detail his journey from China to Persia and his diplomatic mission from the Il-khan court in Persia to Europe.

The thirteenth century was a great era of both maritime and overland travel through-out Eurasia for merchants, missionaries, spies, and diplomats.

ABOVE: Paper money such as this thirteenth-century note was a great curiosity to the Venetian traveler Marco Polo. Made from the bark of the mulberry tree, to his amazement the currency was treated with the reverence accorded gold or silver in his home country.
CHINA PICTORIAL PHOTO SERVICE

bureaucracy, or nomination on the basis of hereditary privilege. Such routes to office were not always open or palatable to Chinese scholars.

The Mongols particularly favored merchants as a group in the Yuan period. Muslim merchants from western and central Asia formed lucrative partnerships with members of the Mongolian imperial family and made fortunes from long-distance trade as well as from money lending at usurious rates among the Chinese population.

The Mongolian rulers' predilection for registering households by virtue of their ethnic background, economic utility, and political reliability is exemplified in their use of four broad categories to classify the entire population of Yuan China. In descending order of privilege (as reflected in administrative regulations) were Mongols, western and central Asians, northern Chinese (including Jurchens and Khitans), and southern Chinese — the last to submit to Mongolian rule and thus at the bottom of the ladder of privilege. In addition to these four categories, there were several subgroupings, such as artisans, merchants, or clergy, to name only a few. Each subgroup had its own fiscal and military responsibilities or exemptions, and each was defined in hereditary terms. Such a system of hereditarily determined social categories did not accord well with

Chinese literati found their path to bureaucratic office blocked. The Mongols chose not to institute the traditional Chinese examination system until 1315. Recruitment into the civil bureaucracy in Yuan times occurred through nontraditional routes: climbing up through the lowly ranks of clerks, crossing over from the military

LEFT: *A horse and groom feel the bite of the bitter northern Chinese wind in this painting by Zhao Mengfu (1254–1322). Despite having been a Song official, he chose to serve the Mongols and became a central figure in the Yuan art world.*
NATIONAL PALACE MUSEUM, TAIBEI, TAIWAN, REPUBLIC OF CHINA

Chinese society, and was abandoned in all but name in the succeeding Ming dynasty (1368–1644).

During the Yuan period popular drama, a relatively new art form, flourished. A total of 171 extant plays date from the Yuan dynasty. The contribution of the Mongols to this literary development was at best indirect. By keeping many Chinese scholars either unemployed or underemployed, the Mongols may have encouraged scholars to turn to writing plays either to earn a living or to occupy leisure time.

Just as the Mongols did not bring about radical changes in Chinese society at large, the Chinese made a relatively short-lived impact upon the Mongols. It is true that by the last decades of the dynasty several members of the Mongolian elite had achieved proficiency in various fields of Chinese art and scholarship. Yet under the pressure of large-scale rebellions in south China, the Yuan dynasty fell in 1368, and those Mongols in Dadu and north China for whom escape was possible fled northward back to the steppes.

The post-Yuan Mongols resumed their nomadic, tribal way of life, and used their acquired knowledge of China to inflict misery upon the succeeding Ming dynasty through continuous frontier raids and skirmishes. The Mongols in their later chronicles looked back to their hegemony over China with pride and longing, but as outsiders who had resisted cultural assimilation.

In Persia, the dynasty of the Il-khans collapsed in the 1330s. Unlike their counterparts in China, the Mongols in Persia and western central Asia had assimilated into the Turkic population and many had converted to Islam. The Golden Horde khanate started to disintegrate in the mid-fourteenth century, but the successor khanates of Kazan, Astrakhan, and Crimea survived for two or more centuries until the expanding Russian empire engulfed them.

BELOW: *Chinggis (Ghengis) Khan's death was kept a secret until the Tangut capital was taken and then, according to legend, his body was taken in a box to be entombed on the sacred mountain called Burkhan Khaldun. The officers of his cortege were instructed to kill anyone who saw it to keep news of his demise from spreading.* LAURIE PLATT WINFREY INC/BRITISH MUSEUM, LONDON

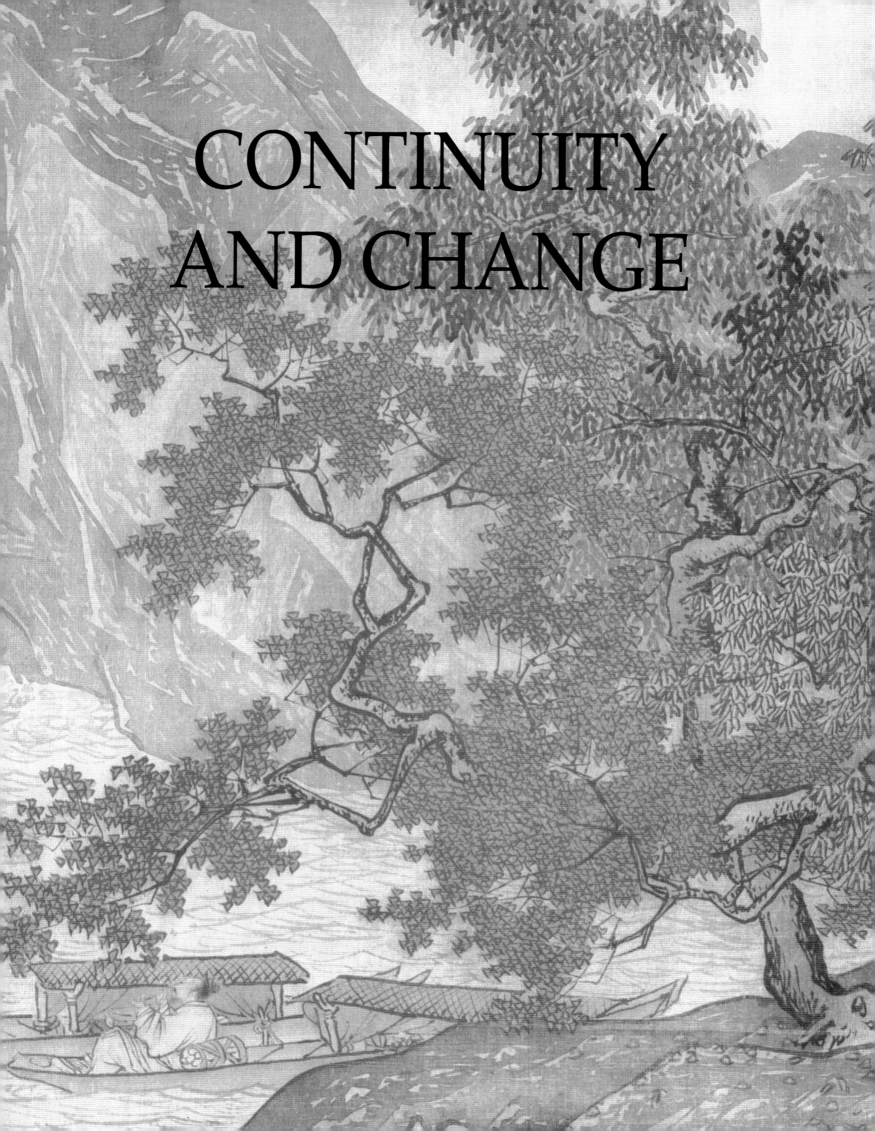

CONTINUITY AND CHANGE

MING AND QING SOCIETY: CHINA AND THE WEST

Richard J. Smith

THE MING AND QING DYNASTIES (1368–1644 and 1644–1912, respectively) happened to coincide with a series of remarkable changes in Western Europe commonly known as the Commercial, Scientific, Democratic and Industrial Revolutions. Contact between China and the West from the late sixteenth century onward brought knowledge of these cataclysmic changes to the Chinese, but they showed remarkably little interest in them until the late nineteenth century.

The founder of the Ming dynasty, Zhu Yuanzhang (1368–98), was a lowly peasant who spent several years in a Buddhist monastery before joining an anti-Mongol religious sect known as the Red Turbans. Eventually he achieved supreme power within the rebel movement and, in 1368, he overthrew the Yuan dynasty. Zhu reigned for thirty years as the Hongwu ("Vast Military Achievement") emperor. Although a friendly, sympathetic, and popular leader in the course of his dramatic rise to power, he became paranoid and tyrannical as emperor of China. Thus, the establishment of the Ming dynasty brought a reassertion of native Chinese rule, but it continued the Mongol trend toward increasingly despotic government.

Zhu Yuanzhang's son, who reigned as the Yongle emperor from 1402 to 1424, continued the aggressive, despotic policies of his father. Ruthless and

powerful, he personally led five large military expeditions against various Mongol tribes in the fourteen years from 1410 to the time of his death. In order to contend more effectively with the Mongols from his former base area in north China, Yongle moved the center of Ming government from Nanjing ("Southern Capital") to Beijing ("Northern Capital"), where he built the huge and impressive palace complex known as the Forbidden City.

Meanwhile, the Yongle emperor also despatched military forces into Vietnam and sent several large naval fleets under the Muslim eunuch–admiral, Zheng He, into Southeast Asia and westward to the shores of India, Arabia, and even Africa. But these impressive voyages of exploration — unlike the better known (yet far more modest) naval expeditions of Europeans such as Vasco de Gama and Columbus — were diplomatic missions, designed primarily to extend the prestige of the Ming dynasty within the framework of the ancient tributary system; and after they were terminated in 1433 China never again engaged in this sort of expansive naval exploration.

Throughout most of the Ming dynasty, the Chinese economy was the most sophisticated and productive in the world, and the Chinese probably enjoyed

ABOVE: *A typical Ming dynasty blue and white ceramic* fu *vase with floral motifs.* WENWU PUBLISHING

OPPOSITE: *Portrait of the Ming dynasty Yongle Emperor (reigned 1402–1424), who was responsible for building the Forbidden City.*
NATIONAL PALACE MUSEUM, TAIBEI, TAIWAN, REPUBLIC OF CHINA

PREVIOUS PAGES: *The material prosperity of the Ming dynasty contributed to a burst of creativity in the arts. This creativity yielded such works as* Secluded Fisherman on an Autumn River, *by Tang Yin (1470–1523), one of the most accomplished painters of the Ming era.*
NATIONAL PALACE MUSEUM, TAIBEI, TAIWAN, REPUBLIC OF CHINA

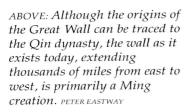

a higher standard of living than any other people on earth. From 1400 to 1600, China's population doubled, from about 80 million to perhaps 160 million. Literary and artistic accomplishments, no less than ambitious public works projects such as the Great Wall, reflected this material prosperity. Novels such as *Sanguo zhi yanyi* ("Romance of the Three Kingdoms"), *Shuihu zhuan* ("Water Margin"), and *Xiyou ji* ("Journey to the West"), brought Chinese vernacular literature to a new level of sophistication, just as the works of painters such as Shen Zhou (1427–1509), one of the "Four Great Masters of the Ming," exemplified the best traditions of the scholar–artist in late imperial times.

During the late Ming a series of important changes began to take place in China: urbanization of the lower Yangzi area, the growth of regional trade, the emergence of a national market in bulk commodities, increased geographical mobility, the expansion of popular literacy, an increase in the size of the elite class, and the professionalization of local managerial activities. These changes, in turn, contributed to transformations in the style of local politics, in patterns of personal and intellectual affiliation, and ultimately in modes of thought. The dominant figure in late Ming intellectual life was Wang Yangming (1472–1529), whose highly intuitive and idealistic approach to moral cultivation, known as

the "teaching of the mind" (*xinxue*), gained widespread currency during the last century of Ming rule. But following the overthrow of the dynasty, empirically oriented Chinese scholars blamed Wang's individualistic and speculative philosophy for the factionalism and other problems of the late Ming era.

Early Western missionary contact with the Ming, initiated by the Italian Jesuit Father Matteo Ricci (1552–1610) at the end of the sixteenth century, brought new Western scientific, technological, and religious knowledge to China. But it did little to alter the character of Ming intellectual life. The Jesuits, who succeeded in accommodating themselves in a deliberate way to the Chinese cultural and social milieu, were able to win a number of high-level converts and even to achieve positions of considerable responsibility within the Ming bureaucracy. But they never came close to achieving any significant political power or intellectual influence.

Dynastic decline came inexorably to the Ming, as it had come to all previous ruling houses. The pattern was a familiar one: reign by weak and self-indulgent emperors, official corruption and bureaucratic factionalism, abuse of power by court eunuchs (a particularly acute problem during the Ming dynasty), fiscal irresponsibility, neglect of public works, natural disasters, and the rise of rebellion.

Meanwhile, outside the Great Wall, in the remote northeastern area of

Liaodong, a tribal confederation of Tungusic peoples known as the Manchus waited in the wings. When the rebel marauder Li Zicheng took the Ming capital of Beijing in 1644, the Manchus joined forces with Ming troops under Wu Sangui (1612–78) to expel the insurgents, declaring that they had come to save China from rebel depredations.

In a self-conscious (and self-interested) effort to demonstrate their devotion to traditional Chinese values, the Manchus not only maintained the political institutions, economic policies, rituals, and religious practices of the fallen dynasty, but they also supported the Ming civil service examination system and its official Confucian orthodoxy. Furthermore, they became ardent patrons of Chinese art, music, literature, and drama. But while the Manchus sought to legitimize themselves as the protectors of China's cultural tradition, they also crystallized their image as "barbarian" conquerors by forcing the Chinese to shave the front of their scalps and grow the Manchu-style queue (*bianzi*) as a sign of submission.

Consolidation of the empire took several decades of fighting in the face of Ming loyalism and resistance to "barbarian rule." But by the 1690s, under the leadership of the dynamic Kangxi emperor (reigned 1662–1722), the Qing established a strong, stable regime.

LEFT: The founder of the Ming dynasty, Zhu Yuanzhang (the Hongwu emperor), reigned for 30 years from 1368.
NATIONAL PALACE MUSEUM, TAIBEI, TAIWAN, REPUBLIC OF CHINA

ABOVE: Lead-glazed, Ming dynasty earthenware incense burner with the dragon motif (Chenghua period), dated 1469. ROYAL ONTARIO MUSEUM

ZHENG HE

Between 1405 and 1433 the Muslim Grand Eunuch Zheng He (an extremely high-ranking court eunuch) led seven great naval voyages into Southeast Asia and westward to India, Persia, Arabia, and Africa. Some of his fleets consisted of over 300 ships manned by about 27,000 sailors. His first three expeditions went no farther than India, but the fourth arrived at the Straits of Hormuz, to the south of what is now Iran, and the last three touched the eastern coast of Africa, as far south as Malindi (just above Mombassa, in modern-day Kenya). In his combined roles as merchant, admiral, and diplomat, Zheng bartered for exotic goods, fought a few

battles, and either established or reaffirmed relationships with some 30 countries — each ostensibly a tributary of China.

Zheng He's voyages, the largest and most impressive displays of naval power in all of Chinese history, took full advantage of many great advances in nautical technology that had occurred in the previous Song and Yuan dynasties. They were not, however, exploratory in the fashion of the more well-known European expeditions undertaken by Vasco de Gama and Columbus. Instead they followed established maritime trade routes. Nor were Zheng He's adventures inspired by any sort of commercial competition or colonizing impulses.

In any case, after his voyages ceased in 1433 they were never again followed up. One of the reasons for curtailing China's naval expeditions was ideological: Confucian-trained bureaucrats vociferously opposed voluntary contact with "barbarians." Another was personal: Chinese officials in Beijing were jealous of eunuch power as exemplified by Zheng He and his influential associates. A third reason was strategic and financial: by the mid-fifteenth century China faced a revival of Mongol power on the northern land frontier at the same time that it confronted a severe financial crisis. China could no longer afford the luxury of costly and impractical overseas adventures.

THE TAIPING REBELLION

The Taiping Rebellion lasted from 1850 to 1864; it spread to all of China's eighteen provinces and resulted in the loss of an estimated 20 million lives. The charismatic founder of the "Heavenly Kingdom of Great Peace" (*Taiping tianguo*) — a brilliant but erratic Chinese scholar named Hong Xiuquan — claimed to be the younger brother of Jesus. Exposed to Protestant missionary tracts at a formative period in his tumultuous life, Hong developed an eclectic ideology that combined certain elements of Confucian utopianism (expressed in the concept of Taiping or "Great Peace") and Christianity (the idea of a "Heavenly Kingdom"). In the first years of the rebel movement, this virulently anti-Manchu ideology proved attractive to millions of peasants who were dissatisfied with Qing rule.

ABOVE: Zeng Guofan (1811–72) was the principal architect of the Taiping defeat. He and his talented protégés, Li Hongzhang (1823–1901) and Zuo Zongtang (1812–85), not only suppressed the rebels but also led China's "self-strengthening" movement during the latter half of the nineteenth century.
NATIONAL PALACE MUSEUM, TAIBEI, TAIWAN, REPUBLIC OF CHINA

Hong's appeal rested on two primary claims. One was theological: that the Manchus were the Devil incarnate, whom God had commanded him to destroy. The other was practical: that Taiping rule would bring a new era of peace and

ABOVE (RIGHT): This Taiping decorative pouch (wai fubao), used as a clothing accessory, is emblazoned with a five-clawed dragon — symbol of imperial power. Despite their iconoclastic, Western-influenced ideology, the Taipings employed many such traditional Chinese symbols.
NATIONAL PALACE MUSEUM, TAIBEI, TAIWAN, REPUBLIC OF CHINA

prosperity to China. Toward this latter end, the rebels tried to implement a number of specific policies designed to distribute wealth and land more equitably to the Chinese people. Their Sacred Treasury system, based on a primitive form of communalism, achieved some early success; but the Taipings were never able to implement their highly idealistic Heavenly Land system.

In the end, the Taiping movement succumbed to its own internal weaknesses as well as to outside forces. In addition to unstable leadership, the intolerance and iconoclasm of the rebels had alienated members of the Chinese scholarly elite. The Taipings also made a series of military mistakes and foreign policy miscalculations during the period from 1856 to 1860. Although the Taipings referred to Westerners as their foreign brothers (wai xiongdi) and sought to establish a fruitful alliance with them at Shanghai, they ultimately left a decidedly negative impression. Their Christianity appeared strange to foreign missionaries; their anti-opium policies gave significant pause to British merchants; and their half-hearted efforts to bring the treaty port of Shanghai to submission in 1860 and 1862 produced a vigorous Western counterattack. Finally, the rise of new-style armies under Zeng Guofan, Li Hongzhang, and others gave the Qing dynasty a potent and ultimately decisive weapon against the Taipings.

LEFT: This illustration depicts the recovery of Ruizhou in Jiangxi province by Zeng Guofan's forces late in the summer of 1857. The beleaguered Taiping garrison abandoned the city after fourteen months of relentless siege. NATIONAL PALACE MUSEUM, TAIBEI, TAIWAN, REPUBLIC OF CHINA

LEFT: *Early seventeenth-century woven bamboo and painted lacquer box. Inlay with colored lacquers and the technique of carving through layers of different colors satisfied the Ming taste for polychrome effects.*
THE AVERY BRUNDAGE COLLECTION/ASIAN ART MUSEUM OF SAN FRANCISCO/B60M427

activities of all the Catholic orders, including the Jesuits.

The expansive Kangxi, Yongzheng, and Qianlong reigns marked the high point of Manchu rule in China. Under the watchful eyes of these three despotic but able and enthusiastic imperial patrons, nearly every aspect of traditional Chinese culture flourished. Teams of scholars, many commissioned by the throne, produced great collections of art and literature, as well as huge reference works of enduring value. Meanwhile, continuing a vernacular tradition begun in Ming times, Qing scholars wrote a number of excellent full-length works of fiction, including the sprawling masterpiece *Honglou meng* ("Dream of the Red Chamber") by Cao Xueqin (died 1763), generally considered to be China's greatest novel. Although the Qing is sometimes described as a period of "academic" painting and artistic stagnation, there were many noteworthy

During this period of consolidation, the pragmatic and accommodating Jesuits easily transferred their allegiance to the Manchus. They also made considerable headway in gaining high-level converts until a controversy between the various Catholic orders in China, centering on the correct interpretation of Confucian rituals, provoked papal interference. When this happened, the Catholic missionary effort became a political matter and not simply a religious one. The Yongzheng (1723–35) and Qianlong (1736–96) emperors responded by branding Christianity as subversive and severely constraining the

FAR LEFT: *Under the leadership of the Kangxi emperor (reigned 1662–1722), the Qing eliminated, or drove underground, the last pockets of anti-Manchu resistance.*
THE PALACE MUSEUM, BEIJING

LEFT: *Portrait of the Qianlong emperor (1736–96), whose expansive reign, which witnessed the ardent patronage of traditional Chinese culture, is regarded as one of the high points of the Manchu (Qing) era.* THE PALACE MUSEUM, BEIJING

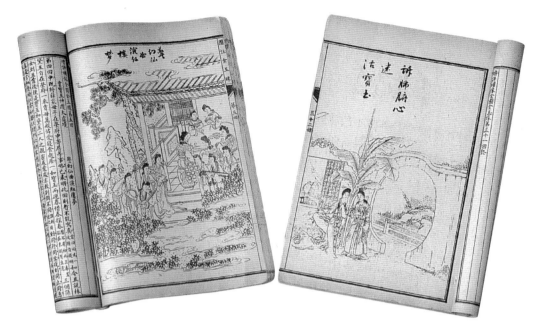

ABOVE: *Illustrations from Honglou Meng ("Dream of the Red Chamber"), by Qing scholar Cao Xueqin (died 1763), which is generally considered to be China's greatest novel.*
CHINA PICTORIAL PHOTO SERVICE

exceptions. Wang Yuanqi (1642–1715), for example, one of the legendary "Six Masters of the Qing," did highly original work, despite his close identification with the orthodoxy of the imperial court.

Qing chroniclers of the eighteenth century referred to their time as "unparalleled in history." Yet even in the midst of the glorious Qianlong reign, the fabric of Chinese society had begun to unravel. From the 1770s onward, riots, banditry, and organized uprisings became frequent in many parts of China. The sectarian White Lotus movement of 1796–1804 was the first in a series of widespread and protracted rebellions that were a product of popular dissatisfaction with Manchu rule.

The inexorable decline of the Qing dynasty was part of a larger process: the breakdown of traditional Chinese civilization itself. This process resulted from the interaction of two unprecedented challenges, one internal and the other external. Domestically, population increased from an estimated 143 million Qing subjects in 1741 to a reported 432 million by the beginning of the Taiping Rebellion — nearly three times more people than had ever lived in China before. This surge of population pressure exacerbated all of the dynasty's political and social problems. Meanwhile, the Western powers, led by Great Britain and quite literally driven by the engines of the Industrial Revolution, sought to open

China to Western commerce and evangelism. Their goal was no longer Jesuit-style accommodation but forceful entry into the Chinese market, with its 400 million customers (and an equal number of souls).

The rise of opium addiction in China during the nineteenth century epitomized China's double bind. On the one hand, widespread social demoralization, brought on by acute population pressure, encouraged opium-use as a means of escape from harsh reality. (Among other things, opium dulled hunger pangs.) On the other hand, Great Britain's interest in keeping India afloat as a colonial proposition led to a concerted effort to promote the sale of Indian opium in China. The conflict that erupted when the Qing government attempted to abolish the opium trade naturally bore the name of the product: the Opium War (1839–42). British technology easily prevailed, and during the period from 1842 to 1860 the Chinese were forced to sign a series of "unequal treaties" which lasted until 1943.

According to the terms of these onerous agreements, Great Britain and the other foreign powers gained the right to

RIGHT: *The female usurper, the Empress Dowager Cixi (1835–1908), seated on the Imperial throne.*
ET ARCHIVE/FREER GALLERY OF ART, WASHINGTON DC

THE FORBIDDEN CITY

LEFT: The Forbidden City, the palace compound of 24 Ming and Qing emperors from 1420–1912, was surrounded by a moat and a 33-feet (10 meter) wide wall. The complex was divided into front halls of government with rear palaces and courts in which the Emperor, his consorts and harem, and thousands of female servants, concubines and eunuchs lived. CHINA PHOTO LIBRARY LTD

BELOW: The Forbidden City, roof detail. HARALD SUND/THE IMAGE BANK

The vast palace compound of the Ming and Qing emperors from 1420 to 1912 was called the Purple Forbidden City (*Zijincheng*) — "purple" to match the designated color of the polestar (the symbolic center of the universe) and "forbidden" because commoners could not enter the complex without special permission. Built on a cosmically mandated north–south axis, and surrounded by a moat 177 feet (54 m) wide and a wall 33 feet (10 m) high, the Forbidden City occupied a total area of about 861,000 square yards (720,000 sq m). Within its majestic confines 24 emperors not only conducted their private affairs but also performed their official duties, which ranged from daily audiences with high officials to the periodic reception of tributary envoys from afar.

The Ming and Qing emperors conducted their personal affairs and more intimate business audiences in the secluded northern section of the Forbidden City, known as the Inner Court. Ceremonial audiences, including the Grand Audience (held on New Year's Day), "ordinary" audiences for officials, and the reception of tributary envoys, took place in the sprawling Outer Court area to the south of the Inner Court.

Following the Republican Revolution of 1911, the new provisional government at Nanjing struck an agreement with the Manchus, guaranteeing that after the young boy emperor, Puyi, abdicated, he and his huge family could continue to live in the Forbidden City on a stipend equivalent to four million US dollars a year. In addition, the family would be granted ownership of the great art treasures that had been collected by previous emperors. Puyi continued to live in the palace until 1924, when a warlord evicted him and forced him to escape to Tianjin. The next year the Forbidden City became a public cultural and historical museum.

At present the Old Palace Museum (*Gugong bowuguan*) is a major tourist attraction. Visitors can stroll freely through the Imperial Garden and enter many palace buildings, including the magnificent Hall of Supreme Harmony in the Outer Court and the Hall of Heavenly Purity in the Inner Court. They can also view displays of paintings, calligraphy, bronzes, jades, and other items from the vast imperial art collection which, despite pillaging by eunuchs, fire damage, and the loss of many items during the Chinese civil war from 1945–49, still numbers over 910,000 items.

BELOW: Bird's eye view of the Forbidden City. The main southern gate (left side of photograph) leads into the Outer Court area, with its three main buildings (center of photograph) and into the Inner Court, with its three corresponding structures surrounded by many smaller buildings. THE PALACE MUSEUM, BEIJING

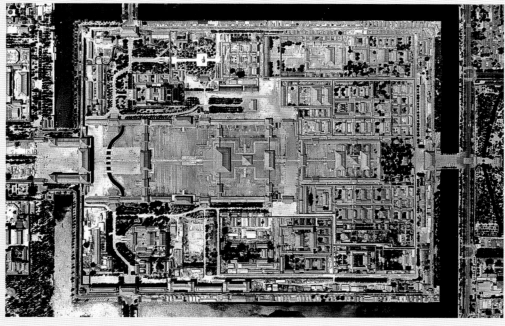

establish self-governing treaty-port settlements for Western residence and trade, to have access to the Chinese interior, to operate foreign ships between the treaty ports on the coast and on inland waterways, to promulgate Christianity without obstruction, to limit Chinese customs duties, and to establish formal diplomatic relations at the capital and in treaty-port areas. Westerners enjoyed immunity from Chinese law (extraterritoriality) and other non-reciprocal privileges.

From 1860 onward, the treaty ports became conduits for the transmission of Western influences of all kinds. Foreign merchants, missionaries, diplomats, and military men collected in the port cities, bringing to China new products, ideas, practices, and skills. At the same time, these Western intruders exerted a disruptive influence on Chinese society, threatening the traditional economic system, elite prerogatives, the Chinese world order, and China's security and sovereignty. The treaty ports were thus both showcases for the modern West and vivid reminders of the challenge of foreign imperialism.

From the 1870s, new ideas began to pour into China. The rise of Western-style Chinese newspapers, together with a growing number of Western literary works translated into Chinese, brought a heightened awareness of the West to China, at least in treaty-port areas.

But until the Sino-Japanese War of 1894–95, change came slowly in China. One important reason was the persistence of the civil service examination system, which relentlessly attracted the best minds of the empire as it had done for over a thousand years. This system remained virtually unchanged in form and content from the early Ming dynasty to the first few years of the twentieth century.

Chinese intellectuals, with a vested interest in their classical studies, were slow to appreciate the need for change, while the Manchus had a political motive for maintaining the examination system. Since they had originally justified their conquest in terms of protecting China's cultural heritage, they could scarcely appear to abandon traditional values, practices, and institutions. Complicating the problem in the late nineteenth century

was the presence of Empress Dowager Cixi (1835–1908) on the throne. She executed a coup d'etat in 1861 to gain power, and then manipulated the dynastic laws of succession to keep it until her death.

But China's crushing defeat in the Sino-Japanese War of 1894–95 unleashed forces for change which neither Cixi nor anyone else could control. This traumatic event not only marked the total destruction of the traditional Chinese world order by a onetime tributary; it also resulted in the loss of Chinese territory (including the entire province of Taiwan!) and the imposition of a costly and humiliating unequal treaty on China by the Japanese themselves. A surge of Chinese nationalism ensued, and with it, a burst of reform sentiment. Ironically,

Japan now became a modernizing model for China. Even so, it took the failure of the famous Reform movement of 1898 and the disastrous Boxer rebellion of 1900 to prompt the Qing government into sponsoring meaningful reforms.

To some nationalistic Chinese, including a growing number of Western-educated individuals such as Dr Sun Zhongshan (Sun Yat-sen, 1866–1925), these reforms were too little, too late. From their standpoint, China's salvation could only be found in revolution. Thus, from 1895 until 1911, Sun Zhongshan and his motley band of supporters devoted themselves single-mindedly to the overthrow of the Manchus and the establishment of a Chinese republic.

The most significant of the late Qing institutional changes were: the establishment of a new, Western-style army; the abolition of the civil service examinations (in order to encourage enrolment in new-style government schools with both Western and Chinese curricula); and the creation of representative assemblies as a prelude to eventual constitutional government on the Japanese pattern. Although designed to preserve the dynasty, these reforms had revolutionary consequences. For example, by terminating the traditional examinations the Manchus dealt a staggering blow to the Confucian concept of rule by virtue and eliminated the institutional re-inforcement of orthodox Confucian values. Representative govern-ment politicized the Chinese elite and gave them a new base of power and the so-called New Army became a revolutionary instrument.

Chinese nationalism no longer permitted alien rulers to claim legitimacy as the protectors of China's cultural heritage, for Chinese intellectuals increasingly saw the need to differentiate between politics and culture in order to achieve the modern goal of "wealth and power" (fuqiang). Thus, the cultural conservatism of the throne, its desperate attempt to maintain Manchu political supremacy, and growing Chinese fears that a vigorous anti-imperialist movement might well result in foreign intervention, all made the Manchus a convenient target for nationalistic advocates of republican revolution. The

mysterious death of the Guangxu emperor (1875–1908) and the installment of an infant emperor under a conservative prince regent destroyed China's best chance for a Japanese-style constitutional monarchy; and in 1911–12, the republican revolutionaries under Sun Zhongshan threw out the imperial baby with the Manchu bathwater. This created a political vacuum and a ritual void that the hastily constructed system of representative institutions could not fill. The Republic of China so on degenerated into warlordism.

ABOVE: Qing dynasty (Qianlong period) porcelain moonflask with a dragon and flaming pearl design. ART GALLERY OF NEW SOUTH WALES, PURCHASED 1954

LEFT: Figure standing in a boat, by artist Ren Bonian, (1840–96). During the nineteenth century Shanghai emerged as a major center of artistic production in China. Ren Bonian, one of the city's most distinguished painters, had a vibrant style inspired not only by Chinese popular art but also by the new bold and restless spirit of the Western-influenced treaty port.
ART GALLERY OF NEW SOUTH WALES, PURCHASED 1988

REVOLUTION, EVOLUTION, AND CONTINUITY

Timothy Cheek

IN MAY, 1989, STUDENTS AND WORKERS demonstrating in Tiananmen Square in central Beijing blamed "feudalism," the continuing pre-modern habits of Chinese culture, for the corruption and errors of the present government. Three decades earlier in the Cultural Revolution Chairman Mao had come to a broadly similar conclusion, and he blamed the Chinese Communist Party (CCP). He used a different term, "capitalism," but it was something bad, rooted in China's peasant culture and it exacerbated the CCP's own "feudal" practices, which Mao called "bureaucratism." Seventy years before students of Tiananmen appeared on worldwide television, their predecessors, also students from Beijing's universities, marched on 4 May 1919 to save China and criticize its government for its old "Confucian" culture. They blamed China's ancient culture for ruining the young Chinese republic of 1911, which had fallen to warlord rule and foreign aggression.

These three important movements from the beginning, middle, and end of the twentieth century each proposed different solutions that were foreign and revolutionary in their own time. The revolutionary solutions changed, but the problem remained the same: China's ancient civilization. In a century that has seen the rise and fall of a republican

revolution and a socialist revolution, the one survivor has been "Chineseness" — that sociocultural substratum of attitudes, values, and social behavior that transmits China's enduring civilization.

China's eventful revolutions have not endured in their original form, but they have contributed to the evolution of social institutions from the role of women, to the family, to how business and religion are conducted, as well as promoting industrialization, the creation of a mass media, and expanded foreign contact and understanding. Finally, these changes rest upon a bedrock of physical realities that dominate life in China. Today over 80 percent of China's population are still peasants. Problems of agricultural production and social order that vexed the emperors and village chiefs of imperial China still confront communist cadres and the rural entrepreneurs of the 1990s.

THE REPUBLICAN REVOLUTION

The first major event of the century was the disastrous Boxer Rebellion (1899–1900). These peasants and rebels marched on Beijing in June 1900 and laid siege to the International Legation district of the capital. In the face of massive foreign military reinforcements two months later, the antiforeign

ABOVE: *Chickens and bicycles, ubiquitous in modern China, mingle in a marketplace by an ancient wall in Xi'an, the capital of Shaanxi province.*
MAGNUM PHOTOS/HIROJI KUBOTA

OPPOSITE: *Construction workers are dwarfed by Mao Zedong's statue in Fuzhou, the capital of Fujian province.*
LIN JIAN/CHINA TOURISM PHOTO LIBRARY

165

ABOVE: Beijing's Tiananmen gate after the Boxer Rebellion of 1900. The foreign armies that counterattacked the rebellion added to the devastation caused by the Boxers. Beijing was stripped and the surrounding countryside and villages pillaged on suspicion of antiforeign sentiment.
THE HULTON DEUTSCH COLLECTION

FAR RIGHT: The Boxers, members of a secret society called the Fists of Righteous Harmony, cut telegraph wires during the 1900 uprising.
MARY EVANS PICTURE LIBRARY/ PETIT JOURNAL

RIGHT: Confrontation during the Sino-Japanese War (1894–95), which resulted from rivalry in Korea and ended with China's ceding Taiwan, the Pescadores, and the Liaodong Peninsula to Japan. THE BRIDGEMAN ART LIBRARY/ VICTORIA AND ALBERT MUSEUM, LONDON

uprising was a complete failure.

By 1911 the nationalism of China's educated elite and growing commercial and urban population had been aroused by the series of military disasters of the Qing, beginning with the Opium Wars of 1842 and 1860. Along with defeat came haughty foreigners who demanded and obtained special rights to trade, preach their religion (Christianity), and avoid Chinese law. Missionaries disturbed the equilibrium of village life by competing with the local Confucian scholar families who had traditionally handled such local administrative tasks as famine relief, education, and public ritual displays.

Western treaty ports and commercial penetration of China's markets had begun with the 1842 Treaty of Nanjing. This promoted a growing Chinese bourgeoisie and, in the 1910s and later, a working proletariat. In the first decade of this century, these newly empowered merchants teamed up with displaced Confucian scholars who found their loyalty to the failing Qing regime weakening and their understanding of the Western challenge growing, based on study abroad. Another result of the crumbling central government was the emergence of regional military commanders. By the 1920s these volatile armies had become the famous warlords.

Alienated scholars, a new bourgeoisie, and regional military leaders formed the social base of the republican revolution of 1911. It was officially led by Dr Sun Zhongshan (Sun Yat-sen, 1866–1925), a charismatic revolutionary. Sun was in

America at the time but returned to become the first president of the new Republic of China in 1912. He was almost instantly replaced by Yuan Shikai, one of the top militarists of the late Qing period. The autocratic Yuan and his brief, failed dynasty died in disgrace in 1916.

THE SEARCH FOR A NEW CHINA

The 1911 revolution began a four-decade period of near constant warfare and territorial disintegration for China. Although a national government of the republic was established in Nanjing in 1927, China was not reintegrated either

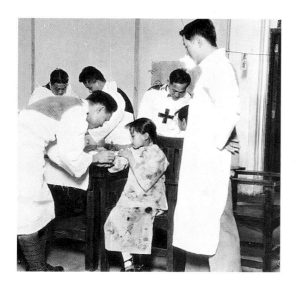

territorially or socially until the 1950s. However, economically, socially, and culturally these were creative years.

Economically, China consolidated its industrial revolution in the teens, twenties and thirties. Chinese textile companies rose from 22 in 1911 to 54 in 1919 to 109 in 1921; modern banks rose from seven in 1911 to 131 by 1923. Similar growth came in coal production, flour mills, steamships, and iron production. Railroads expanded considerably, linking China's markets. China had about 5,700 miles (9,000 km) of track by 1911. By the 1940s this had more than doubled to 14,000 miles (22,500 km) of track and by the 1980s there were 38,000 miles (61,000 km).

Industrialization and factory production transformed two of the traditional four Confucian classes — merchants and laborers. Merchants were traditionally despised in Confucian China. Western impact increased the power and status of Chinese business people. Although a tiny portion of China's population, they provided a bridge between the European world order and the interior of China.

Equally important were the workers, the industrial proletariat, who operated the factories. Shanghai was the center with 36,000 factory workers in 1894 and 182,000 in 1919. Almost half of these worked in Shanghai's 26 cotton mills. Women accounted for over 70 percent of the workers of this key industry. The impact on the role of women and family life was profound, yet "Chineseness" survived. Women from the poor villages north of Shanghai were more or less sold to brokers to work in the factories in the

same system that procured women for prostitution. While women were paid, it was difficult for them to keep their pay and dispose of it according to their wishes. Still, the sisterhoods such women developed to protect themselves evolved, with the aid of the missionary organization, the YWCA, into study groups and, for some, further studies and a new life in urban China.

The other two traditional social classes were peasants and scholars. Real poverty set in during the 1930s and provided a powder keg of misery and revolutionary potential which the Nationalist government failed to defuse (because it was dependent on local landlords for tax support) and which the Communists tapped for support.

The last of the traditional social classes, the *shi* or scholar, changed profoundly during the period of disunion (1911–49). The traditional role of the educated man was service to the state and ritual ordering of local society. The scholar class was forcibly cut off from the state by the abolition of the state exams in 1905 and the fall of the last Confucian dynasty in 1911. China's scholars began the slow transformation to professionals, studying in military schools with a curriculum of mathematics and the sciences and new Western-style comprehensive universities, such as Beijing University. A small but significant group of students studied overseas (by 1915 some 15,000 a year, most in Japan), bringing new ideas to the cultural life of China — Darwinism,

LEFT: Volunteer Chinese doctors of the Young Men's Christian Association give free smallpox vaccinations to residents in Hong Kong in the early 1920s. This and other medical education campaigns greatly reduced many diseases in China, and enhanced the reputation of the YMCA and other missionary groups there.
YMCA CHINA COMMITTEE, HARVARD-YENCHING LIBRARY, HARVARD UNIVERSITY

ABOVE: Statue of Yuan Shikai, the militarist who usurped the presidency of the new Republic and ultimately declared himself emperor. He and his brief dynasty died in 1916.
ROBERT E. MUROWCHICK

BELOW: A warlord army on the march in Yunnan province. The rule of China fell to militarists during the 1920s.
PEABODY MUSEUM, HARVARD UNIVERSITY, PHOTOGRAPH BY F. R. WULSIN

ABOVE: *The Bund, Shanghai's Western business district in the 1920s. In the center is the dome of the Hong Kong and Shanghai Bank.* POPPERFOTO

RIGHT: *Dr Sun Zhongshan (Sun Yat-sen) inspects the troops in front of the Memorial Tablets at Nanjing as part of the celebrations at the Ming tombs over the abdication of the Manchu Qing dynasty. Remembered as the father of the Republic of China, he was a charismatic rebel and a tireless organizer, though a political failure for most of his life. His philosophy, the Three People's Principles, is still the state ideology of the Kuomintang (KMT) government of Taiwan.* THE HULTON DEUTSCH COLLECTION

anarchism, John Dewey's pragmatism, Marxism–Leninism.

The key cultural development of this period was the introduction of *baihua*, the Chinese vernacular. Until 1919 the language used in schools, offices, and government had been classical Chinese, broadly equivalent to Latin in medieval Europe. The power of *baihua* was strengthened by another development of industrialization — the creation of a national media market of newspapers and magazines. By 1917, 10 million Chinese had received some sort of modern education, becoming the audience for

China's reformers and revolutionaries.

Out of the warlord period emerged a competition between two political parties and two leaders for the hearts and minds of China. Both the Nationalists (Kuomintang, or KMT) and the Communists (Chinese Communist Party, or CCP) were modern Bolshevik-style political parties. The KMT was the republican successor to Sun Zhongshan's earlier political parties. One of his generals, Jiang Jieshi (Chiang Kai-shek), led the "Northern Expedition" which by 1927 had recaptured half of China from the warlords for the republic. Over the

RIGHT: *The typical silk filature mill in Shanghai in the early 20th century employed large numbers of women and girls, often overseen by a foreign floor supervisor. The workers labored in sweatshop conditions for twelve hours per day — harsh conditions that helped to foster the growth of labor unions in China's major cities.* YMCA CHINA COMMITTEE, HARVARD-YENCHING LIBRARY, HARVARD UNIVERSITY

years for the CCP to become a real contender for national leadership.

THE SOCIALIST REVOLUTION

The CCP hammered out its successful program for government in the dusty hills of northwest China. This is called the Yan'an period for the name of the county town in Shaanxi province that the CCP made their capital from 1937–47.

The CCP and its ideology, Mao Zedong Thought, answered the perennial needs of governing China and addressed the new challenges of the modern world. Land reform, in which land was redistributed from landlords to the tillers, was enforced by the People's Liberation Army (PLA) and gained the support of China's peasants, its largest population group. Rectification, a careful and harshly emotional study program "remolded" the attitudes of CCP cadres to accept Mao's policy of "mass line" service to the people (officials consulted commoners about their needs, and incorporated them into CCP policy), thus providing a disciplined and loyal leadership group around the country. Finally, the United Front promised to tolerate and work with non-Communist "patriotic Chinese."

From the mid-1950s to the present, the CCP has confronted problems that have faced all governments in China since the First Emperor of Qin in the third century BC.

next 50 years Jiang would stand for the KMT and during the 1940s he was China's hero in its fight against Japan.

The KMT had an agreement known as the "United Front" with the fledgling CCP. Founded in 1921, the CCP advocated radical revolution based on the model of the Soviet revolution in Russia. Before 1925 it was not a serious contender for government. Nonetheless, the CCP helped the KMT in the Northern Expedition. One of the CCP participants was a former peasant from Hunan, Mao Zedong (Mao Tse-tung, 1893–1976). By the late 1930s he became the spokesman and later the supreme leader of the CCP. The KMT and CCP had a violent split in April 1927 when Jiang launched a surprise attack on CCP cadres and union activists in Shanghai. The ensuing slaughter decimated the CCP. It took another 20

ABOVE: *Lu Xun's 1919 antihero "Ah Q" captured not only the failure of the Republican revolution but also epitomized the faults of traditional Chinese culture as seen by May Fourth critics: ignorance of science, slavishness, and selfdeluding pride.* LIU YI/CHINA TOURISM PHOTO LIBRARY

LEFT: *Jiang Jieshi (Chiang Kai-shek), leader of the Nationalist Kuomintang (KMT), visiting troops.* POPPERFOTO

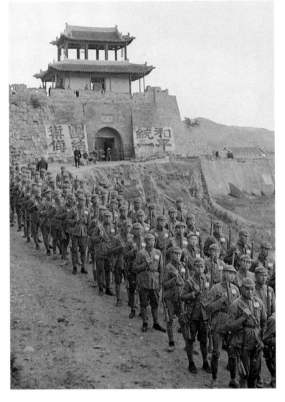

The state had to organize economic production, keep the peace, and bring culture to its citizens. The twentieth century brought new content to these enduring challenges. Economic issues now included industrialization; security included the Korean War and the Cold War; and culture meant a struggle between enduring Chinese practices and Mao's version of Marxism–Leninism.

Mao launched three great campaigns to make China achieve the utopic state of "communism" before anyone else. In 1956–57, he called upon the intellectual elite to "Let a hundred flowers bloom," to criticize and improve the CCP. The party, however, was shocked at the antisocialist and liberal tone of many suggestions. Mao gave up on the intellectuals and the anti-Rightist campaign of 1957–59 sent hundreds of thousands of them to labor in poor villages and labor camps.

Mao next turned to the peasants of China in a stupendous production campaign, the Great Leap Forward (1958–60). It was an unmitigated disaster, causing the deaths of some 30 million rural folk in the man-made famines of 1959 and 1960. Because of a hurry-up mentality and because recently criticized intellectuals were unwilling to contradict local cadres eager to impress their superiors, most projects lacked sound engineering and took labor away from the fields, causing major harvest failures. At the same time, Mao pushed the commune movement, which took away the land recently given to peasants and gave control of farming to collectives about the size of the old counties. By 1960 the policies of the Great Leap Forward had to be abandoned, in fact if not in name.

The fall-out of the Great Leap Forward for China cannot be overstated. Before the Great Leap Forward the CCP was an almost messianic movement that had reunified the nation. During the Great Leap Forward the Communists battled the realities of agriculture and the habits of village family life and were defeated. It fractured the CCP and began its decline. It also led to the Sino-Soviet split in 1960 and put an end to Soviet economic aid to China. No Soviet leader visited China again until Gorbachev in 1989.

Mao's final major attempt to make China great was a war against human nature. He wanted to create the pure socialist man. The Cultural Revolution of 1966–76 instead became a vicious party purge and the excuse for horrible violence at the hands of student Red Guards.

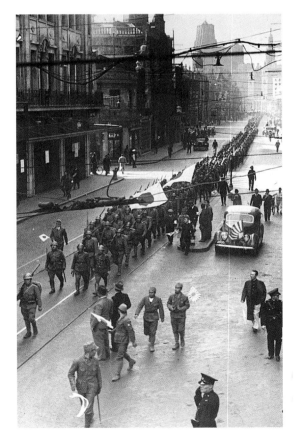

Attacks centered on current local party leaders and intellectuals in general. Almost all were sent for three to ten years of labor in poor villages.

Today although the Cultural Revolution is acknowledged to have been a tragedy it has had important consequences. A generation of intellectuals was reintroduced (albeit involuntarily) to the realities of rural life. This generation still understands the rural heartland of China better than the young students of Tiananmen in 1989 who looked down on "stupid peasants." The Cultural Revolution also burst the bubble of charismatic authority for most Chinese intellectuals and armed a generation with the tools of independent thinking and political dissent.

After Mao's death in 1976 there was a struggle for a successor. By late 1978 Deng Xiaoping emerged as the de facto victor. Deng and his protégés initiated a series of reforms in the "reform decade" up to 1989. The two keys of the reform have been opening China to the world and introducing a market economy to replace the communes and state industry of Maoist China. The first goal has been largely successful, with China gaining recognition in the United Nations (actually in 1972 under Mao) and diplomatic recognition from its old nemesis, the

United States, in 1979. Foreign capital and technology has cascaded into China, often more quickly than it can be sensibly absorbed. By the late 1980s nearly a hundred thousand Chinese students and citizens had studied in and visited foreign countries.

Economic reform has proven more difficult. In the early 1980s, the CCP once again returned land to the tiller and reaped another windfall bonus of increased agricultural production. However, urban price reform and the

MAO ZEDONG – BANDIT HERO AND HARSH EMPEROR

Born to a rich peasant family in central China, Mao Zedong was one of the May Fourth generation who sought radical answers to China's ancient ills. Although he did not study overseas, he adopted Marxism–Leninism and became an early member of the CCP. Mao always stressed the revolutionary potential of the oppressed, especially the peasants. He did not rise to central power until the Yan'an period (1937–47) where his practicality, strategic genius, and charismatic common touch rocketed him to supreme leadership of the CCP.

BELOW: *Painting of Mao Zedong engaged in strategic planning.* ROBERT E. MUROWCHICK

Mao was genuinely admired and adored for leading the establishment of "New China" in 1949. By the mid-1950s, however, Mao had become dictatorial and increasingly unreasonable. Having made him the supreme leader, the CCP proved incapable of controlling their "Great Helmsman." Mao initiated a series of disastrous campaigns such as the Great Leap Forward (1958–60) and the Great Proletarian Cultural Revolution (1966–76), and by his death in 1976 he had left the CCP mortally damaged. In 1981 the CCP officially admitted some of Mao's mistakes but distinguished between "Mao the Man" and "Mao Zedong Thought." The man made mistakes but, the Party maintains, the Thought remains infallible.

Mao is thus remembered in terms of traditional Chinese lore as both a bandit hero and a harsh emperor. His legacy is a complicated one. His greatest legacies are his high regard for common people and their sufferings and his spectacular abuse of autocratic power. One of the unusual social phenomena of

the 1990s, particularly since the Tiananmen massacre of 1989, has been a nostalgia craze for the departed Chairman among youth who could never have known what life was like under Mao.

While Mao is now acknowledged in the PRC as having made errors, he remains a model of personal integrity and dedication to the interest of all China in contrast to the petty corruption and self-interest of current leaders.

ABOVE: *Statue of Mao Zedong in Lijiang in northwest Yunnan province.* ROBERT E. MUROWCHICK

ABOVE: *Mao Zedong traveling in an open car to review student Red Guards from all over China in 1966 at the start of the Great Proletarian Cultural Revolution.* GREENHILL–S.A.C.U.

LEFT: *Zhou Enlai and Mao Zedong at the Chinese Communist Party (CCP) base at Yan'an in Shaanxi province during the late 1930s.* PEABODY MUSEUM, HARVARD UNIVERSITY, PHOTOGRAPH BY OWEN LATTIMORE

management of factories and businesses have proven much more difficult to achieve and produced corruption and inflation. Part of being open to the world has meant that China's citizens have seen, at least through the media and reports of friends and neighbors who had traveled overseas, that China is underdeveloped still. Taiwan especially looms as an economic and political success against which the achievements of the CCP begin to pale.

THE RISE OF TAIWAN

When the defeated KMT forces scrambled to the large island off the coast of Fujian province in 1949 many thought the regime would not last. These "Northerners" were not welcome among a southern Chinese population that had been under Japanese colonial rule since 1895. Yet the KMT has presided over an economic and political success story. Taiwan is still ruled by the KMT and claims to be the sole government, the "Republic of China."

The twin successes of Taiwan have been its economic growth and political democratization. In the 1950s Taiwan's economic growth was the same as the PRC's, but in the 1960s growth took off. In 1992 Taiwan's per capita income for its 20 million inhabitants was about US$10,000 — a level matched in Asia only by Japan.

The three sources of Taiwanese economic success were an end to the disastrous inflation that had crippled the KMT regime in China in the 1940s, a policy of land-to-the-tiller, and government promotion of key industries. The most successful technique was the "export processing zone" first tried at the southern city of Kaohsiung in 1966. These tax-free zones attracted foreign capital and technology and were copied by the PRC in 1979 when it set up its "special economic zones" around Hong Kong and other former treaty ports.

Politically, Taiwan has made the difficult transition from one-party rule to parliamentary democracy. Through the 1970s the KMT government struggled with the emerging Taiwan Independence movement and its representatives such as the Democratic Progressive Party (DPP). Opposition parties were finally legalized in 1986. In 1992 a full parliamentary election was successfully held in which the KMT lost nearly half its seats to opposition parties.

CHINA'S PROSPECTS FOR THE TWENTY-FIRST CENTURY

The inheritors of China's ancient civilization are not just the CCP in Beijing or the KMT in Taibei (Taipei). Important Chinese communities exist in Hong Kong

ABOVE: A military guard watches over the statue of President Jiang Jieshi (Chiang Kai-shek) at his memorial in Taibei, Taiwan.
ROBERT E. MUROWCHICK

LEFT: Slogans come bellowing from a loudspeaker-laden truck at a "one-child-per-family" rally at a market in Zhengzhou in Henan province. ROBERT E. MUROWCHICK

TIANANMEN — POPULAR PROTESTS AND REPRESSION OF 1989

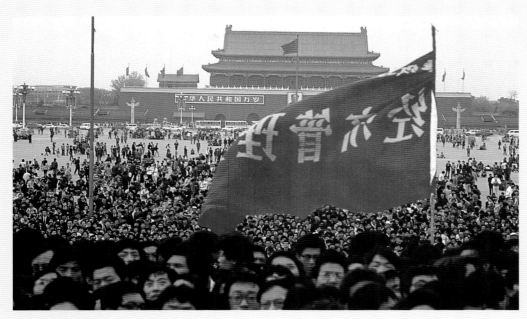

LEFT: The mass of students assembled in Tiananmen Square during the protests of April 1989.
RENE BURRI/MAGNUM PHOTOS

T ensions of the reform decade came to a breaking point in the spring of 1989. After the sudden death on 15 April of Hu Yaobang (the popular reformist party chief who had been fired in 1987), student marches to mourn his passing quickly became protests against inflation, government corruption, and restrictions on public expression. Protests were led by Beijing's students who claimed the mantle of the famous May Fourth student demonstrations of 1919. Thousands of students filled Tiananmen square in central Beijing on 17 April 1989 and over the next six weeks the demonstrations grew (and emerged in other cities) despite official prohibitions,

the state visit of Gorbachev (which inadvertently brought world television to Tiananmen — a propaganda source students used to good effect), and direct military threats by the government.

The widespread nature of these demonstrations around the country reflected a broad dissatisfaction in China's urban population (some 100 million people in the major cities) with the social results of the reform decade. Two issues stood at the forefront: personal economic security which was threatened by inflation and job insecurity and a sense of unfairness generated by popular perceptions of government patronage

and unscrupulous business people. The breaking of the "iron rice bowl," the prospect of being fired from one's job in government enterprises, severely threatened workers. Inflation not only hit at those on fixed salary incomes, but carried the powerful negative picture of the failed Nationalist government of the late 1940s, which had allowed inflation to ruin urban life. Added to these economic concerns in the public mind, the reforms also produced powerful resentments about unfair access to wealth and power. The two guilty parties have been high officials and their children and the *getihu* or private entrepreneurs. Chinese who studied long and hard to pass the university entrance exams resented seeing the best professional jobs going to children of high cadres, regardless of that child's quality of education. They also resented the economic wealth of the relatively uneducated street entrepreneurs. Citizens who played by the rules were sick and tired of seeing pampered cadre kids flying off to America and swaggering *getihu* driving around Beijing in expensive imported cars.

Three social groups articulated this general malaise: university students, older intellectuals, and workers. The students were the leading voice, but students alone could not have generated such a massive popular protest movement. Rather, they continued

FAR LEFT: The defiant young man, shown atop the lead tank heading for Tiananmen Square, repeatedly stood in their path in an effort to halt their advance.
S. FRANKLIN/MAGNUM PHOTOS

LEFT: Protesters erecting the Goddess of Democracy statue during the Tiananmen demonstrations. PATRICK ZACHMANN/MAGNUM PHOTOS

RIGHT: Troops forced an end to the protests, resulting in the loss of more than 2,000 lives in Beijing alone.
S. FRANKLIN/MAGNUM PHOTOS

the role of Confucian literati and the speakers for the public mind. Finally, older intellectuals (many of whom had been riotous "Red Guards" of the Cultural Revolution in the1960s) advised the students and provided them with information and rationale in their negotiations with the government. Unfortunately, the young and idealistic students were not inclined to take the cautious counsel of older intellectuals who knew that the government would eventually use force to end the demonstrations. Just days before the bloody crackdown, the students denounced older intellectuals as cowards for advising the students to abandon Tiananmen Square immediately.

The confrontation ended in tragedy on 4 June 1989 when PLA units from the provinces fired on unarmed protesters, killing over 2,000 in Beijing alone. The results of the popular protests and government repression have been mixed. The killings brought immediate international condemnation and sanctions from the U.S. and several European countries. Since the "June Fourth Massacre" the Chinese democracy movement has continued overseas. Nonetheless, both the government, led by Li Peng, and the CCP, and the economic reforms continue in the 1990s. The long-term results are difficult to gauge, but at minimum China's government has been served notice by its citizens that political life in China must include the interests of more people and the international community is now more aware of the complex realities of China as it enters the twenty-first century.

(which will revert to PRC administration in 1997 as a "special zone"), Singapore, and in Chinatowns ranging from San Francisco to Melbourne to London to Vancouver.

Overseas Chinese form a powerful economic community, particularly in Southeast Asia. The impact of China on world culture in the twenty-first century will thus not be limited to Asia or to the nation states that represent most Chinese. Nonetheless, China will remain the center of "Chineseness" in the next century and the home of one and a quarter billion Chinese. Three major problems confront China today — population, pollution, and the CCP. Population is the most intractable problem. The land mass of China supported at most 160 million souls for all of China's history until the eighteenth century. Now it must feed eight times as many mouths. Population control in the 1980s has been only marginally successful because the birth of a son is still the only reliable form of social security for China's 900 million rural inhabitants.

Along with overpopulation have come pollution and environmental degradation. Already Japan is complaining of acid rain from the smoke stacks of north China. The DDT level in Shanghai drinking water is ten times above the limits set in most developed countries. Pollution in both mainland China and Taiwan is not so much a quality of life issue, as it is a survival issue for agriculture, timber, and water control.

Finally, China has the problem of the CCP. The party that led China to "stand up" at mid-century threatens to bring the state to its knees by this century's end because the Leninist system has failed to address the key problems of population and pollution.

From the long-term perspective a pattern is evident: revolutionary efforts of Chinese leaders in the twentieth century have collided with the continuities of material life in China to produce an evolution of Chinese society and culture. China is likely to try some form of democracy in the twenty-first century — it will not be a simple copy of the Western model, but a democracy with uniquely Chinese characteristics that draws from the land and culture of China's civilization.

ABOVE: Skyscrapers and other construction replace traditional Chinese architecture in Penang, Malaysia, a major overseas Chinese community since the tin-mining heyday during the late nineteenth century.
ROBERT E. MUROWCHICK

PAST, PRESENT, AND FUTURE

James L. Watson

"CHINA" IS AS MUCH A STATE OF MIND as it is a concrete, geopolitical entity. After so many centuries of disruption and revolution, do we still speak of China as a unified whole? Why hasn't this vast country dissolved into the Republic of Guangdong, the independent state of Shanghai, and the United Yellow River States (to mention only a few possibilities)? What is it about China that runs so counter to the dominant social trends of the modern world?

The answer to these questions lies in the complexity of Chinese culture, beginning with the spoken language. What linguists categorize as Chinese is, in fact, a set of separate, mutually unintelligible languages. We are often misled by the common use of the term "dialect" to distinguish varieties of spoken Chinese; people who speak dialects of English, for example, may live in separate areas (Boston, Sydney, Oxford) but they can understand each other with a minimum of difficulty. This is not at all the case in China: Cantonese is as distant from Mandarin as is English from Swedish — these languages are, of course, related but one has to work at learning them just like any other remote tongue.

China's linguistic diversity is paralleled by vast differences in geographical settings and human ecosystems. The semitropical zone in south China is so lush that a single field can support two crops of rice, plus a crop of vegetables each year. Not surprisingly, this region has also produced one of the world's most complex systems of patrilineages and clans. In Guangdong province, entire communities are comprised of male descendants of a single founding ancestor who settled in this southern riceland nearly a thousand years ago. In effect, the irrigated fields became economic magnets, holding subsequent generations together in one location.

On the North China Plain, by contrast, the ecology is very different and the agricultural system could not sustain such a high concentration of population. As a consequence, complex lineages and clans did not dominate the north China cultural scene. Rather than building their social world on descent from common (male) ancestors, north China farmers relied more on ties to relatives created by marriage — that is, their in-laws (affines).

It is, therefore, almost impossible to make generalizations about Chinese social organization that hold true for every region and for every subethnic category of Han peoples. All of the social diagnostics that anthropologists normally use to distinguish one culture from another (for example, variations in kinship, family, marriage, adoption, and inheritance) fail

ABOVE: *This rural scene in Fengluo, northern Guangxi, contrasts sharply with the sophisticated life in urban coastal areas.*
ROBERT HARDING PICTURE LIBRARY

OPPOSITE: *Miao woman from southern Guangxi, near China's border with Vietnam.*
GUIDO ALBERTO ROSSI/THE IMAGE BANK

when applied to China. China is a continental-sized system, of the order of Europe or Africa: Swedes and Sicilians do not share the same patterns of marriage and family organization; we should not be surprised then to learn that Cantonese and Shandongese differ in similar ways.

Discoveries of this nature are surprising largely because the majority of Chinese — both elite and nonelite — have gone to such lengths for so many centuries to deny that significant cultural differences could possibly exist among them. A unique feature of the Chinese cultural system, in contrast to the European and the south Asian, is that among Chinese the very idea of unity has become a hallmark of their civilization. The Chinese recognize cultural diversity and internal difference, but do not celebrate them as central features of life. The entire dynamic of Chinese culture and history has been centripetal rather than centrifugal: for the past thousand years the center has held in China.

Explanations of China's cultural longevity depend largely on the perspective of the observer. Many scholars have stressed the role of the ideographic (that is, nonphonetic) script as the key to the puzzle. Chinese characters may be pronounced in different ways by Cantonese or Shanghainese, but the meaning does not change. Mastering the complex written script thus allowed educated people from remote corners of the empire to communicate, even if they could not comprehend each other's speech. A unified script also encouraged the development of a common literary and

LANGUAGE IN CHINA

LEFT: Uighur woman from Kashi reading a newspaper. ANNE RIPPY / THE IMAGE BANK.

Depending upon the criteria used, there are at least seven major language families in China: Mandarin, Cantonese, Wu, Hakka, Gan, Xiang, and Min (including Taiwanese). Each of these language families can be divided into dialects and subdialects which are themselves mutually incomprehensible. Speakers of standard Cantonese who grow up in Hong Kong can barely understand Sze-yap Cantonese spoken by older residents of San Francisco's Chinatown. One could make similar observations about Wu dialects in the Shanghai region or Gan dialects in Jiangxi province.

Beginning in the early twentieth century, Chinese central governments have pushed Mandarin, notably the version dominant in Beijing, as the national spoken language.

During the imperial era (pre-1911) a Mandarin dialect known as *guanhua* (officials' speech) was promoted among top civil servants who came from remote corners of the empire. Until the 1950s, however, ordinary people rarely spoke or understood anything other than their local language. Both the Communists on the mainland and the Nationalists (KMT, or Kuomintang Party) on Taiwan enforced the use of Mandarin in the schools, on radio and television, and in government offices. By the 1970s and 1980s the majority of people on both sides of the Taiwan Straits could converse in Mandarin. Today, people may continue to speak Gan or Wu at home or on the streets, but most Chinese are now bilingual. To comprehend the enormity of this accomplishment, one must imagine a unified Europe in which all citizens speak a modernized form of Latin, while speaking varieties of French, German, and Spanish among friends. It is not surprising, therefore, that what outsiders call Mandarin is known in China as *putonghua* (common speech).

It is important to note that the language families outlined above are all specific to the dominant ethnic group, the Han Chinese. The term Han refers to people who speak versions of Chinese, use written Chinese, and adhere to certain cultural patterns. The Han are distinguished from non-Han peoples who live within the political boundaries of China but often speak languages other than Chinese (for example, Miao, Mongol, and Tibetan) and follow marriage or funeral customs that set them apart from the Han. The Communist state officially recognizes 55 non-Han ethnic groups and grants special privileges to people in these categories, including dispensation from the "one-child-per-family" birth control policy and extra quotas for university admissions.

ABOVE: Reading a Beijing newspaper. Unlike the Chinese spoken word, the written form does not vary between dialects. LEO MEIER / WELDONS

philosophical tradition that is unparalleled among world cultures.

While Europe was gradually moving away from Latin as a foundation for ideological unity, successive Chinese governments have reinforced and refined their ancient ideographic system. During the past century there have been organized movements to abandon Chinese characters in favor of various Romanized (alphabetic) systems, but all such campaigns have failed the test of mass acceptance. The Communist government introduced a comprehensive set of simplified characters in the 1950s and 1960s, but these innovations did not transform the structure

nor the inherent complexity of China's unique writing system.

Communist efforts to simplify the written language are the latest in a long series of state interventions aimed at

LEFT: Taxi in Xi'an, the capital of modern Shaanxi province and the site of the ancient Tang dynasty capital of Chang'an. Today this city is bustling with foreign and local tourists, due to its wealth of archaeological sites, particularly the mausoleum of the First emperor of Qin with its entombed terracotta army. PETER EASTWAY

unifying Chinese society and culture. The overarching role of the state is, in fact, an essential feature of Chinese civilization: for as long as we have written records there has been a centralized, autocratic state system in China. During the frequent periods when central control broke down, the idea of unity always served to pull the centralized state back together. It is significant that, in Chinese, China is called *Zhongguo* or "the Central (or Middle) Kingdom" implying not only its singularity among competing states but also its role in the cosmos as a centripetal, or centering force.

As the year 2000 approaches, China is rapidly emerging as a world economic power. The reforms initiated by Deng Xiaoping and his supporters have had a dramatic effect on the agricultural sector and in the realm of small business; state industry remains a problem but even this sector is responding to market reforms. Perhaps the most obvious feature of this economic boom is that it is concentrated in coastal provinces, precisely those areas that display the most linguistic and

ROMANIZATION SYSTEMS FOR MANDARIN CHINESE

Over the centuries, there have been repeated efforts to render Chinese characters into alphabetic script to aid foreigners in their learning of that language and to facilitate communication. In the thirteenth-century Yuan dynasty, for example, the Mongols wrote Chinese characters in their own "Phags-pa" alphabet, and in the sixteenth century the Jesuit scholar Matteo Ricci devised his own transcription system to aid his fellow foreigners in China. These early attempts were followed by those of various nineteenth-century Christian missionaries and Chinese and foreign linguists, resulting in a bewildering variety of spellings; for example, the capital city of China has been variously romanized as Pekin, Peking, Peiking, Pei-ching, and Beijing.

The most popular method of romanization in the West — the Wade-Giles system — was devised in the mid-nineteenth century by the British diplomat Thomas Wade (who later became Professor of Chinese at Cambridge University) and was revised a half-century later by Herbert Giles, another British diplomat-Sinologist. Like other systems, theirs attempted to offer official Beijing Mandarin pronunciations of Chinese words, with many

sounds only approximated with the use of variations of vowels and consonants and apostrophes to indicate aspirated sounds. The Wade-Giles system has given us spellings that many readers will find familiar, such as Mao Tse-tung and Chou En-lai. However, other names, from a variety of romanization systems, proved so durable that they continued to be used as a matter of convenience along with Wade-Giles even though they did not follow the "rules" of that romanization system, for example, Peking, Chiang Kai-shek, and Taiwan. The Wade-Giles system was the preferred method of transcription throughout Western governments and universities for most of this century, and several generations of Western scholars learned it as they studied Chinese.

The 1920s saw the development in China of *Guoyu Luomazi*, or "National Language Romanization," which used internal spelling variations to denote the four tones of spoken Mandarin. This remarkable system has all but disappeared due to a lack of official support and the inherent difficulties of learning it. With the 1930s came another system, known as *Latinxua sin wenz*, which was developed for Chinese speakers in the USSR and then spread

to China. In the late 1930s and early 1940s, this system was supported by Mao Zedong and his followers as a possible means of reducing illiteracy in China's poor northwest. The *Latinxua* system was modified to become the mainland's official *Hanyu pinyin,* or "Phonetic Spelling of Chinese" since the late 1950s, and reflects the national effort to establish Mandarin as the official pronunciation across the mosaic of dialects and sub dialects that makes up modern China.

Since the reopening of China to the outside world after the end of the Cultural Revolution in the mid-1970s, *Hanyu pinyin* has been widely adopted internationally, although the Wade-Giles system remains the favored romanization in Taiwan, in overseas Chinese communities, and among many older scholars in the West. The choice of romanization system has involved more than just ease of use: an early issue was whether adoption of *pinyin* implied political recognition of the mainland, and an ongoing concern is the huge cost of conversion, especially for government and university libraries with millions of card catalog entries already written in Wade-Giles. These problems continue to reflect the complex nature of the issue of romanization.

viewpoint. Taiwanese investments and popular culture have swept through Fujian province with breathtaking speed, and continue a triumphal march through adjoining provinces. Meanwhile Taiwan is rapidly becoming a full-fledged democratic state, the first ever in the Chinese world. Nationalist (Kuomintang) dreams of "returning to the mainland" as military conquerors have long since disappeared. Moreover, recent relaxations in visa procedures on both sides of the Taiwan Straits have meant that huge numbers of Taiwanese tourists and entrepreneurs are now able to wander at will in China to visit family members, ancestral villages, tourist sites, and to pursue business ventures, discovering in the process just how far the two societies have drifted apart in the past 40 years. Taiwan is moving rapidly toward de facto independence from the mainland, even though de jure independence is considered (even by many opposition politicians) to be too risky — at least until the last of the old revolutionaries, including Deng Xiaoping, are gone on both sides of the Taiwan Straits. The irony is that at the end of their long lives, the elders of the Communist and the Nationalist parties have more in common with each other than they do with their nominal successors.

LEFT: Women from the Yi minority group, from Sichuan province, at a torch festival.
NEVADA WIER/THE IMAGE BANK

ABOVE: Burning incense and offering oranges are part of the ritual observed by a possession cult in Hong Kong's New Territories. JAMES L. WATSON

subcultural diversity: Guangdong (Cantonese), Fujian and Taiwan (Min), and Zhejiang and Jiangsu (Wu/Shanghainese). In the 1990s Beijing authorities began to complain that these linguistically separate regions were becoming "too arrogant" and "too independent." The Communist party periodically tries to crack down on coastal provinces and enforce central authority over regional economics, but to little avail. The growth of Hong Kong and Taiwan as dominant players in the mainland economy has exacerbated this trend toward economic independence. During the past decade (1983–93) economic development in the Pearl River Delta — an ecozone that incorporates Hong Kong — has taken off at a dizzying pace. Before long, the entire delta region will resemble Hong Kong's New Territories, an area that was transformed into a modern, urbanized environment in the 1970s.

From the perspective of ordinary citizens living in south China, the 1997 merger of Hong Kong into the People's Republic has already occurred, and there is little question which side is dominant. Hong Kong is like a beacon on the horizon, sending out strobe flashes of light that promise affluence, enlightenment, and personal freedom. Reunification with Taiwan is another issue that is largely moot from the economic and social

LEFT: Dressed as a guardian deity for the City God Procession, Taibei, Taiwan.
JAMES L. WATSON

ANTHROPOLOGICAL PERSPECTIVES

From an anthropological perspective there are two particular features of Chinese culture that foster a sense of unity. One is the idea of history itself: for centuries Chinese people, both elite and nonelite, have celebrated the fact that their society has had two, three, four, even five thousand years of unbroken history, thus setting China apart from all other cultural systems (for example, Pharaonic Egypt, the Aztecs, the Roman, British, and Ottoman Empires). This reverence for a lineal connection to a grand and glorious tradition has acted as a kind of social adhesive, leading successful rebels to draw on the past when they rise to power as opposed to embracing new, iconoclastic cultural ideas. If one examines the actual sequence and structure of the Chinese political economy over the past two thousand years it is apparent that Chinese history is no more unified or unbroken than say, that of western Europe or Russia. Nonetheless, the important point to note is that the majority of Chinese people believe that their history is special and unlike any other.

ABOVE: People worshipping Huangdi (known as the common ancestor of the Chinese race) at Huangdi's mausoleum at Huangling in Shaanxi province. YANG LI MIN/CHINA TOURISM PHOTO LIBRARY

BELOW: Mourning scene in a farming community in Shaanxi province. WANG MIAO/CHINA TOURISM PHOTO LIBRARY

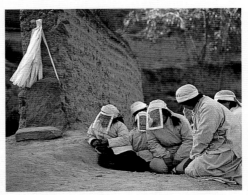

The second anthropological perspective on this problem is the overarching concern in Chinese culture for what might be called proper behavior in social relations. In Chinese the relevant term is li, perhaps best translated as ritual, etiquette, or correct behavior. In order to be accepted as a member of the dominant Han ethnic group people had to conform to accepted ritual form, especially in the domain of family rites: weddings, birth celebrations, funerals, and ancestor worship. There was, in other words, a more or less clear set of ritual prescriptions for the performance of weddings and funerals. These prescriptions were set out in published texts for the literate and in highly visible public performances for the illiterate. There was little ambiguity in this realm of culture: a wedding either was or was not a Han Chinese wedding. People who chose to follow other, competing ritual forms were defined as non-Han ethnic minorities or worse, sectarian rebels. In fact, the surest way for adherents of a new religion to attract the attention of imperial officials was to begin performing funerals or weddings in aberrant form; such boldness was tempting fate, however, and could easily lead to annihilation.

Prior to the introduction of Communism it is clear that Chinese state officials were primarily concerned with the public behavior of their subjects rather than the content of their beliefs. People of all descriptions were permitted to believe anything they wished about religion or the afterlife, as long as they adhered to proper ritual conduct in public observances. The imperial state promoted specific deities and suppressed others, and defined what was and what was not a proper funeral. But state officials rarely, if ever, engaged in inquisitions or investigations regarding the content of peoples beliefs.

This preoccupation with orthopraxy (correct behavior) as opposed to orthodoxy (correct belief) was an important key to the problem of cultural unity in China. By focusing on the performance of public rituals, officials did not feel the need to probe too deeply into subcultural differences regarding religious interpretations or conflicting beliefs. Groups of people could be accepted as Han Chinese if they behaved according to received ritual prescriptions. In other societies, notably those deriving from Christian or Islamic origins, a preoccupation with proper belief has led to increasing cultural disintegration and fragmentation. The genius of the Chinese system was that it allowed for a surprisingly high degree of religious diversity within a united overall structure. In this China may very well have been unique among world civilizations.

BELOW: Members of a clan in Fujian province pay respect to their ancestor on the first day of Lunar New Year. CHAPMAN LEE/CHINA TOURISM PHOTO LIBRARY

The most serious question in China's future is not the resolution of the Taiwan issue or the prospects of international confrontation. The growing gap between China's wealthy, sophisticated coastal regions and the less developed inland areas presents more danger for social unity. Communist party officials are extremely worried about the prospects of disorder in the provinces of Sichuan, Hunan, and Shaanxi (among others) where farmers have been paid for their requisitional grain with "white papers," promissory notes that may or may not be convertible to cash. Industrial workers and professionals in inland areas are growing increasingly disillusioned with economic reforms that have "broken the iron rice bowl" (job tenure) and effectively lowered their real income. Meanwhile there has been what some Chinese observers call a "consumer frenzy" as people fear that their savings will dissolve as inflation rises. To add to the party's anxiety, internal controls on migration (a hallmark of Maoist autocracy) have completely collapsed and China's coastal regions are awash with job seekers from inland provinces. In rural areas of Guangdong, for instance, squatter huts and mat-sheds of the type that existed in Hong Kong's New Territories during the 1960s have appeared. The difference is that today (1993), these huts are inhabited by Mandarin speakers from as far away as Heilongjiang on the Russian border. These migrants do not speak Cantonese and work as day laborers for wages that are one-fourth the rate for local workers — and they still keep coming, packed into China's overcrowded railway cars. Unless the state finds a solution to this and other imbalances in the economy, China faces a future in which there are essentially two societies: one increasingly rich, sophisticated, and plugged-in to the world system; the other poor, backward, and locked into authoritarian patterns of centralized state control. The revolution was fought to rectify just such a set of conditions that prevailed in China during

the 1930s and 1940s. Has the Communist party brought China the full circle in only 40 years, or will a new era of democratic reforms and true "liberation" finally take root in China? The answer, as always, lies in the Chinese countryside where the majority of *laobaixing* (ordinary people) have always lived. Only when these ordinary citizens — not the intellectuals, not the bureaucrats, not the new millionaires — gain control over their own lives will Sun Yixiang's (Sun Yat-sen) great dream of political unity (as opposed to cultural unity) be realized. And, as in so many other parts of the postsocialist, post-Cold War world, it is the economic sphere (not the political arena) that will define the future of Chinese society.

HONG KONG

H ong Kong has had a massive impact on southern China's economic, cultural, and social system — such that many Cantonese maintain that "China is not going to eat Hong Kong, Hong Kong is eating China."

Hong Kong has become what many anthropologists would call the ultimate postmodern social system. "Postmodern" has a specialized meaning in anthropological jargon, referring to social and economic adaptations that are marked by a characteristic lack of boundaries. This emerging cultural system defies older definitions that anthropologists and sociologists have taken for granted. Corporations, services, and personnel move effortlessly through national boundaries, and linguistic and social barriers; frontiers of etiquette, culture, ethnic identity, and even cuisine dissolve.

In today's Hong Kong social and cultural categories are slippery. It is difficult to define people with any finality because what they are today they aren't tomorrow. Everything and everyone is in the process of becoming something new and different. Hong Kong in the 1990s has become a determinedly

transnational, transcultural, and translinguistic environment. People of this type are in the forefront of Hong Kong's development, which is marked by a technological sophistication that is breathtaking when one first encounters it. Perhaps Hong Kong is what China could become, depending on its future leadership. This is why, no doubt, China's aging autocrats find Hong Kong so alluring, and yet so dangerous.

RIGHT: Portrait of a British Crown Colony — the Peak tram provides sweeping views of Hong Kong and Kowloon across the harbor in 1964.
AUSTRALIAN PICTURE LIBRARY/ THE BETTMANN ARCHIVE, INC

ABOVE: Postmodern Hong Kong of 1994 is a transnational, transcultural, translinguistic environment.
HORIZON/ADINA AMSEL TOVY

Further Reading

The Land

Andersson, J. G. *Children of the Yellow Earth* MIT Press, Cambridge, Mass, 1973

Fairbank, J. K. *The United States and China* Harvard University Press, Cambridge, Mass, 1983

Fitzgerald, C. P. *China: A Short Cultural History* Praeger, New York, 1961

Gernet, Jacques *A History of Chinese Civilization* J. R. Foster (trans.), Cambridge University Press, Cambridge, 1982

Hermann, Albert *Historical Atlas of China* Aldine, Chicago, 1966

Meskill, John (ed.) *An Introduction to Chinese Civilization* Heath, Lexington, Mass, 1973

Tregear, T. R. *A Geography of China* Aldine, Chicago, 1965

The People

—*The Times Atlas of China* Times Books, London, 1974

Chao, Kang *Man and Land in Chinese History* University of Chicago Press, Chicago, 1986

Gourou, Pierre *L'Asie* Hachette, Paris, 1953

He, Bochuan *China on the Edge: The Crisis of Ecology and Development* China Books, San Francisco, 1991

Shabad, Theodore *China's Changing Map* Praeger, New York, 1972

Smil, Vaclav *China's Environmental Crisis* M. E. Sharpe, White Plains, New York, 1993

Rediscovering the Past

Chang, Kwang-chih "Archaeology and Chinese historiography" *World Archaeology* 13.2 (1981): 156–69

Chang, Kwang-chih *The Archaeology of Ancient China* 4th ed., Yale University Press, New Haven and London, 1986

Cohen, Warren I. *East Asian Art and American Culture: A Study in International Relations* Columbia University Press, New York, 1992

Elman, Benjamin A. *From Philosophy to Philology: Intellectual and Social Aspects of Change in Late Imperial China* Harvard University Press, Cambridge, Mass, 1984

Hopkirk, Peter *Foreign Devils on the Silk Road: The Search for the Lost Treasures and Cities of Chinese Central Asia* Murray, London, 1980

Li Chi *Anyang* University of Washington Press, Seattle, 1977

Olsen, John W. "Archaeology in China Today" *China Exchange News* 20.2 (1992): 3–6

Owen, Stephen *Remembrances: The Experience of the Past in Classical Chinese Literature* Harvard University Press, Cambridge, Mass, 1986

Pulleyblank, Edwin G. "The Historiographical Tradition" in Dawson, Raymond (ed.) *The Legacy of China* 143–64, Oxford University Press, London, 1964

Rudolph, Richard C. "Preliminary Notes on Sung Archaeology" *Journal of Asian Studies* 22 (1963): 169–77

Schneider, Lawrence A. *Ku Chieh-kang and China's New History: Nationalism and the Quest for Alternative Traditions* University of California Press, Berkeley and Los Angeles, 1971

Wang Gungwu "Loving the Ancient in China" in Isabel MacBryde (ed.) *Who Owns the Past?* Oxford University Press, Melbourne, 1985, 175–95

Xia Nai "What is Archaeology?" in Gregory E. Guldin (ed.) *Anthropology in China* M. E. Sharpe, Armonk, New York and London, 1990, 59–67

The Beginnings of Settled Life

Chang, Kwang-chih *Art, Myth and Ritual: The Path to Political Authority in Ancient China* Harvard University Press, Cambridge, Mass, 1983

Chang, Kwang-chih *The Archaeology of Ancient China* 4th revised edition, Yale University Press, New Haven and London, 1986

Ritual and Power

Chang, Kwang-chih *Art, Myth, and Ritual: The Path to Political Authority in Ancient China* Harvard University Press, Cambridge, Mass, 1983

Chang, Kwang-chih *The Archaeology of Ancient China* 4th revised edition, Yale University Press, New Haven and London, 1986

Chang, Kwang-chih 1989 "An Essay on *Cong*" *Orientations* Vol. 20, No. 6 (June 1989): 37–43

Sacred Characters

Allan, Sarah *The Shape of the Turtle: Myth, Art and Cosmos in Early China* State University Press of New York, Albany, 1991

Boltz, William G. "Early Chinese Writing" *World Archaeology* 17, (1986): 420–36

Boltz, William G. *The Origin and Evolution of the Chinese Writing System* American Oriental Society, New Haven, 1993

Keightley, David N. *Sources of Shang History: The Oracle-Bone Inscriptions of Bronze Age China* University of California Press, Berkeley, 1978

Keightley, David N. "The Origins of Writing in China: Scripts and Cultural Contexts" in Wayne M. Senner (ed.) *The Origins of Writing* University of Nebraska Press, Lincoln, 1989, 171–202

Wu Hung "Bird Motifs in Eastern Yi Art" *Orientations* 16.10 (October 1985): 30–41

The Early Literary Traditions

de Bary, William T. (ed.) *Sources of Chinese Tradition* Vol. 1. Columbia University Press, New York, 1960

Hawkes, David (trans.) *The Songs of the South: An Anthology of Ancient Chinese Poetry by Qu Yuan and Other Poets* Penguin Books, Harmondsworth, Middlesex, 1985

Schneider, Laurence A. *A Madman of Ch'u: The Chinese Myth of Loyalty and Dissent* University of California Press, Berkeley, 1980

Waley, Arthur (trans.) *The Book of Songs* Evergreen Edition, Grove Press, New York, 1960

Watson, Burton (trans.) *Records of the Historian: Chapters from the Shih Chi of Ssu-ma Ch'ien* Columbia University Press, New York, 1969

Watson, Burton *Early Chinese Literature* Columbia University Press, New York, 1969

Watson, Burton *Ssu-ma Ch'ien: Grand Historian of China* Columbia University Press, New York, 1958

Watson, Burton (trans.) *The Complete Works of Chuang-tzu* Columbia University Press, New York, 1968

Yu, Pauline *The Reading of Imagery in the Chinese Poetic Tradition* Princeton University Press, Princeton, 1987

Philosophers and Statesmen

Graham, A. C. *Disputers of the Tao: Philosophical Argument in Ancient China* Open Court, La Salle, 1989

Hansen, Chad *A Daoist Theory of Chinese Thought: A Philosophical Interpretation* Oxford University Press, New York and Oxford, 1992

Hsu, Cho-yun *Ancient China in Transition: An Analysis of Social Mobility, 722–222 BC* Stanford University Press, Stanford, 1965

Hsu, Cho-yun and Linduff, Katheryn *Western Chou Civilization* Yale University Press, New Haven and London, 1988

Lawton, Thomas *Chinese Art of the Warring States Period: Change and Continuity 480–222 BC* Smithsonian Institution, Freer Gallery of Art, Washington DC, 1982

Li, Xueqin *Eastern Zhou and Qin Civilizations* (trans. Chang, Kwang-chih) Yale University Press, New Haven and London, 1985

Schwartz, Benjamin I. *The World of Thought in Ancient China* Harvard University Press, Cambridge, Mass, 1985

The Birth of Imperial China

Bodde, Derk *China's First Unifier: A Study of the Ch'in Dynasty as Seen in the Life of Li Ssu 280?–208 BC* Hong Kong University Press, Hong Kong, 1967

Cotterell, Arthur *The First Emperor of China* Macmillan, London, 1981

Duyvendak, J. J. L. (trans.) *The Book of Lord Shang* University of Chicago Press, Chicago, 1963 (1928)

Guisso, R. W. L. and Pagani, Catherine with Miller, David *The First Emperor of China* Birch Lane Press, New York, 1989

Hulsewé, A. F. P. *Remnants of Ch'in Law* E.J. Brill, Leiden, 1985

China's Growing Strength: The Han Dynasty

Bodde, Derk *Festivals in Classical China: New Year and Other Annual Observances During the Han Dynasty 206 BC–AD 220* Princeton University Press, Princeton, 1975

Hsu, Cho-yun *Han Agriculture: The Formation of Early Chinese Agrarian Economy* University of Washington Press, Seattle and London, 1980

Knechtges, David R. *The Han Rhapsody* Cambridge University Press, Cambridge, 1976

Loewe, Michael *Chinese Ideas of Life and Death: Faith, Myth and Reason in the Han Period (202 BC–AD 220)* George Allen and Unwin Ltd, London, 1982; reprinted SMC, Taipei, 1993

Loewe, Michael *Everyday Life in Early Imperial China During the Han Period* B.T. Batsford Ltd, London, G. P. Putnam's Sons, New York, 1968; reprinted Dorset Press, New York, 1988

Pirazzoli-t'Serstevens, Michèle *The Han Dynasty* (trans. Seligman, Janet), Rizzoli, New York, 1982

Twitchett, Denis and Loewe, Michael (eds), *The Cambridge History of China Volume I: The Ch'in and Han Empires*, Cambridge University Press, Cambridge, 1986

Watson, Burton *Ssu-ma Ch'ien: Grand Historian of China* Columbia University Press, New York, 1958

Yü, Ying-shih *Trade and Expansion in Han China* University of California Press, Berkeley and Los Angeles, 1967

The Florescence of Buddhism

Ch'en, K. *Buddhism in China: A Historical Survey* Princeton University Press, Princeton, 1964

Dien, Albert E. (ed.) *State and Society in Early Medieval China* Stanford University Press, Stanford, 1991

Kohn, Livia *Early Chinese Mysticism: Philosophy and Soteriology in the Taoist Tradition* Princeton University Press, Princeton, 1992

Welch, Holmes and Seidel, Anna (eds) *Facets of Taoism* Yale University Press, New Haven, 1979

Zürcher, E. *The Buddhist Conquest of China* 2 vols. E. J. Brill, Leiden, 1959

The Golden Age of Tang and Song

Bol, Peter K. *'This Culture of Ours': Intellectual Transitions in T'ang and Sung China* Stanford University Press, Stanford, 1992

Chaffee, John W. *The Thorny Gates of Learning in Sung China: A Social History of Examinations* Cambridge University Press, Cambridge, 1985

Chaves, Jonathan *Mei Yao-ch'en and the Development of Early Sung Poetry* Columbia University Press, New York, 1976

Ebrey, Patricia Buckley *The Aristocratic Families of Early Imperial China: A Case Study of the Po-ling Ts'ui Family* Cambridge University Press, Cambridge, 1978

Ebrey, Patricia Buckley *The Inner Quarters: Marriage and the Lives of Chinese Women in the Song Period* University of California Press, Berkeley, 1993

Gernet, Jacques *Daily Life in China on the Eve of the Mongol Invasion, 1250–76* Wright, H. M. (trans.), Stanford University Press, Stanford, 1962

Graham, A. C. *Two Chinese Philosophers: Ch'eng Ming-tao and Ch'eng Yi-ch'uan* Lund Humphries, London, 1958

Hartman, Charles *Han Yü and the T'ang Search for Unity* Princeton University Press, Princeton, 1985

Hung, William *Tu Fu: China's Greatest Poet* Harvard University Press, Cambridge, Mass, 1952

Hymes, Robert P. *Statesmen and Gentlemen: The Elite of Fu-chou, Chiang-hsi, in Northern and Southern Sung* Cambridge University Press, Cambridge, 1986

Kracke, Edward Jr *Civil Service in Sung China: 960–1076* Harvard University Press, Cambridge, Mass, 1953

Liu, James T. C. *Reform in Sung China: Wang An-Shih (1021–1086) and His New Policies* Harvard University Press, Cambridge, Mass, 1957

Liu, James T. C. *Ou-yang Hsiu: An Eleventh-Century Neo-Confucianist* Stanford University Press, Stanford, 1967

McMullen, David *State and Scholars in T'ang China* Cambridge University Press, Cambridge, 1988

Owen, Stephen *The Great Age of Chinese Poetry: the High T'ang* Yale University Press, New Haven, 1981

Perry, John Curtis and Smith, Bardwell (eds) *Essays on T'ang Society: The Interplay of Social, Political, and Economic Forces* E. J. Brill, Leiden, 1976

Pulleyblank, Edwin G. *The Background of the Rebellion of An Lu-shan* Oxford University Press, London, 1955

Reischauer, Edwin O. *Ennin's Travels in T'ang China* Ronald Press Co., New York, 1955

Schafer, Edward H. *The Golden Peaches of Samarkand: A Study of T'ang Exotica* University of California Press, Berkeley, 1963

Shiba, Yoshinobu *Commerce and Society in Sung China* Elvin, Mark (trans.) The University of Michigan Center for Chinese Studies, Ann Arbor , 1970

Waley, Arthur *The Life and Times of Po Chu-i, 772–846 AD* George Allen & Unwin Ltd, London, 1949

Wright, Arthur and Twitchett, Denis (eds) *Perspectives on the T'ang* Yale University Press, New Haven, 1973

Invaders from the North

Jackson, Peter, (trans.) *The Mission of Friar William of Rubruck. His Journey to the Court of the Great Khan Möngke 1253–1255* (Introduction, notes and appendices by Peter Jackson with David Morgan) The Hakluyt Society, London, 1990

Langois, John D. Jr (ed.) *China under Mongol Rule* Princeton University Press, Princeton, 1981

Morgan, David *The Mongols* Basil Blackwell, New York, 1987

Ratchnevsky, Paul *Genghis Khan: His Life and Legacy* Haining, Thomas Nivison (trans. and ed.) Basil Blackwell, Cambridge, Mass, 1992

Rossabi, Morris *Khubilai Khan: His Life and Times* University of California Press, Berkeley, 1988

Rossabi, Morris *Voyager from Xanadu: Rabban Sauma and the First Journey from China to the West* Kodansha, New York, 1992

Ming and Qing Society: China and the West

Crossley, Pamela Kyle *Orphan Warriors: Three Manchu Generations and the End of the Qing World* Princeton University Press, Princeton, 1990

de Bary, William T. *The Message of the Mind in Neo-Confucian Thought* Columbia University Press, New York, 1989

Dreyer, Edward *Early Ming China: A Political History, 1355–1435* Stanford University Press, Stanford, 1982

Fairbank, John K. (ed) *The Cambridge History of China vol. 10: Late Ch'ing, 1800–1911*, Part 1, Cambridge University Press, Cambridge, 1978

Gernet, Jacques *China and the Christian Impact: A Conflict of Cultures* (trans. Lloyd, Janet) Cambridge University Press, Cambridge, 1985

Johnson, David, et al. (eds) *Popular Culture in Late Imperial China* University of California Press, Berkeley, 1985

Mote, Frederic and Twitchett, Denis (eds) *The Cambridge History of China vol. 7: Ming China, 1368–1644*, Part 1, Cambridge University Press, Cambridge, 1988

Naquin, Susan and Evelyn Rawski *Eighteenth Century China* Yale University Press, New Haven, 1987

Smith, Richard J. *China's Cultural Heritage: The Ch'ing Dynasty, 1644–1912* Westview Press, Boulder, 1983; 2nd edition forthcoming 1994

Smith, Richard J. et al. (eds) *Robert Hart and China's Modernization* Harvard University Press, Cambridge, Mass, 1991

Spence, Jonathan *The Search for Modern China* Norton, New York, 1990

Sullivan, Michael *Symbols of Eternity: The Art of Landscape Painting in China* Stanford University Press, Stanford, 1979

Wakeman, Frederic Jr *The Great Enterprise: The Manchu Reconstruction of Imperial Order in Seventeenth-Century China* University of California Press, Berkeley, 1984

Revolution, Evolution, and Continuity

Eastman, Lloyd E. *Family, Fields, and Ancestors: Constancy and Change in China's Social and Economic History, 1550–1949* Oxford University Press, New York, 1988

Honig, Emily *Sisters and Strangers: Women in the Shanghai Cotton Mills, 1919–1949* Stanford University Press, Stanford, 1986

MacFarquhar, Roderick and Fairbank, John K. (eds) *The Cambridge History of China* Cambridge University Press, Cambridge, 1987

Spence, Jonathan *The Search for Modern China* Norton, New York, 1990

Van Slyke, Lyman P. *Yangtze: Nature, History, and the River* Addison-Wesley, New York, 1988

Wasserstrom, Jeffrey, and Perry, Elizabeth (eds) *Popular Protest and Political Culture in Modern China: Lessons from 1989* Westview Press, Boulder, 1992

Past, Present, and Future

Johnson, David et al. (eds) *Popular Culture in Late Imperial China* University of California Press, Berkeley, 1990

Liu, Kwang-ching *Orthodoxy in Late Imperial China* University of California Press, Berkeley, 1990

Vogel, Ezra F. *One Step Ahead in China: Guangdong under Reform* Harvard University Press, Cambridge, Mass, 1989

Walder, Andrew G. *Communist Neo-Traditionalism: Work and Authority in Chinese Industry* University of California Press, Berkeley, 1986

Watson, James L. *Class and Social Stratification in Post-Revolution China* Cambridge University Press, Cambridge, 1984

Watson, James L. "Rites or Beliefs? The Construction of a Unified Culture in Late Imperial China" in Dittmer, Lowell and Kim, Samuel S. (eds) *China's Quest for National Identity* Cornell University Press, Ithaca, NY, 1993

Watson, James L. and Rawski, Evelyn S. (eds) *Death Ritual in Late Imperial and Modern China* University of California Press, Berkeley, 1988

Watson, Rubie S. and Ebrey, Patricia B. (eds) *Marriage and Inequality in Chinese Society* University of California Press, Berkeley, 1991

Notes on Contributors

TIMOTHY H. BARRETT received his BA and MA in Oriental Studies from Cambridge University and in 1979 gained his PhD in *Buddhism, Taoism and Confucianism in the Thought of Li Ao* from Yale University. He is the author of *Singular Listlessness: A Short History of Chinese Books and British Scholars* (1989), and *Li Ao: Buddhist, Taoist or Neo-Confucian* (1992), and has contributed to the *Cambridge History of China*, and various academic journals. Since 1986 he has been Professor of East Asian History at London University.

KWANG-CHIH CHANG was educated at the National Taiwan University and Harvard University. He taught at Yale for 16 years before moving in 1977 to his current position of John E. Hudson Professor of Archaeology at Harvard. His field research has taken him to France, Taiwan, and China, and he is particularly interested in archaeological theory and the formation of civilizations in ancient China. He is the author of several books including *The Archaeology of Ancient China* and *Art, Myth, and Ritual: The Path to Political Authority in Ancient China*.

TIMOTHY CHEEK received his BA in Asian Studies (Honours) at the Australian National University in 1978, his MA in History at the University of Virginia in 1980, and his PhD in History and East Asian Languages at Harvard in 1986. His research focuses on the role of intellectuals in the modern transformations of China, particularly their role in the Chinese Communist Party. He has published widely on these topics, including several translations of Chinese studies and documents. His books include *The Secret Speeches of Chairman Mao* (1989), written jointly with Roderick MacFarquhar and Eugene Wu, and the biography *Between Priest and Professional: Deng Tuo and Intellectual Service in Mao's China*.

PATRICIA EBREY has taught at the University of Illinois since 1973 and is currently Professor of East Asian Languages and Cultures and of History. She has specialized in the social and cultural history of premodern China, with her first book, *The Aristocratic Families of Early Imperial China: A Case Study of the Po-ling Ts'ui Family* (1978), tracing an elite descent group from the Han through the Tang dynasties. After writing a few articles on Later Han social history, she researched the Song dynasty, writing several studies concerning family and kinship. In addition to co-editing three books and translating two twelfth-century books, she has also written *Confucianism and Family Rituals: A Social History of Writing About Rites* (1991) and *The Inner Quarters: Marriage and the Lives of Chinese Women in the Sung Period* (1993).

ELIZABETH ENDICOTT-WEST received her PhD in East Asian Studies from Princeton University. She is a specialist in the history of the Yuan Dynasty in China and has published many pieces including a monograph entitled *Mongolian Rule in China; Local Administration in the Yuan Dynasty* (1989) and several articles on Sino-Mongolian history. She is also co-author of *The Modernization of Inner Asia* (1991). From 1986 to 1993, she held the position of Assistant, then Associate Professor of Chinese and Inner Asian History, Department of East Asian Languages and Civilizations, Harvard University.

LOTHAR VON FALKENHAUSEN, PhD studied Sinology and Art History at the University of Bonn. From 1979–81 he specialized in Chinese archaeology at Beijing University. He later did two years of research in Japan on a Monbusho Fellowship, and participated in two field seasons of archaeological excavations in Korea. In 1988 he received a PhD in anthropology from Harvard University. He has taught at Stanford University and the University of California, Riverside, and he spent the 1990–91 academic year as a research fellow at the Institute of Archaeology, Chinese Academy of Social Sciences, in Beijing. He is presently Associate Professor of Chinese art and archaeology at the University of California, Los Angeles, and is author of *Suspended Music: Chime-bells in the Culture of Bronze Age China* (1993).

GRACE S. FONG received both her BA and MA from the University of Toronto and her PhD in Chinese literature from the University of British Columbia. She has taught at the University of Massachusetts and Smith College, and is currently Associate Professor, Department of East Asian Languages and Literatures at McGill University. Her research areas include classical Chinese poetry, women's writings in late imperial China, and literary theory. She has published extensively on Chinese poetry, in particular on the song lyric genre, and is currently preparing a book on critical issues in the interaction between gender and genre in premodern Chinese poetry.

CHRISTOPHER FUNG received his BA in anthropology and his BSc from the University of Auckland in 1984 and 1986 respectively. Between 1985 and 1987 he was a New Zealand–China Government exchange scholar studying Chinese archaeology at Beijing University. He has participated in several excavations, and his research interests include the origins of social hierarchy, household archaeology, gender, race and class, and anthropological perspectives and the

social and ritual uses of art and food. He is currently a doctoral candidate in the Anthropology Department, Harvard University.

DAVID N. KEIGHTLEY is a Professor of History at the University of California, Berkeley, where he has taught since 1969. One of the editors and founders of the journal *Early China*, he received a Guggenheim Fellowship in 1978 and a MacArthur fellowship in 1986. He is the author of *Sources of Shang History: The Oracle-Bone Inscriptions of Bronze Age China* (1978), editor of *The Origins of Chinese Civilization* (1983), and is currently working on a book entitled *Divination and Kingship in Late Shang China*.

MICHAEL LOEWE held university lectureships at the universities of London and Cambridge until retiring in 1990. His professional interests have been with the history of the early Chinese empires, including their religious, intellectual and institutional aspects. He has written a number of books including *Records of Han Administration* (1967), *Everyday Life in Early Imperial China* (1968), *Crisis and Conflict in Han China* (1974); *Ways to Paradise: The Chinese Quest for Immortality* (1979), *Chinese Ideas of Life and Death: Faith, Myth and Ritual in the Han Period* (1982), and was co-editor of *The Cambridge History of China, Volume 1, The Ch'in and Han Empires*.

RHOADS MURPHEY studied history at Harvard University, receiving his BA and MA in 1941 and 1942 respectively. In 1948 he received an M.A. in Regional Studies: China and gained a PhD in 1950 in Far Eastern Languages and History. He was Assistant Professor to Professor at the University of Washington from 1952–63, and since 1964 has been Professor of History and Asian Studies at the University of Michigan. He has written a dozen books, predominantly on Chinese history, as well as over 60 articles in scholarly journals.

RICHARD J. SMITH, former Master of Hanszen College, Rice University, is a Professor of History and Chair of Asian Studies at Rice, where he has won nine teaching awards, including the George R. Brown Certificate of Highest Merit. He has written numerous articles on China, and several books, including *Mercenaries and Mandarins* (1978), *Traditional Chinese Culture* (1978), *China's Cultural Heritage* (1983), *Fortune-tellers and Philosophers* (1991) and *Chinese Almanacs* (1992). He is also co-editor or co-author of *Chinese Walled Cities* (1979), *Entering China's Service* (1986), *Robert Hart and China's Early Modernization* (1991), and *Cosmology, Ontology, and Human Efficacy* (1993).

JAMES L. WATSON is Fairbank Professor of Chinese Society and Professor of Anthropology, Harvard University. He holds a PhD in anthropology from the University of California, Berkeley, and has taught previously at the School of Oriental and African Studies, University of London and at the University of Pittsburgh. He has conducted ethnographic field research in Hong Kong, Guangdong, Jiangxi, and the Beijing region; and has published on family life, kinship, ancestor worship, migration, ritual, and food systems. He currently serves as Director of the Fairbank Center for East Asian Research, Harvard.

ROBIN D. S. YATES was educated at Oxford University and the University of California before joining the Society of Fellows, Harvard University, where he received his doctorate in Chinese History in 1980. He has taught at Harvard, the Massachusetts Institute of Technology, and Dartmouth College, and is currently Director of the Centre for East Asian Studies, Chair of the Department of East Asian Languages and Literatures, and Professor of History and of East Asian Languages and Literatures at McGill University. He has written extensively on Eastern Zhou and Qin history in the light of the new archaeological finds, Chinese military technology, and Chinese poetry.

Acknowledgments

Weldon Russell would like to acknowledge the following people for permission to include copyright material: *The Mission of Friar William of Rubruck—His Journey to the Court of the Great Khan Mongke, 1253–1255* edited by Peter Jackson and David Morgan 1990 © Hakluyt Society; *The Songs of the South: An Anthology of Ancient Chinese Poetry by Qu Yuan and Other Poets* David Hawkes (translator) 1985 © Penguin Books London; *The Complete Works of Chuang-tzu* Burton Watson (translator) 1968 © Columbia University Press, New York; *The Travels of Marco Polo* Ronald Latham (translator) 1980 © Penguin Books, London.

Weldon Russell would also like to thank Jacqueline Voo for her help with translating correspondence and communicating with Chinese picture sources.

Index

Page numbers in italics indicate illustrations